Microsoft® SharePoint® 2010: Creating and Implementing Real-World Projects

Jennifer Mason
Christian Buckley
Brian T. Jackett
Wes Preston

Published with the authorization of Microsoft Corporation by:
O'Reilly Media, Inc.
1005 Gravenstein Highway North
Sebastopol, California 95472

ISBN: 978-0-7356-6282-7

1 2 3 4 5 6 7 8 9 LSI 7 6 5 4 3 2

Printed and bound in the United States of America.

Microsoft Press books are available through booksellers and distributors worldwide. If you need support related to this book, email Microsoft Press Book Support at mspinput@microsoft.com. Please tell us what you think of this book at *http://www.microsoft.com/learning/booksurvey*.

The example companies, organizations, products, domain names, email addresses, logos, people, places, and events depicted herein are fictitious. No association with any real company, organization, product, domain name, email address, logo, person, place, or event is intended or should be inferred.

Acquistions and Developmental Editor: Kenyon Brown

Production Editor: Kristen Borg

Editorial Production: Curtis Philips

Technical Reviewers: Shannon Bray and Geoff Evelyn

Copyeditor: John Pierce

Indexer: Lucie Haskins

Cover Design: Twist Creative • Seattle

Cover Composition: Karen Montgomery

I would like to dedicate this book to Chris Maiers. The idea for this book came from many of the conversations we have had over the past year. Thanks for being such a great client and friend!

—Jennifer Mason

I'd like to dedicate this book to my old echoTechnology team of Garry Smith, Sergio Otoya, Darshan Dalwadi (and team), Luis Juarez, Nick Kellett, and latecomer Mark McGovern. Thanks guys for all your support!

—Christian Buckley

I would like to dedicate this book to my family—Tom, Debbie, Dave, and Jay—and my girlfriend, Sarah, for all of your support through the writing process and beyond. Thanks for your support; it hasn't gone unnoticed.

—Brian T. Jackett

My work on this book is dedicated to my parents, who founded, owned, and operated the oldest computer store in Milwaukee, Wisconsin, for 17 years and forever instilled in me a love of technology and of helping others to embrace and benefit from it as well. Thanks Mom and Dad!

—Wes Preston

Contents at a Glance

Contents

What do you think of this book? We want to hear from you!

Microsoft is interested in hearing your feedback so we can continually improve our
books and learning resources for you. To participate in a brief online survey, please visit:

microsoft.com/learning/booksurvey

Chapter 4   Building a Learning Center   151

Chapter 5   Building a Help Desk Solution   179

Chapter 6   Building a Remote Teams Activity Site   205

What do you think of this book? We want to hear from you!

Microsoft is interested in hearing your feedback so we can continually improve our
books and learning resources for you. To participate in a brief online survey, please visit:

microsoft.com/learning/booksurvey

Introduction

If you are reading *Microsoft SharePoint 2010: Creating and Implementing Real-World Projects*, it is likely that you are experienced with SharePoint but looking for ways to really get the most from the out-of-the-box tools. Let's face it; the truth is that SharePoint is a large platform, with many different tools and methods for building and creating solutions. For someone who is getting started, there is much to take in and learn. That is where this book will come in handy! In the pages of this book, you will be working through and examining many different everyday examples that you are likely to have encountered at your organization.

This book is designed so that you can examine the business problems and then pull together the various tools and techniques available for building solutions within SharePoint to address the given business needs. We have quite a bit of ground to cover, so let's get started.

Who Should Read This Book

Before jumping into the chapters, you should be aware that we are expecting you to have a general understanding of the basics of SharePoint. This means that you should be somewhat familiar with common site administrator tasks. This allows us to focus more on why and how to do some advanced configurations. If you aren't familiar with some of these techniques, you can still continue with the book, and you will still gain lots of knowledge, but you might want to supplement your reading with some of the resources that we recommend in the resource appendix at the end of this book.

Assumptions

To help you understand the level of experience that is prerequisite for this book, the following is a list of common tasks that we expect you to be familiar with:

- Creating sites and webs (subsites)
- Creating lists and libraries
- Managing site permissions
- Creating and customizing list views

- Working with web parts

- Customizing a site with Microsoft SharePoint Designer 2010

- Customizing list forms with Microsoft InfoPath 2010

- SharePoint and Office integration

We define *familiar* as knowing the general concepts, not necessarily knowing how to configure and manage everything on the list. For example, in a chapter we might provide an instruction such as "Create a new view for this list." We expect that you know what a SharePoint view is, and our examples for the view will be specific to the solution at hand and won't really be focused on the general concept of a SharePoint view. If you are unfamiliar with any of the following items, don't worry, because it should be easy for you to get up to speed so that you are familiar enough to work through the chapters. Besides, if you are reading a chapter and run into something that you aren't familiar with, Bing is only a few clicks away!

Another assumption that we have made in the writing of this book is that all of our solutions have been built in separate and unique site collections. This was done as a way to provide a clean slate for each new solution. As you consider implementing the ideas within the book in your organization, it is important for you to review with your SharePoint team the governance in place, which determines when you should use a site collection and when you should use a site. You can easily adapt the solutions in this book so they can be created as a site in an existing site collection. There are many considerations to think about as you look at the best location to add these solutions within your organization. If your organization does not have any existing governance plans surrounding the creation of sites or site collections, we recommend you read "Plan sites and site collections (SharePoint Server 2010)" at *http://technet.microsoft.com/en-us/library/cc263267.aspx* to help you determine the best solution for your needs.

Organization of This Book

When you read each of this book's chapters, you should look for ways that you can apply the same solutions within your environment. Each chapter is structured in a way that allows you to start from the business problems and work through the implementation, followed by a discussion about maintaining the solution over time. This format is consistent across all chapters, so you gain experience in the process of evaluating business problems and applying SharePoint solutions to address specific needs. Because this book is intended to be read by a large, diverse audience, it is not likely that all scenarios will apply specifically to your needs. It might also be that your scenarios match only part of our solutions. What happens then? It is our intention in this book that you should be able to pull the pieces that apply specifically to your needs and then make adjustments as needed to meet your specific requirements. The chapters should be considered as starting points. If you are a master chef, you might follow a recipe but add your own spices to really enhance the meal you are creating. In the same way, you can think of this book as a collection of recipes. You might follow the recipe exactly, or you might enhance or make substitutions. In fact, you might very well combine the techniques from different chapters into a single solution. The point is, where you are able to, look at the different solutions proposed and then adapt them for your specific environment.

Here is a quick summary of what you can find in each of the chapters:

Chapter 1, "Building a Project Management Solution," explores a project management solution that provides a way for the project team to collaborate and for the project manager to report project status to the management team.

Chapter 2, "Building a Training Registration Management System," provides a solution that allows users to view a calendar of courses and then register for those courses directly from the calendar. This solution is built using many of the rich enterprise features in SharePoint, especially InfoPath.

Chapter 3, "Building a Basic FAQ Solution," provides a solution that utilizes SharePoint Foundation to create a centralized location to store and manage FAQs. This solution highlights the rich feature set within SharePoint Foundation and guides you through making the most of the customizations available to you.

Chapter 4, "Building a Learning Center," focuses on designing and implementing a learning center site that aggregates classes and the related documents, discussions, and links to external resources. SharePoint Foundation elements such as lists, lookup columns, and simple SharePoint Designer workflows are utilized to build the solution.

Chapter 5, "Building a Help Desk Solution," focuses on designing and implementing a help desk solution for creating and tracking service requests for a departmental organization. SharePoint Server Standard elements such as more complex Visio to SharePoint Designer workflows, document libraries, and wiki pages are used to build the solution.

Chapter 6, "Building a Remote Teams Activity Site," takes a look at a simple way to keep geographically dispersed teams connected and their schedules aligned by providing a shared calendar solution. The chapter also offers suggestions for further aligning tasks and documents.

Chapter 7, "Building a Team Blog Platform," walks through the building of a team blog platform, with all the expected blog components, and outlines a method for reviewing and approving content in a secure and managed way.

Chapter 8, "Building an RFP Response Solution," walks through the design and steps to build a solution for consulting or services organizations that respond to requests for proposals or bids. The solution enables consistent communication across the organization and manages bid-creation tasks across multiple teams. The solution can be built using any version of SharePoint 2010 or SharePoint Online (Office 365).

Chapter 9, "Building a Contact Management Solution," steps through the design and building of a contact management solution using core SharePoint functionality available in any version of SharePoint or SharePoint Online (Office 365). The solution extends the out-of-the-box contacts list and starts down the path of presenting multiple facets of data regarding contact management and activities.

Chapter 10, "Building a Resource Scheduling Solution," walks through the design and steps required to build a resource scheduling solution. This solution uses a relatively underutilized feature built into SharePoint sites, called Group Work Lists. The solution can be built using any version of SharePoint 2010 or SharePoint Online (Office 365).

Setting Expectations

The best thing we can do for our readers is to help them understand the expectations we have from this book. This way, as you are reading the book, you can get the most from it. When the team of authors started discussing this book, one of the key things we kept focusing on was the desire for the audience to be able to read through the chapters and use the information within the chapters to build solutions within their organization. While you learn lots of techniques in the pages of this book, the overall purpose is not to teach you how to create a workflow or how to configure a library, but instead to convey why you would want to perform those tasks. After reading this book, you should have the tools needed to look at business solutions objectively and then pick and choose the different approaches within SharePoint for building solutions that address the problems at hand.

What Is a Real-World Scenario?

In the title of the book we use the term *real-world* projects. Because this term can be slightly overused and underexplained at times, we want to be sure to define what we mean when we use it. In the context of this book, *real world* is defined as various scenarios encountered by the authors as we have used SharePoint as a tool to build solutions that address business needs. As the authors came together for this book, each of us submitted ideas based on concepts we have built solutions for. Each of the solutions has been implemented within one or more organizations. The solutions we selected are ones that we feel address a large audience. This approach allows us to offer solutions that most readers can relate to in their everyday work experiences.

Introduction to SharePoint

No SharePoint book would be complete without an introduction to each of the platforms. The term SharePoint is tossed around quite a bit in general, and at times it can be hard to understand whether a particular discussion applies to your environment. Later in this chapter, in the section "Different SharePoint Versions," we give you a high-level summary of each of the available platforms in SharePoint. This section can serve as a reference point if you have questions later in the book about the different platforms we use.

What Is SharePoint?

So what is SharePoint? There are two ways you can look at SharePoint—what it is and what you do with it. Think of the process of building a house. There are many different tools and materials that are combined for the final product. Each of the materials alone might or might not be anything by itself, but once they are combined with the proper use of tools, you have a strong, reliable structure that fulfills a purpose. In the same way, SharePoint is like the various tools and materials, and the final business solutions you build are like the house. There are many features and tools in SharePoint, and within this book you will see different ways to combine and structure them into business solutions.

If you head over to the official Microsoft SharePoint website (*SharePoint.com*), you will see a discussion of six capabilities that SharePoint provides. In the following sections, we summarize each of them.

Sites

Within SharePoint you can use sites to store and manage data in many different forms. You can create a site that publishes content internally for users: this is typically referred to as your corporate intranet. You can also push information to the web for public, anonymous access, which is referred to as your Internet site. You can also use sites to store and manage data that is used and referenced by a group of named users who have access to the sites. These are typically referred to as collaboration sites. Some common types of collaboration sites include project sites, team sites, and department sites. In some cases these collaboration sites are extended outside the corporation, and vendor and third-party users are invited to join in the collaboration. These types of sites are typically referred to as extranet sites.

Communities

Communities are the various social features that allow us to collaborate more efficiently. These features can help you locate other users within your organization on the basis of information about them or their areas of expertise. Once you are connected, you can easily communicate and collaborate with them through their My Sites. Communities also provide some tagging and rating features. These features allow you to quickly classify content, and these classifications are shared across the organization and used by others as they try to locate content.

Composites

Composites define the way that you can interact with various line of business systems within your organization. Using the composite features, you can easily incorporate business data into SharePoint. The two primary features within the composites structure are Access Services and Business Connectivity Services (BCS). Access Services allow you to use Microsoft Access to build and configure applications that can be published to SharePoint. Users will have visibility to the data within SharePoint, through the browser alone, without needing to have the Access client installed. BCS is used to configure connections to external data. Once the connection is configured, the external data is available within SharePoint through the standard features of lists, metadata, and external content types.

Content

Within the content features of SharePoint, some of the most common features are records management, document management, web content management, and search. The records and document management features allow you to manage how data is added to the environment and let you create policies to manage data compliance.

Insights

Insights are considered the business intelligence features within SharePoint and include the following technologies: Excel Services, Visio Services, Chart web part, key performance indicators (KPIs), and PerformancePoint Services. These services provide the capabilities for you to use common tools such as Visio and Excel to manage and report on data, while allowing users to access the content without needing a client application. The chart and KPI features can connect to the data that is published through the services, giving you another way to present the data to your users through SharePoint. PerformancePoint is a downloadable application that allows you to create rich charts, graphs, and reports on data that is stored within SharePoint, Excel Services, or SQL Server. As with the other tools mentioned earlier, the reports are generated within the PerformancePoint dashboard builder and published to the SharePoint sites, allowing users to have clientless access to the data.

Search

The search features within SharePoint allow you to easily find and locate relevant content. Since search is configured for both content and people, users within the organization can rely on search to help them quickly find what they need. The search experience is completely configurable, allowing for each organization to provide a search experience that best works for its users.

So now that we have covered some of the primary functionality available within SharePoint, let's dive into the different versions of the product. There are several versions of the product, and it is important to understand what version you are working with so that you can fully understand the features that are available for you to use in your solutions.

Different SharePoint Versions

We could write books dedicated to mapping out the differences in the various versions of SharePoint. But since we are ready to get started building our solutions, we have decided to offer just very quick overviews and point you to locations online where you can get the most up-to-date information.

SharePoint Online

SharePoint Online is the newest SharePoint offering provided by Microsoft. This version comes with Office 365 as part of the SharePoint hosted model. There are several different versions of SharePoint Online, including ones for small businesses and ones for enterprises.

See Also *For more information on the specific features included in SharePoint Online, refer to the Microsoft website* technet.microsoft.com/en-us/sharepoint/gg144571.

SharePoint Foundation Server

SharePoint Foundation Server is the free version of SharePoint that comes with Windows Server 2008. This version allows you to create and manage sites, but it does not include any of the enterprise features or services.

See Also *For more information on the specific features included in SharePoint Foundation Server, refer to the Microsoft website* technet.microsoft.com/en-us/sharepoint/ee263910.

SharePoint Server

SharePoint Server comes in two different versions, Standard and Enterprise. Both versions include the features required for web content management and search. The Enterprise version, however, includes all the enterprise services, such as Visio Services, Excel Services, Access Services, and InfoPath Form Services.

See Also *For more information on the specific features included in SharePoint Server, refer to the Microsoft website* technet.microsoft.com/en-us/sharepoint/ee263917.

SharePoint Environment Used for This Book

Throughout this book, we use all the versions of SharePoint as examples. Each chapter's solution, depending on its topic, is built in a single environment. At the beginning of each chapter, we outline what environment we are using, as well as what decisions we made for selecting that environment. At the end of each chapter, we review the different environments and highlight how the solution would be different in each of them. In some cases this means we explain the limitations and workarounds required if you aren't running the same set of services, or we explain the different enhancements that you can make to the solution if you are running additional services. The authors have selected this approach to create a holistic approach to building solutions using SharePoint. By looking at each of the solutions based on different environments, you will be able to get a broad understanding of the different features available. If you are currently running in an environment with fewer features, you will be able to gain some practical insight and valid business justification for upgrading to more services. If you are running with all the features, you will see that sometimes "less is more." There might be cases where you are going out of your way to use all the features available when only some are required.

Acknowledgments

God has blessed me beyond belief, and I am so thankful for all the opportunities I have been presented with. With each book I finish, it is exciting to look back and see all that went into the process. In doing that, it is impossible to not be thankful to those around me who help make the process possible! In this small section I want to thank those who have influenced me along the way. While it is impossible to thank everyone, I will give it my best shot.

First off, I need to thank Shane and Nicola and all my wonderful crew at SharePoint911. I can honestly say that you have become like a family to me. Life would be boring without you, and I would be lost if I had to work without you. Thanks for being the best coworkers anyone could ask for!

Second, I want to thank my coauthors for such a fun journey discussing the need for this book and then seeing it come to life. Christian, Brian, and Wes, I am honored to get to work with you.

Third, I need to thank Shannon, our tech editor. I appreciate your insight and your additions to the book. In my book, you are the best MCM there is. Thanks for everything!

Fourth, I want to thank the community that makes all of this so much fun. There are far too many of you to name, but each of you makes my days so much more enjoyable. I look forward to continuing this journey together.

And finally, a group that needs to be thanked is the team at Microsoft Press who made this book happen. Ken Brown, there is no way this would be done without your organization and coordination. Thanks for all you did to make this come together. Working with authors is never easy, but we appreciate all you do for us.

—*Jennifer Mason*

I'd like to thank a few of my former Microsoft team members for their contributions to my SharePoint career path, whether they recognize their influence or not, and for making things a little more sane during the early days of my Microsoft tenure. Specifically, I'd like to thank Mike Watson, Joel Oleson, Bill Baer, Charles Ofori, Sean Livingston, Derek O'Loughlin, and Kimberley Ward. I'd also like to say thank you to Jennifer for inviting me to participate in this project, to Wes and Brian for the team support, and to friends in the SharePoint community who are always there to answer my questions and share their ideas—people like Geoff Varosky, Jason Himmelstein, Laura Docherty, Michael Doyle, Chris Beckett, Nedra Allmond, Jeff Shuey, Owen Allen, Paul Culmsee, Becky Isserman, and so many others. Thanks.

—*Christian Buckley*

I would like to thank my friends, family, and girlfriend, Sarah, for being supportive throughout the writing process. I would also like to thank those who helped me become who I am today: Frank Fernandez for introducing me to SharePoint, Kelly Jones for mentoring me during my early SharePoint days and beyond, Jeff Blankenburg for encouraging me to start a blog, Jennifer Mason for getting me more involved in the SharePoint community and getting this book concept started, Eric Harlan for providing career guidance, and Sean McDonough for helping with community events and numerous miscellaneous other things. I also thank my coauthors Wes and Christian for providing great content and support during the writing process. Lastly, I would like to thank God for all of the graces and blessings He gives to me each and every day.

—*Brian T. Jackett*

I would like to thank my wife, Kirsten, and boys, Connor and Ryan, for their unwavering support while I wrote this book. Making the time to commit to the project would have been impossible without their support. I'd like to thank Jennifer for inviting me to contribute to this project, as well as Christian and Brian. I also need to thank my cohorts Raymond Mitchell (the other half of "Wesmond") and Phil Jirsa for helping with lots of input, feedback, and gap filling. Finally, I'd like to thank the SharePoint community. There are so many great contributors out there who deserve a lot more credit than they are often given. It's difficult to name a few without including everyone, but a few standouts are Sarah Haase, Mark Rackley, Chris Geier, Kris Wagner, and Bill English.

—*Wes Preston*

Errata & Book Support

We've made every effort to ensure the accuracy of this book and its companion content. Any errors that have been reported since this book was published are listed on our Microsoft Press site at oreilly.com:

http://go.microsoft.com/FWLink/?Linkid=241462

If you find an error that is not already listed, you can report it to us through the same page.

If you need additional support, email Microsoft Press Book Support at mspinput@ microsoft.com.

Please note that product support for Microsoft software is not offered through the addresses above.

We Want to Hear from You

At Microsoft Press, your satisfaction is our top priority and your feedback our most valuable asset. Please tell us what you think of this book at

http://www.microsoft.com/learning/booksurvey

The survey is short, and we read every one of your comments and ideas. Thanks in advance for your input!

Stay in Touch

Let's keep the conversation going! We're on Twitter: *http://twitter.com/MicrosoftPress*.

CHAPTER 1

Building a Project Management Solution

Finding ways to better manage projects is a key concern for many different organizations. Projects are typically the heart of any company, and the success of how projects are managed determines the success of the company. Finding tools that enable you to better manage your projects can have a direct impact on the success of the organization.

Many great tools are available in the market that you can use to help manage projects, and some of them, like Microsoft Project, even integrate with Microsoft SharePoint. But not all organizations are ready to manage projects at the level required to successfully implement those solutions. Some organizations are looking for straightforward ways to better manage current processes and improve current communications. In this chapter, you will work through the process of creating a simple SharePoint solution for managing projects. You will start by reviewing the business problem, then you will work through the design phase, and finally you will implement the solution. Once you complete the implementation, you will look at the different steps you need to take in the future to manage the solution.

Have You Read the Book's Introduction?

This book is organized in a way that allows you to find topics quickly. Each chapter is structured in the same way, allowing you to read about a particular business scenario, from the requirements to the solution. If you haven't read the book's introduction, you should do that before reading this chapter. This will help you understand the flow of the topics in chapters.

In this chapter you will take on the role of a business analyst building a solution that your organization will use to manage projects. This means that you are on the outside looking in to the ways that projects are managed in your organization. To get the most out of this chapter, you should try hard to look at the process from the outside and not from your current role on projects.

Identifying the Business Problem

For any solution you build in SharePoint, the place to start is to identify the business problem. You want to fully define and understand the issues that users face, as well as understand the overall goals of the organization. You want to look at the problem from all perspectives to ensure that you build a solution that will truly address the needs of the organization. After all, you could spend a lot of time building the perfect solution, but if no one uses it, then your time spent developing it has been wasted.

When it comes to project management, several common complaints exist within different organizations. In the next section you are going to look at several of the common issues that organizations try to address when they build a solution for project management. You will use these common complaints as the requirements for the solution you will build in the remainder of this chapter.

> **Important** As you read about the issues that are identified, take some time to think about how they apply to your organization. Do you see the same issues? Can you identify additional issues that your organization faces that might not be discussed here?

Data, Data, and More Data

Many of us struggle with information overload. We have access to so much content that it is often hard to determine what is most important and relevant. Content comes in many shapes and formats and can be defined as the information and data that is accessed while we perform our jobs. We access content online, in documents, in the form of personal meetings, and even more in the form of email. We often work with content in various phases and often save copies of the content at each phase. Saving different versions is important because you need to understand how the content progressed from draft to final, but an issue comes up later in the same project when you have to go back and reference the data. Which version is the latest version? Who last made updates? When users were working on the project, it was easy to keep up with the chain of control, but three months later it can be hard to remember.

In addition, having many versions of the content, users have a lot of places to store them. They typically have access to several shared drives, a few personal drives, various SharePoint sites, a local hard drive, and, of course, email storage. Storing content in so many different locations can easily create a large web of disorganized content. While one user or one group might have a very detailed, structured way to store content, what happens when the organization realigns and users move to different groups or departments? What happens to the content then?

The following list identifies specific content management issues you will address in the SharePoint solution that you build in this chapter:

- Clearly identified locations to access project data.

- Ability to manage multiple versions of the same content.

For each additional topic discussed in this section, a new list of issues will be presented. These will then be used in the design section of the chapter as checkpoints to ensure that the solution proposed addresses the issues discussed.

It's All in Our Minds

The next issue to explore involves the amount of process information that is contained within our resources. Spend a few minutes thinking about the people who work at your organization. Think about the people who have been there the longest. Now think about what would be lost if they left the organization. How much data would they take with them when they walked out the door? The data I am referring to is not physical documentation or files but an understanding of how the organization does business. Longtime employees understand the ins and the outs, and they understand how to get things done, and without them your organization will likely suffer a loss of productivity and efficiency. An organization's resources are vital to its operations, and your organization will always rely on the minds of its resources, but there are definitely some mechanisms you can put in place to help ensure that practices are recorded and knowledge is retained. This way you are relying on a defined process and not the resources themselves. Having a structure like this in place will provide an easier way to switch out employees and to mentor new employees when they are brought onboard.

But here is where it gets tricky. While there are many standard processes, there are just as many unique processes for each organization. The following list describes some of the general processes that can be put in place, but to really make the most out of this solution, you will want to spend some time thinking about various processes that are unique to your organization and how your organization manages projects. There may be some additional processes that you will want to incorporate into your solution as you build it:

- Clearly identified process for determining where to store project data.

- Clearly identified process for managing different versions of project data.

- Clearly identified approval processes for project data.

- Clearly identified matrix for identifying who has access to project data.

I Don't Have Time to Learn New Products

The final area to discuss is usability. I am not sure I could count the number of times I have heard from users about the difficulty they have learning and using new systems. Phrases like "Just when I started to learn to do it this way, they changed it" or "Why do all the new ways have to be so hard? This isn't broken, so why fix it?" are very common sentiments among users. I am sure that as you read this, you can relate to these statements, as well as add others you have heard from your users. While these complaints are not specific to project management, they should definitely be taken into consideration while you develop your solution. The following list summarizes some of the common pain points that you will address in the solution:

- The solution must be intuitive and easy to use without in-depth training.

- The solution should allow users to navigate easily to different areas.

- The solution should integrate with tools and applications that are familiar and known by the user base.

Summarizing the Business Problem

In this section, three different areas of common business problems surrounding projects have been discussed. In summary, the following areas were identified as key points of consideration:

- Location of data

- Process for interacting with data

- Providing easy and intuitive solutions for users to work with data

Now that you have the data that identifies current pain points, it is time to start gathering some more information. So far, only a very high-level description of common issues and pain points has been identified. The next step in the process is to look deeper into each of the issues and clearly determine specific requirements. You might be tempted to skip over this next section and get right to the meat of things, but I assure you that you won't want to miss the next few sections. Sure, you could take what you have learned so far and build a solution that satisfied the requirements at hand, but how effective would that solution be? Do you even fully understand the requirements at this point? Now is the time to drill down to that next level and really start to gather those requirements. This is where you spend time talking with different users to learn about what they are currently doing and develop an understanding of their pain points. The high-level issues identified earlier will serve as our starting point for the requirements gathering phase.

Gathering Information

During this step of building the project management solution, you are going to look in more detail at the specific requirements of the system. You will start by evaluating each group of users who will use the system to get a good understanding of what they will use the system for. As you meet with users and look at their needs, you will be able to identify the specific requirements that need to be included in the solution.

System Users

Our solution is going to be built based on the requirements of three types of users. Each group will interact with the solution differently, and to ensure that the solution is as effective and usable as possible, it is important to understand the specific needs of each user group.

Project Committee

The project committee, in our example, is a group of users who are directly responsible for the strategic direction of projects within the organization. They provide oversight, direction, and approval for projects and are responsible for understanding how projects relate to the direction of the organization. They approve the start of all new projects and provide strategic direction for the completion of projects. While project managers work directly with the organization throughout the project process, they are also responsible for communicating status to this oversight committee.

In terms of our solution, the project committee would require the following level of functionality:

- Ability to access a real-time summary for all projects, which includes the following items:

  - Scope

  - Budget

  - Schedule

- Ability to review, as needed, the following items for a specific project:

  - Project tasks

  - Project calendar

  - Project issues

  - Project documentation

Project Managers

In our example, project managers are directly responsible for the day-to-day management of any given project, based on the scope, budget, and timeline. Depending on the scope of the project, a project manager might be responsible for only a single project or for multiple projects. Project managers are responsible for assigning and directing resources, as well as for reporting on project status to the various stakeholders.

In terms of our solution, project managers require the following level of functionality:

- Ability to get real-time status on any of the project elements, including the following items:
  - Project tasks
  - Project calendar
  - Project issues
  - Project documentation
- Ability to easily report on the current project status to the project stakeholders.
- Ability to easily communicate with various project resources on project issues and tasks.

Project Resources

In our example, project resources are the people directly responsible for completing project tasks. They work together as a team and rely on each other to complete the project. Most resources will be assigned to specific project tasks, but in general the project is considered a team effort and will require a level of input from everyone as tasks are completed.

In terms of our solution, project resources require the following level of functionality:

- Ability to get real-time status on any of the project elements, including the following items:
  - Project tasks
  - Project calendar
  - Project issues
  - Project documentation
- Ability to easily interact with other project resources on any project components.
- Ability to create additional project tasks for project team members.
- Ability to easily communicate with various project resources on project issues and tasks.
- Ability to easily update the project manager on project tasks and assignments.

Different Users Working Together

So far, we have outlined three different types of users who will be accessing our solution, and we have identified the primary requirements that each type has for the solution. If we mapped out the relationship of users, it would look similar to the illustration shown here.

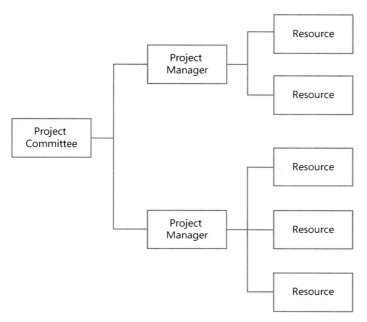

In this diagram, you can see a relationship between the three user groups. Each group works together in a slightly different way but is still part of a larger solution. As you look at building this solution, it is important that you understand the requirements of each of the user groups and how they are incorporated into the solution as a whole. Any solution that you build needs to address the requirements of all three unique types of users and still provide one consistent solution. The best way to determine how to achieve this goal is to spend some time identifying how the different users interact with each other. The following illustration shows the relationships between the different users.

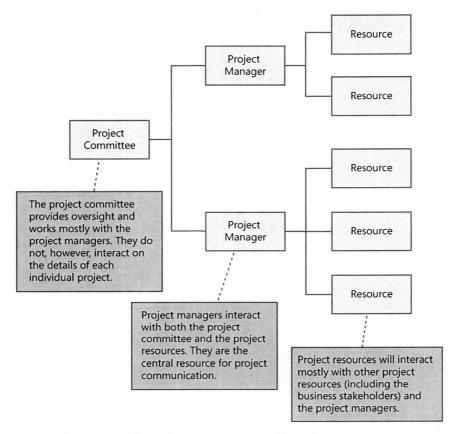

The project committee provides oversight and works mostly with the project managers. They do not, however, interact on the details of each individual project.

Project managers interact with both the project committee and the project resources. They are the central resource for project communication.

Project resources will interact mostly with other project resources (including the business stakeholders) and the project managers.

This diagram provides a high-level overview of how the different roles are related to each other. This information will be used to help design a solution that best facilitates this relationship. Understanding how the solution's users are related helps ensure that our solution includes these relationships in the overall design.

Solution Data

Now that we have identified the different users who will be working with our solution, it is time to look at the different types of information that will be stored within the solution. The following list describes the different items that have been identified so far:

- Project summary reports
- Project documents (this includes Microsoft Word, Microsoft PowerPoint, Microsoft Excel, and PDF files)
- Project contacts
- Project tasks

- Project discussions

- Project calendars

Just knowing the data types, however, is not enough for us to really understand how to incorporate them into our project management solution. At this point you need to take time to understand how each of the user groups works with the data. How do users currently create and store documentation and project artifacts? Doing this will help you get a clear understanding of each group's current processes and any pain points they have with their current solution. The following table identifies the assumptions for the sample solution within this chapter. The table identifies the current information in our chapter's example. You can see that we are assuming that various types of content are created differently for each group. Whenever Office documents (such as Word, Excel, or PowerPoint) are mentioned, you can assume that these files are stored within a shared drive or an organization file share.

Required Solution Data	Current Location
Project summary reports	Excel and Word documents stored in a shared drive that the project managers and project committee members can access.
Project documents (includes Word, PowerPoint, Excel, and PDF files)	Stored in various shared drives and network locations. Each project team determines the storage location and structure for its project documentation.
Project contacts	Some teams keep an Excel document with contacts on a shared drive, while others use a contact list in Outlook.
Project tasks	Each project team stores its tasks differently. Some use an Excel worksheet, some use a Word document, and some use tasks in Outlook.
Project discussions	Most of the project teams had a hard time defining what a discussion included, but most agreed that all discussions about projects happened in meetings and were recorded in the meeting notes or happened through email messages.
Project calendars	Each project team manages its calendar differently. Some have a shared calendar in Outlook, and some keep a calendar list in Excel or Word. In some cases, the project team relied on everyone keeping their own personal calendars up to date and had no team calendar.

Summarizing the Requirements Gathering Process

The process of looking at users and the data they are accessing during project work is now complete, and it is time to start designing the solution. Before we start the next phase, it would be good to summarize the information collected so far:

1. The business problem was reviewed at a high level to identify the key requirements for our solution.

2. The different users of the solution were identified along with their relationship to each other.

3. The different types of data and information that are used by the solution's users were identified.

This chapter is dedicated to a project management solution, but the process completed to this point can be followed for any type of solution you are trying to create. Next up, you will look at ways to translate requirements into a working design.

Designing the Solution

Now that the requirements have been identified, it is time to translate them into a working SharePoint site design. The first step includes reviewing some of our design decisions. (Remember when reviewing them that this is a sample chapter and the design decisions within your environment could vary.) Following the review of the design decisions, wireframes will be created to show the overall look of the site. Wireframes are a great tool for getting a project's business stakeholders to understand what the final solution will look like. A picture can be worth a thousand words, so this is one of the most important steps in building out the site design. The project's business stakeholders are required to approve the wireframes prior to the actual creation of the solution. Having their approval helps ensure that we are building the solution they are expecting. In our chapter example, the approval would likely come from a collection of users that represents each of the identified user groups. Once approval has been given to the wireframes, the process of constructing the solution will begin.

What Is Your Solution Build Approach?

Take a few minutes and think through the last solution you built for your organization. This can be a solution within SharePoint or any other application. Looking back at your process, how would things have changed if you followed the steps outlined earlier? Would your end results have been different or would the process to get to the end results have been different?

Design Decisions

Before you start to build a solution, there are key decisions to be made that impact how the solution is created. In our example, we have several of these decisions. Each of the decisions is identified in the following sections, along with an explanation of why the decision was made.

Single Site Collection

The solution in this chapter will be built using a single site collection. This approach was chosen so that the following SharePoint features could be used:

- Shared solutions

- Shared templates

- Shared navigation

- Content query rollups

- Shared permission groups

When making this decision, one of the main items that needs to be addressed is the overall size of our solution. SharePoint implements site quotas to allow SharePoint site collections to grow only to a certain size. The quota is configured by the system administrators and should be included in your organization's governance plan. In this chapter, the guideline is that no single site collection can contain more than 100 gigabytes (GB) of content. The site collection will start with a small, manageable quota, such as 20 GB, but over time it can be expanded to meet the solution's needs. This information is provided to help set the stage for the solution we will build in this chapter, and it should be evaluated against the restrictions within your environment.

See Also *For more information about how to properly size your SharePoint environment, refer to the article "Capacity Management and Sizing Overview for SharePoint Server 2010" at* technet.microsoft.com/en-us/library/ff758647.aspx.

Site-Level Permissions Management

All permissions will be managed at the site level using SharePoint groups. This practice ensures that content is managed in a consistent manner that is easy to maintain and administer. Based on the earlier user statements, it has been difficult to find content and to understand who has access to the content. Managing item-level and list-level permissions can add a high degree of overheard to projects and is something that could cause potential confusion to users as they access the sites.

See Also *For more information on understanding SharePoint permissions, refer to "User Permissions and Permission Levels (SharePoint Server 2010)" at* technet.microsoft.com/en-us/library/cc721640.aspx.

Solution Templates

This solution will be built using SharePoint site templates. This will allow for the configuration of a single project site that can then be used as the basis for all future project sites. The template will be agreed upon by the project team and will be evaluated quarterly for any required updates. The following table describes the template that will be created in this chapter.

Required Solution Data	Current Location
Project sites	When a new project is started, the Project Site template will be used to create a site in the Project site collection. The following content will be included in this template: Project announcements Project documents Project tasks Project events Project team Project discussions

In addition to the Project Site template, a single site will be created as a location for the project committee to collaborate on the status of projects. This site will not need to be based on a template because it will be needed only once. The following list shows the items that will be included in this site:

- Project status summary

- PMO (project management office) announcements

- PMO links

Project Site Modifications

The solution in this chapter allows anyone with the proper rights to add customizations to their project site after the site is created from the template. To manage this, an administrator will be identified, who will complete the required training and then be given administrative access to manage the project site. This approach allows for the template to be used as a common starting point as well as for project team members to make modifications to increase their value to the project team. Only approved users who have completed training will be eligible for elevated permissions on the project sites. When a project site administrator completes training, she will need to agree to live by a common set of principles for their site. Random audits will be conducted on the project sites to ensure that each project team remains in compliance with the agreed upon standards that are included in the governance plan.

Solution Navigation

For our solution, we will not require that all sites use a common or inherited navigation structure. Since each site will have a link to the root site collection in the breadcrumbs, users will be trained to use the breadcrumbs to navigate back to the main site collection. This decision was made because most users of the solution will be confined to a single area.

See Also *To learn more about all of the different navigation options in SharePoint, refer to "Site Navigation Overview (SharePoint Server 2010)" at* technet.microsoft.com/en-us/library/ee695757.aspx.

Solution Content Metadata

Within our solution templates, the project document libraries will contain a collection of metadata that will be required for classifying content. Using this approach helps ensure that content can be easily found across all projects. The metadata being used is outlined in the following table.

Metadata	Column Type	Required	Default Value
Project Number	Lookup	Yes	Will have a default value configured for the current project. This means users will not have to update this value when adding content; instead it will be preconfigured with the current value.
Document Type	Managed Metadata	Yes	No default value.
Description	Multiple Lines of Text	No	No default value.
Keyword	Managed Metadata	No	No default value.

To best manage the metadata, a content type will be created at the root site collection and will be made available to all sites within the site collection. Since each new document library will use the same content type, a custom document library template that is configured with this content type will be created. Site administrators will learn in training that they should create all new document libraries using this custom template.

Solution Branding

Our project management solution will use the default corporate branding. Site administrators will be instructed not to modify the master pages, themes, or logos applied to the project sites.

But What About?

Remember that this chapter is just a sample chapter. Your organization may have different rules, requirements, or governance in place. These design decisions are provided to give you a framework for the sample environment, along with any assumptions that this chapter is including in the design. As you read this section, don't get worried about the small details; focus instead on the end goal of being sure to review your design requirements prior to implementing any solution. Doing this will save you from potentially reworking a solution down the road.

Site Wireframes

Once all the site design decisions have been made, the site wireframes need to be created. These wireframes are a representation of what the final product will look like. Having this representation allows users to validate their requirements and provide us with additional feedback if required. When creating wireframes, you should create a range of layouts for review, based on the needs of the current solution. For this project, we will create two wireframes. Since our requirements are fairly simple in nature, we can use Microsoft Visio to create wireframes for the project management landing page and the project home page.

Project Management Landing Page

The first wireframe shows the landing page used to access all projects. The users of this page are the project committee and project managers. Other users can access this page to view project summary data and to access links to any of the project sites, but it is likely that the users who collaborate on project content directly will use their own favorites and shortcuts to access the project sites.

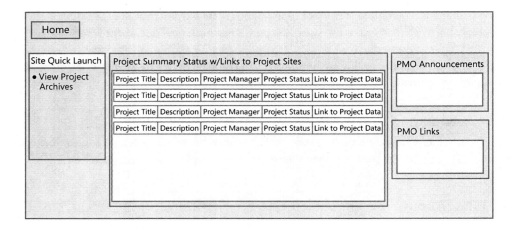

Project Template

The project template is the base template that will be created for each project site. The primary users of this wireframe are project managers and project resources.

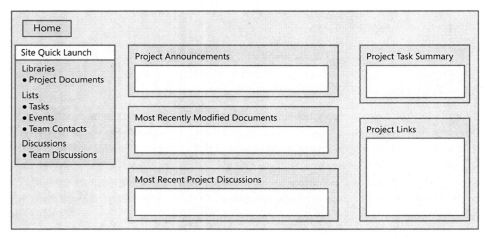

Once the wireframes have been completed, they should be reviewed and approved by the project's business stakeholders. In our chapter example, this would likely include a representation of users from all three user groups. They would review the different wireframes to ensure that our design matched their expectations. The wireframes are used to verify that the solution is proceeding in the right direction to satisfy their needs.

Building the Solution

It is now time to build the solution. The first step is to build the Project site collection and configure the project landing page. Following that, we will create the site template. Site collections are created in SharePoint 2010 Central Administration. If you do not have access to create site collections, you can ask your administrator for a new site collection and then follow the remaining steps in the section.

Assumptions About the Reader

This book is written for users who have experience with SharePoint but are looking to combine what they know into working solutions. It is assumed that you already have a basic understanding of SharePoint and that you are familiar with creating some content. If you find that you need additional information on the topic covered, please refer to the Office Help and How-To site for assistance (*office.microsoft.com/en-us/support/?CTT=97*).

Projects Home Page: Project Central

The first step is to create the site collection.

Create the Site Collection

The following table provides the information needed to create this site collection. If you do not see the values in your environment that are listed in this table, you need to work with your server administrator to adjust the values to something that can be used in your environment.

Field	Value
Web Application	http://www.tailspintoys.com
Title	Project Central
Description	Central location for management, collaboration, and reporting for all Tailspin Toys projects.
URL	.../sites/PCentral
Template Selection	Collaboration: Team Site
Primary Site Collection Owner	Wallace, Anne
Secondary Site Collection Owner	Duncan, Bart
Quota Template	20 GB

Important Now would be a good time to start keeping track of the way you are implementing this solution within your environment. The values in the preceding table are specific for the environment I am using and will need to be updated with values from your environment.

1. On the Central Admin home page, click Create Site Collections to display the Create Site Collection page.

2. Enter the required information, and click OK to provision the site collection. The preceding table provides examples of the values you enter. Remember that they need to be modified to match your specific environment.

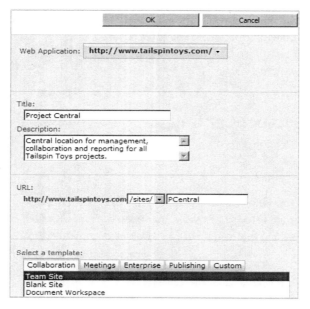

3. Once the site collection has been provisioned, follow the link provided to open it. A screenshot of the provisioned site collection is shown here.

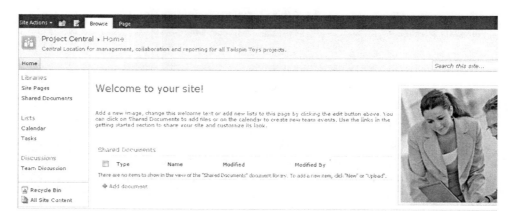

Create Site Lists and Libraries

One of the great things about SharePoint is the ability it gives you to easily create new sites based on a template. The solution in this chapter is based on one of the default SharePoint site templates. Some items that are included in the template aren't needed in our solution, and those items will be deleted. To remove any confusion in the next steps, take a few minutes to delete the unused content. Since new lists and libraries can be created at any time, there is no danger in deleting something now that might need to be added back later.

Before you start, from the Site Actions menu, select the option View All Site Content.

Take a few moments to review the lists that have been created by default. Notice that different descriptions are provided with each list. Some lists included in the default template should not be modified. Most of these can be identified by the wording in the description. For example, the Customized Report folder's description indicates that the library has the templates needed to create custom reports for the site collection, and the Form Templates library's description identifies it as the container of administrator-approved reports. It is clear by these descriptions that other items are dependent on these libraries. The following table identifies the lists and libraries that we will be deleting and provides our reasoning for deleting the items.

List or Library	Justification for Deleting the List
Shared Documents	All project documents will be stored in the individual project subsites. Because it would be very easy for users to accidently add content to this library if it remained, it should be deleted. At a later point, if it is determined that documents are required at this level, a new library can easily be created.
Calendar	We will not be creating a calendar for this solution, so it can be deleted from our site.
Tasks	Project tasks will be stored in the individual project sites, so we can delete this list.
Team discussions	Team discussions will not exist at this level of the project management solution, so we can remove this team discussion board.

For each of the lists or libraries identified in the preceding table, you need to access the List Settings page and delete the list.

1. From the Site Actions menu, open the All Site Content page.

2. Locate the library or list, and then click the title to open the item.

3. On the ribbon, select the Library (or List) Settings icon. This icon is located on the Library or List tab, depending on the specific item being deleted.

4. In the Permissions And Management group, select the option to delete this item. In the warning message that is displayed, click OK.

You will return to the All Site Content page, and from there you can repeat these steps for each item that is detailed in the previous table.

Two of the lists included in the template will be used in the chapter's solution, but first they need to be modified. The following table identifies the two lists that will be updated, as well as the configuration settings that will be changed.

List	Updated Title	Updated Description	Additional Changes
Announcements	PMO Announcements	All general PMO announcements will be added to this list. To be notified of new items, be sure to add an alert for this list.	By default, the announcements list has an announcement welcoming you to the site. You will want to delete this sample announcement from the list.
Links	PMO Links	All general PMO links will be added to this list. To be notified when new items are added, be sure to create an alert.	NA

To update these lists, use the ribbon's option for modifying the list settings. This is the same menu accessed in the steps for deleting the lists that weren't needed. A sample of the list's general settings is shown here for your reference.

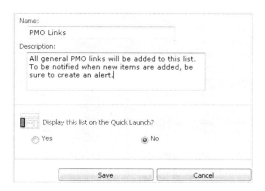

You are now ready to add the custom list and libraries to the site. The following table identifies the specific list that is needed in our solution, as well as the details needed for configuration.

List	Name	Template	Description	Navigation
Project Status Report	PSR	Custom List	This list keeps a record of the current status of all projects. This list will be updated on a regular basis by project managers. To be notified when changes are made, create an alert for the list.	No

You can create the list from the Site Actions menu by selecting the More Options command. This will open the Create dialog box, which allows you to search for and locate the templates that are available for creating lists and libraries. The first list you are creating is a custom list, so you should search on "custom" so that the template is easy to locate.

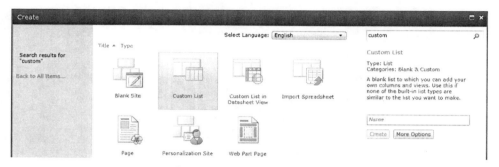

Once you locate the Custom List template, select the template and click the More Options button. When the Create dialog box is displayed, enter the information from the preceding table and then click Create.

Customizing Site Lists and Libraries

In the steps in the previous section, you created your list, but now you need to customize it. This is where you create the columns and views that are required for the solution. You will update the title to a more friendly one, activate versioning, and create several columns and custom views.

1. Use the ribbon to open the List Settings page.

2. Click the Link, Title And Description link in the General Settings section.

3. Change the title from PSR to Project Status Report.

Why Didn't You Use the Friendly Name When Creating the List?

The title of the list was changed after the list was created so that the list could be created with no spaces in the URL. By default, when you create a list, the name given becomes the URL and it cannot be changed once it is created. You should always create short, space-free names and then update them to friendly names once the list is created.

The next configuration change is around versioning. The list in this solution will be using a feature that requires versioning. Use the following steps to configure this list to allow versioning:

1. Use the ribbon to open the List Settings page.

2. Click the Versioning Settings link in the General Settings section.

3. Select the Yes option button to create a version each time you edit the item. Click OK to save your changes.

The next configuration you need to make to the list is to create the list columns. Click on the Library (or List) tab on the ribbon, and then click Create Column. Examples of what you need to select are provided in the following screenshots.

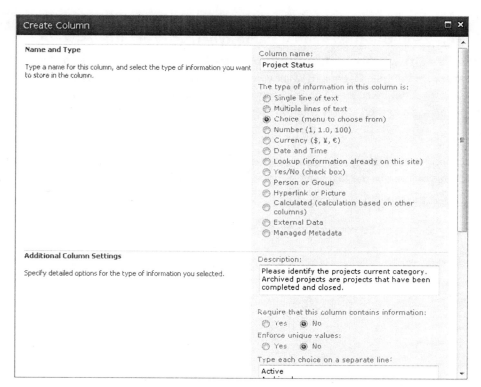

Use the values in the following table to fill in the column information for each of the columns in the list.

Column Name	Field	Value
Description	Type	Multiple Lines of Text
	Description	(Leave blank since the column title is self-descriptive.)
	Specify Type of Text	Plain Text
	Required	Yes
	Append Changes to Existing Text	No
	Add to Default View	Yes
Summary	Type	Multiple Lines of Text
	Description	(Leave blank since the column title is self-descriptive.)
	Specify Type of Text	Enhanced Rich Text
	Required	Yes
	Append Changes to Existing Text	Yes
	Add to Default View	Yes

Column Name	Field	Value
Project Manager	Type	Person or Group
	Description	(Leave blank since the column title is self-descriptive.)
	Required	Yes
	Allow Multiple Selections	No
	Allow Selection Of	People Only
	Choose From	All Users
	Show Field	Name (with presence)
	Add to Default View	Yes
Link To Project Site	Type	Hyperlink or Picture
	Description	The link provided takes you to the project collaboration site for this project. The link has restricted permission. If you feel you should have access and do not, contact the project manager for assistance.
	Required	No
	Format URL As	Hyperlink
	Add to Default View	Yes
Project Status	Type	Choice
	Description	Please identify the project's current category. Archived projects are projects that have been completed and closed.
	Values	Active Archived
	Required	No
	Enforce Unique Values	No
	Default Value	Active
	Add to Default View	Yes
	Column Validation	NA

With the columns created, the final step is the creation of the custom views for the list. These views will allow users to easily find the relevant content within the solution.

1. Click the Library (or List) tab on the ribbon.

2. Select Create Views.

3. Select Standard View as the view format.

4. Use the values in the following table to fill in the view information. You can see an example in the screenshot that follows the table.

View Name	Field	Value
My Projects	View Type	Public
	Columns	Attachments Title Description Status Link to Project Site
	Sort	Title
	Filter	Project Manager = [Me]
	Inline Editing	No
	Tabular View	Yes
	Group By	None
	Totals	None
	Style	Shaded
	Folders	Show Items in Folders
	Item Limit	30, Display in Batches
	Mobile	Enable, 3, Field = Name (linked to document with Edit menu)
Active Projects	View Type	Public
	Columns	Title Description Status Link to Project Site
	Sort	Project
	Filter	Project Phase = Active
	Inline Editing	No
	Tabular View	No
	Group By	None

View Name	Field	Value
Active Projects, *continued*	Totals	None
	Style	Shaded
	Folders	Show Items in Folders
	Item Limit	30, Display in Batches
	Mobile	Enable, 3, Field = Name (linked to document with Edit menu)
Archived Projects	View Type	Public
	Columns	Title Description Status Link to Project Site
	Sort	Project
	Filter	Project Phase = Archived
	Inline Editing	No
	Tabular View	No
	Group By	None
	Totals	None
	Style	Newsletter
	Folders	Show Items in Folders
	Item Limit	30, Display in Batches
	Mobile	Enable, 3, Field = Name (linked to document with Edit menu)

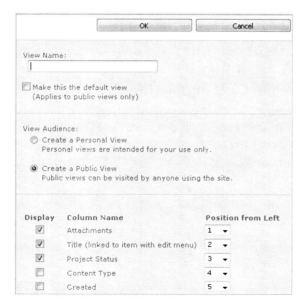

5. Click OK to save the view.

InfoPath Customizations

One way to quickly improve the usability of our sites is to customize our list views using InfoPath Forms services. By using Microsoft InfoPath 2010, you can create different forms that can be easily formatted for usability and ease of use. For this solution you will make several customizations to the Project Status Report list. The main purpose of these customizations is to make it easier for the users of the sites to quickly identify the relevant information from the list.

1. On the List tab, select Customize Form.

    This opens the current list form in InfoPath 2010.

2. Use the options on the InfoPath client ribbon to customize the list.

3. Click the Quick Publish button to save the changes to the SharePoint list. The following screenshot highlights the location of this option on the Quick Access Toolbar.

The following screenshot provides some sample customizations that can be made to the list. For this list, the customizations are related to updating the page design and grouping the different fields into sections.

Need More Help with InfoPath Customizations?

InfoPath is a large topic area, and unfortunately there isn't enough space in this book to go into depth on the different things you can do with the program. For a great resource, check out *Using Microsoft InfoPath 2010 with Microsoft SharePoint 2010 Step by Step* by Darvish Shadravan and Laura Rogers (Microsoft Press, 2011; ISBN 9780735662063).

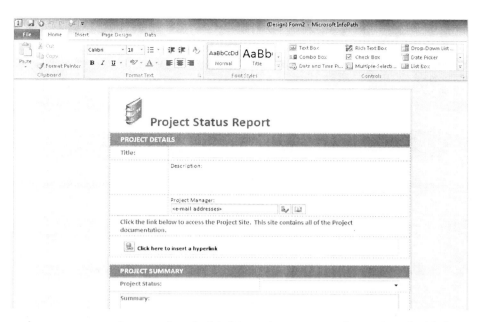

Now, whenever you create a new item in this list or whenever you view an item in this list, you will access the customized list form instead of the standard list form.

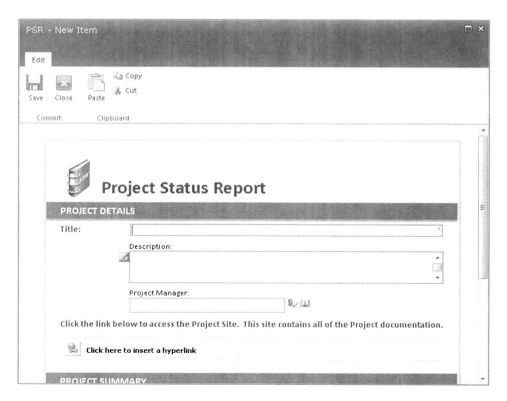

Design the Site

It is now time to add a few design elements to the site. The changes are simple for this project and are limited to updating the theme and adding a site logo.

Since all sites within our site collection need to use the same theme, the Publishing feature will be activated. By activating this feature, you can apply a theme to a site and all of its subsites.

1. Navigate to the Site Settings page.

2. Click the Site Collections Features link in the Site Collection Administration group.

3. Locate the SharePoint Server Publishing Infrastructure feature and click the button to activate it.

4. Navigate to the Site Settings page and click the Site Theme option in the Look And Feel group.

5. Select the theme called Construct. In the Apply Theme options, select the option for applying the theme to the current site and all the subsites, and then select Apply.

6. From the Site Actions menu, select View All Site Content.

7. Open the Site Assets library. Using the List tab, select the option Upload Document. When prompted, enter the path to upload the company logo. We will be referencing this file later to use as our site icon.

8. When the image has been uploaded to the library, right-click the image title and select Copy Shortcut. You will paste this link in a future step.

9. Using the Site Actions menu, navigate to the Site Settings page. Under the Look And Feel section, click the link to customize the title, description, and icon.

10. In the URL field, paste the value you copied in step 8 and then click OK.

11. When you navigate back to the home page, you should see the logo displayed in the top-right corner of the site.

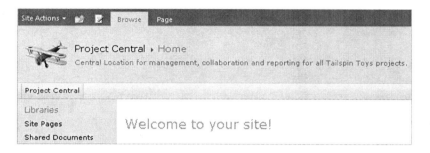

Customize the Quick Launch

To make the site as easy as possible for the user to navigate, we will customize the Quick Launch to remove unused links. Since the majority of the content is displayed on the home page, there is no reason to also display it on the Quick Launch.

1. From the Site Actions menu, navigate to the Site Settings page.

2. In the Look And Feel section, select the Navigation option.

3. In the Navigation Editing And Sorting properties area, remove all links in the Current Navigation group.

4. With the Current Navigation group selected, click Add Link.

5. Use the information in the following table to create the navigation link.

Column Name	Value
Title	View Project Archives
URL	/sites/PCentral/Lists/PSR/archived.aspx

6. Click OK, and navigate back to the Project Central home page. You will see that the link you created is now the only link displayed in the Quick Launch.

Add and Configure Web Parts

Now that our site is almost complete, you are ready to add web parts to the home page. You will add them based on the wireframes created earlier in the process. You will first select the text layout that best matches the wireframe, and then you will add and configure the web parts one by one.

1. From the Site Actions menu, select the Edit Page option.

   The page is already formatted for two columns, so you do not need to update the text layout.

2. Highlight and delete the existing page content.

3. With the cursor in the main section, select the Insert tab on the ribbon. In the Web Parts group, select the Existing List option.

4. When the existing lists are displayed, select the Project Status Report list and then click Add.

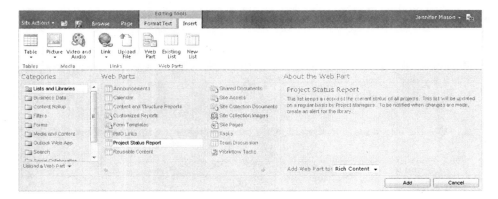

5. Once the web part is displayed on the page, select the option on the Web Part menu to edit the web part.

6. In the web part tool pane, configure the following web part properties:

Property	Value
Selected View	Active
Toolbar Type	None
Title	Project Summary Status w/ Links to Project Sites

7. Move your cursor to the Right web part zone, and repeat the process for adding a web part and configuring web part properties for the following two lists:

- For PMO Announcements:

Property	Value
Selected View	Summary View
Toolbar Type	None
Title	PMO Announcements

- For PMO Links:

Property	Value
Selected View	Summary View
Toolbar Type	None
Title	Project Summary Status w/ Links to Project Sites

8. When all the changes have been made, select the Save & Close option on the Page tab.

Your home page should now look similar to the following:

Configure Site Permissions

You are now ready to add permissions. For this solution you are going to use the groups that were created by default when SharePoint configured the site collection. Based on our requirements, the project managers and project stakeholders will be added to the Members group, and the project resources will be added to the Visitors group.

1. On the Site Actions menu, select the Site Permissions link.

2. On the Users page, you should see all the groups currently associated with the site.

3. Select the Project Central Members group, and when the group is displayed, select the option on the New menu to add new users.

4. Add all project managers and project committee members to this group.

5. Repeat these steps for the Project Central Visitors group, and add the project team members to this group.

Project Site Template

Now you are ready to configure the site you will be using as a template for all future projects. You will start by creating a site called Project Template. Once this site is configured correctly, it will be saved as a template. By doing this, you can use the site as a base template that will provide a consistent look and feel across all project sites.

Create Template Site

You will be creating this site as a subsite in our existing site collection.

1. Select the New Site option on the Site Actions menu.

2. Use the Collaboration filter in the Create dialog box to locate the Team Site template.

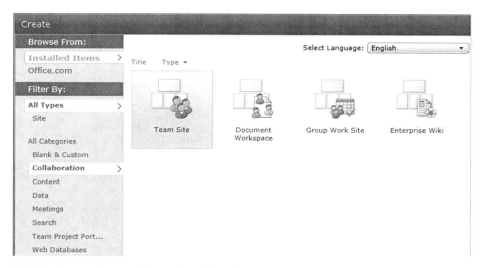

3. With the Team Site template selected, click More Options and use the following data to create the site:

Field	Value
Title	Project Template
Description	(Leave blank)
URL	.../sites/PTemplate
User Permissions	Use Unique Permissions
Use the Top Link Bar from the Parent Site?	No

4. On the permissions page that is displayed, select the option to create a new group for Visitors, Members, and Owners.

Delete Unused Content and Update Existing Lists

In creating the Project Central site, one of the first steps was to delete all the content that was created by default so that it wouldn't be used in our solution. You also need to do this for the Project Template site:

1. From the List Settings page, delete the list referenced in the following table. If you need additional instructions on the steps, you can refer to the steps provided earlier in the chapter.

List or Library	Justification for Deleting List
Shared Documents	Our solution will be using a custom document library template. Since we want to watch for spaces in the URL, we will delete the default library and create our own library.

2. For each of the lists referenced in the following table, update the settings to match the configurations that are described. If you need additional information on the exact steps to follow, refer to the steps described earlier on page 18.

List	Updated Title	Updated Description	Additional Changes
Announcements	Announcements	(Leave the description blank.)	By default, the announcements list has an announcement welcoming you to the site. You will want to delete this sample announcement.
Calendar	Project Calendar	This calendar contains all the important project milestones and meetings.	NA

Create Custom Content Types for Project Documents

In the process of gathering requirements, the need to tag all project documents in a consistent format was identified. Since it is likely that these tagging requirements will change over time, a content type will be used to allow for future modifications. For our solution, you will be creating this content type for the Project Central site collection. This means that all sites created within this site collection will have access to this content type.

1. Use the site breadcrumbs to navigate back to the Project Central site.

2. On the Site Actions menu, click the Site Settings link.

3. In the Galleries section, select Site Content Types.

4. Select the Create option on the Site Contents Type page, and use the following information to create the new content type:

Property	Value
Name	Project Document
Description	Project documents are created during different phases of the project life cycle. Each document remains a permanent part of the project archive.
Select Parent Content Type From	Document Content Types
Parent Content Type	Document
Put This Site Content Type Into:	New Group: Project

5. Click OK. The Content Type Information page will be displayed.

   Now you need to create the custom columns associated with the content type.

6. In the Columns section on the Content Type Information page, click the link Add From New Site Column. Use the following information to create the various columns needed for our content type:

Column Name	Field	Value
Document Type	Type	Managed Metadata
	Group	New Group: Project
	Description	(Leave blank since the column title is self-descriptive.)
	Enforce Unique Values	No
	Allow Multiple Values	No
	Customize Your Term Set	Yes
	Term Set Values	Reports Status Budget Task Deliverable Misc
	Allow Fill-In Choices	No
Description	Type	Multiple Lines of Test
	Group	Existing Group: Project
	Description	(Leave blank since the column title is self-descriptive.)
	Specify Type of Text	Plain Text
	Required	No
	Append Changes to Existing Text	No

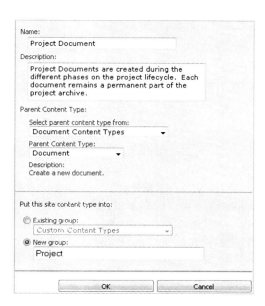

For the final column, you will want to configure this content type to use the SharePoint default keywords field. This is the Enterprise Keywords field that is created and shared for the entire web application. This means that instead of creating this column, you will use the option that allows you to add a column from existing site columns.

7. In the existing site column page, select the Enterprise Keywords column from the Enterprise Keywords group and then click OK.

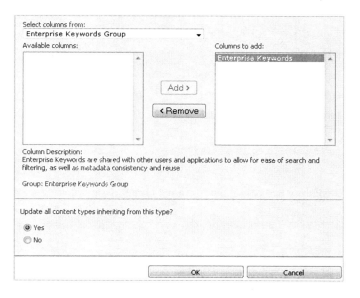

You should now see the columns associated with our content type.

Columns

A column stores information about each document in the document library. Because this document library allows multiple content types, some column settings, such as whether information is required or optional for a column, are now specified by the content type of the document. The following columns are currently available in this document library:

Column (click to edit)	Type	Used in
Description	Multiple lines of text	Project Document
Document Type	Managed Metadata	Project Document
Enterprise Keywords	Managed Metadata	Project Document
Title	Single line of text	Project Document
Created By	Person or Group	
Modified By	Person or Group	
Checked Out To	Person or Group	

Create column
Add from existing site columns
Indexed columns

Because there aren't really any default templates or workflows that need to be associated with the content type, you don't need to make any additional customizations. You can now navigate back to our template site and create the new document library.

Create Custom List Template for Project Documents

Now that our content type has been created, it is time to create our custom document library for our project documents.

1. Open the Project Template site.

2. On the Site Actions menu, select the More Options link.

3. Select the Document Library template, and click More Options. Use the following information to create the library:

Library Name	Field	Value
ProjDocs	Description	(Leave blank since the column title is self-descriptive.)
	Navigation	Quick Launch: Yes
	Version History	Yes
	Document Template	Microsoft Word Document

Once the list has been created, you need to update some of the list settings, including the title and the versioning settings.

1. Update the title of the library to **Project Documents**. (See the examples earlier if you need more instructions.)

2. From the List Settings page, open the versioning settings and verify that the library is configured for major versions and also require that documents be checked out prior to edits. An example of the configuration is shown in the following screenshot.

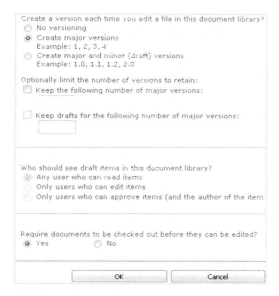

3. Click the Advanced Settings link, and select Yes for the option that allows the list to use custom content types. Click OK to return to the List Settings page.

Once this option has been enabled, an additional section called Content Types will be displayed on the List Settings page.

4. Select the Add From Existing Site Content Types link in this section to add the custom content type to the list.

5. Select the Project Document content type from the Project group and add it to the library. Click OK to return to the List Settings page.

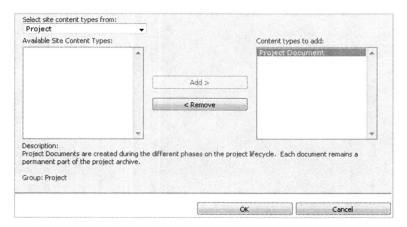

6. In the Content Types section, select the content type called Document, and then delete this content type. This will remove the default content type from the library and allow only project documents to be added.

Since managed metadata is used in our content type, managed metadata navigation can be configured to provide a rich navigation experience. This allows us to have a tree view for filtering the content in the library. In the General Settings area for the list, select the metadata navigation settings.

7. Add the Document Type field to the Selected Hierarchy fields, and click OK.

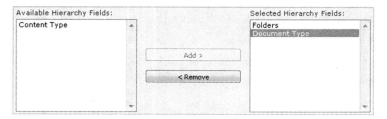

8. Using the breadcrumbs, navigate to the Project Documents library. Notice that you now see some additional navigation elements under the Quick Launch.

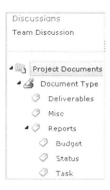

Also notice that when you use the New Document option on the ribbon the Project Document content type is now associated with this library. An example is shown in the following screenshot.

Create Lists

For this template you are able to use most of the lists that are included with the default Team Site template. The only list that needs to be created is a team contacts list.

1. On the Site Actions menu, select the More Options link.

2. Locate the Contacts template, and click More Options to create the contacts list.

3. Use the following information when creating the new list:

Field	Value
Name	Contacts
Description	(Leave blank)
Navigation	Yes

Organize the Home Page Layout

Just as you did with the Project Central site, you need to take some time to customize the home page. You need to delete the default content and add the web parts based on our site mock-ups.

1. On the Project Template site home page, select Edit Page on the Site Actions menu.

2. Remove the default content from the page.

Now you are ready to add the web parts based on the site wireframe. Notice on the wireframe that most of the web parts are showing the most recent items. Because the default views for the web parts are not set to filter by date to show the most recent items, you need to configure the web part to show this information.

1. With your cursor in the main rich content area, select the ribbon option to insert an Existing List web part. Insert the Announcements, Project Documents, and Team Discussions web parts.

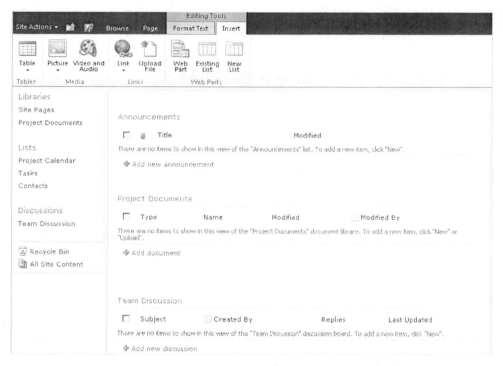

2. Open the web part tool pane for the Announcements web part and update the following settings:

Property	Value
Selected View	Summary View
Toolbar Type	No Toolbar
Title	Announcements

3. When you are finished, click Apply to save the changes.

4. Open the web part tool pane for the Project Documents web part and update the following settings:

Property	Value
Selected View	Edit the Current View (see the following instructions)
Toolbar Type	No Toolbar
Title	Most Recently Modified Project Documents

5. To modify the web part's current view, click the Edit The Current View link directly below the Selected View list in the web part tool pane.

6. When the view is displayed, update the following settings:

Property	Value
Sort	Modified (Show Items in Descending Order)
Tabular View	No
Style	Newsletter
Item Limit	3 (display in batches of specified size)

7. When you are finished, click Apply to save the changes.

8. Open the web part tool pane for the Team Discussions web part and update the following settings:

Property	Value
Selected View	Edit the Current View (see the following instructions)
Toolbar Type	No Toolbar
Title	Most Recent Team Discussion

9. To modify the web part's current view, click the Edit The Current View link directly below the Selected View list in the web part tool pane.

10. When the view is displayed, update the following settings:

Property	Value
Sort	Modified (Show Items in Descending Order)
Tabular View	No
Style	Default
Item Limit	1 (display in batches of specified size)

11. When you are finished, click Apply to save the changes.

Once you have completed the center web parts, you can add the web parts to the right side of the page.

1. With the page in edit mode and your cursor in the right column, insert the web parts for the Links list and for the Tasks list.

2. Open the web part tool pane for the Tasks web part and update the following settings:

Property	Value
Selected View	Active Tasks Edit the Current View (see the following instructions)
Toolbar Type	No Toolbar
Title	Active Tasks

3. To modify the web part's current view, click the Edit The Current View link directly below the Selected View list in the web part tool pane.

4. When the view is displayed, update the following settings:

Property	Value
Columns	Title, Due Date
Sort	Due Date (Show Items in Ascending Order)
Tabular View	No
Style	Newsletter
Item Limit	6 (display in batches of specified size)

5. When you are finished, click Apply to save the changes.

6. Open the web part tool pane for the Links web part and update the following settings:

Property	Value
Selected View	Summary
Toolbar Type	No Toolbar
Title	Links

7. When you are finished, click Apply to save the changes.

8. Once you have completed the web parts configuration, navigate back to the home page.

Your home page should look like the following screenshot.

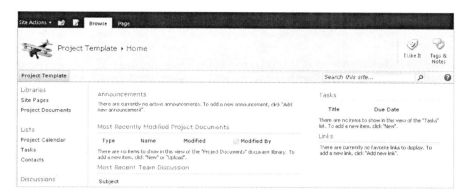

Customize the Active Tasks Web Part

In our solution, it will be important to bring attention to the status of active tasks. Using the browser, all active tasks can be displayed on the home page, but what if more details are required? In this step you are going to add an icon next to the task title that shows the current status of the task. You will be using three different icons, each representing a different task status: an on-time task (green check-mark), a task due today (yellow triangle), and a task that is late (red flag).

> **Note** All images used for this example were downloaded from the Microsoft Office Image repository. This is a great resource for images that you can use within your site. You can access the site at *office.microsoft.com/en-us/images/*.

1. From the home page, on the Site Actions menu, select the option Edit Using SharePoint Designer.

2. When SharePoint Designer opens, navigate to the Site Pages library.

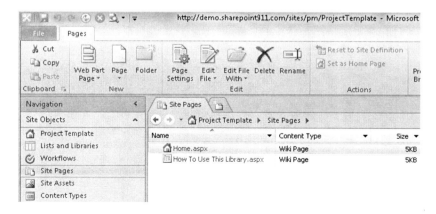

Access to SharePoint Designer

This exercise assumes that you have access to SharePoint Designer. If you do not have Share-Point Designer installed or you are unable to open the site, you need to work with your server administrator to resolve your access issues.

3. Double-click the Home.aspx link to open the properties page. In the Customization section, click Edit File to open the Home.aspx page in edit mode.

4. When the page loads, select the Active Tasks web part.

   Notice that a message is displayed informing you that there is no content in the list.

5. Click the Design tab on the ribbon, and select the option to view sample data. Notice that the view now displays data. An example is shown in the following screenshot. Selecting this option allows you to configure conditional formatting without having to enter test data.

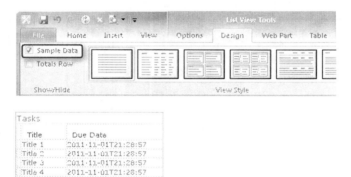

6. Place your cursor in the field that contains Title 1. From the ribbon, insert a new column to the left of the current column.

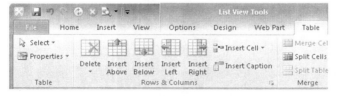

7. In the new column, you will add three different images and then apply conditional formatting to the images so that they are displayed only under certain conditions. The images represent tasks that are on time, tasks that are due today, and tasks that are overdue.

8. With your cursor in the new column, use the ribbon to insert the three images you selected.

For consistency you should be sure that all the images are the same size. Examples of the images used for this chapter are shown in the following screenshot.

9. Select one of the icons, and then use the Options tab under List View Tools to apply conditional formatting to show content. Here is an example:

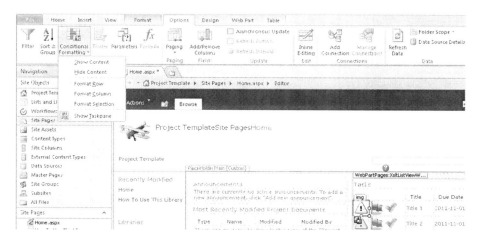

10. In the criteria condition window, enter the conditions that show a specific icon. In our example, you are going to display the check mark whenever the task due date is greater than today.

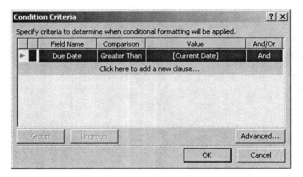

11. Repeat the process for the remaining icons. The flag icon will be displayed whenever the due date is less than today, and the triangle will be displayed whenever the due date is equal to today. By updating this view you are creating a way for users to easily see the current status of open tasks.

12. Once you have formatted the icons, select the Save option on the ribbon.

13. To test, navigate to the home page in the browser. Add several test items with different due dates. Once you have completed testing, be sure to delete the test items.

Update Site Theme

All sites will use the same theme to provide a similar look and feel. The last step we need to take before saving our site as a template is to update the theme to match the theme configured in the Project Central site. Once you configure the setting within the template, you won't have to configure it for each new site.

1. Navigate to the Site Settings page and select the Site Theme option in the Look And Feel section.

2. Click the theme called Construct. In the Apply Theme options, select the option for applying the theme to the current site and all subsites, and then click Apply.

Save Site as Template

You are now ready to save this site as a template so that you can use it as the basis to create new project sites.

1. Access the Site Settings page from the Site Actions menu.

2. In the Site Actions section, select the Save Site As Template link.

3. Use the information provided in the following table to create the site template. Click OK to save your changes.

Field	Value
File Name	TailspinProjects
Template Name	Tailspin Projects
Template Description	This template should be used as the base template for all new Tailspin projects. It includes all the different lists and libraries needed for project management.
Include Content	No

4. Click OK in the Operation Completed Successfully message box.

> ### What Do You Do with the Site Once You Have the Template Built?
>
> In theory, once the site template has been built, the site used to build the template can be deleted. In most cases, however, my preference is to leave the template site and use it when modifications need to be made in the future. Since you can restrict access to the template site, no users will ever see this site.

Creating a New Project

With the completion of our template, you are now ready to start creating project sites. The process for creating sites occurs in two steps. First you create a site by using the template, and then you add an entry to the project list on the Project Central site. Since there is no easy way to automate the creation of sites, we are opting to use this manual approach, which can be managed by the team of project managers. In the future, if this becomes too much of a burden, we can look at further automating the solution with custom code.

Create a New Site

Whenever you need to create a new project site, the first step is to create the subsite. You do this from the Project Central home page.

1. On the Site Actions menu, select the New Site option.

2. Use the Blank & Custom filter to display all the custom templates. Select the Tailspin Projects template, and then click More Options.

3. Use the following settings for configuring the new site:

Field	Value
Title	Project 1
Description	(Leave blank)
URL	P1
User Permissions	Use Unique Permissions
Use the Top Link Bar from the Parent Site?	No

4. On the permissions page that is displayed, select the option to create a new group for Visitors, Members, and Owners.

5. When the new site loads, copy the URL in the address bar.

6. Use the breadcrumbs to return to the Project Central site.

Add a New Entry to the Project Status List

To provide an easy way to access this site, you can add a link to the project from the Project Status list.

1. Click the web part title for the Project Summary w/ Links to Project Sites web part to open the Project Status list.

2. Using the Items tab on the ribbon, select the option to add a new item to the list. Enter the data for your project site, and then click Save on the ribbon.

3. Navigate back to the home page. You should now see your item displayed within the web part on the home page.

Solution in Action

Our solution is now ready to use. At this point you should be adding users to the sites and training them on how to work with the solution. It is likely, however, that before you dive in, you will want to spend some time adding test data and really learning how the sites work. In this section you'll see several screenshots that reference what the site will look like once sample content has been added. (Depending on the content you add, your sites might look a little different.)

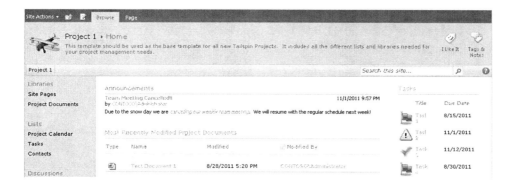

Managing the Solution

Once this solution is configured, a few items need to occur to ensure that the solution is managed properly over time. These are standard items that are required in any software solution. For our solution, project managers are responsible for ensuring that these items are maintained.

Permissions Management

The project managers need to be diligent in managing the permissions to the project sites. As a project team changes or as new members are added to the team, the project manager is responsible for updating the security on the project sites.

Content Management

After a project is completed, the project manager is responsible for indicating that the item is archived in the projects list. Since the project manager is already using this list to provide regular updates to the project stakeholders, this should be an easy task to manage.

Updating the Template

Over time, it is very likely that the template used as the starting point for all projects will need to be updated. The process for updating the template includes accessing the template site, incorporating the changes, and then saving the site as a template. If you use the same name for the template, you can save over the existing template. Any changes you make to the template will be applied to all new project sites.

Other Potential Concerns

The other item that needs to be monitored is the use of storage space for the Project Central solution. Since our solution was created with a quota, the site owner should be notified when the quota limit is being reached. Based on our design, we should not have issues with the quota, but this is an item you will want to pay careful attention to in your environment. It is best practice to keep your SharePoint content databases smaller than 100 GB. If you find that you are reaching that limit, you should take a look at the next section for some different ideas on how you can add structure to your solution.

Reviewing the Platform

In this chapter, we built a project management solution by using the enterprise features in Share-Point. Within our solution, some significant design decisions revolved around the use of a single site collection. Since SharePoint is such a widely used tool, it is likely that you could encounter a scenario in which you need to use a project management solution but don't have access to the enterprise features or do not have the ability to use a single site collection. This section outlines some of the options you have for implementation without using the enterprise features.

Multiple Site Collections Required

If in your scenario you require multiple site collections, you need to take a different approach on several items. These are minor tweaks to the process that require a little additional management, but in the long run they shouldn't require too much overhead.

The following table addresses each of our design decisions and outlines what you would need to adjust if you have a scenario that requires multiple site collections.

Design Decision	Alternative Approach
Single site collection	Since you identified that you need multiple site collections, you now need to determine the best way to structure the solution. Two common approaches I have seen are: ■ A site collection is created as a landing page for accessing all project sites, but each new project is created in a site collection. A list is kept on the project landing page that allows you to easily access the other project site collections. ■ Projects are divided into different categories or types. Each of the different categories is created within a separate site collection. As new projects are created, they are created as subsites in the associated category.
Site-level permissions management	Since you cannot share People groups across site collections, you should be sure that you develop a good naming convention and standard for creating new groups. All site collections should enforce this standard so that it will be easier to manage across site collections.
Solution templates	You will still be able to create different site templates, but you will need to manually deploy these templates to each site collection that needs to use them. You do this by adding templates to the solution gallery of the site collection. Whenever updates are made to the templates, the templates need to be redeployed to each of the site collections. Since this approach requires extra overhead and management, it is highly recommended that you also develop an approach for managing template changes according to a predetermined schedule. You will want to ensure that you have a plan in place that does not require too many updates to the templates, but instead allows for the collection of change requests that are all implemented at one time.

Design Decision	Alternative Approach
Project site modifications	This design decision shouldn't be greatly affected by using multiple site collections.
Solution navigation	Since navigation cannot be shared across site collections, you need a way for users to easily navigate back to the primary landing page for projects. A good way to do this is to use the Portal Site connection feature available for site collections. This allows users to use the site breadcrumbs to navigate back to the primary landing page. This feature would need to be configured as each new site collection is created.
Solution content tagging	Since you want to share a single content type across site collections, you should use a content type hub to publish your content type. Using this approach allows you to manage the content type in one location. Your server administrator should be able to provide information on accessing the content type hub site collection, where the content type will need to be created. The steps for creating the content type in the hub are the same as the steps provided in this chapter; the only difference is the location you use when you create the content type.
Solution branding	This design decision shouldn't be greatly affected by using multiple site collections.

Using SharePoint Foundation

If you are using SharePoint Foundation you will not have access to several of the features that were used in the creation of this solution. Most notable are the features included with the Publishing feature and InfoPath. To address these two areas, you would need to make minor adjustments when you create your solution. For the Publishing feature, you could still manually update the Quick Launch. The interface for configuring the navigation will be different; but the end results will be the same. For customizing list forms in InfoPath, you would be limited to working with the out-of-the-box tools or to customizing the form by using SharePoint Designer.

Using SharePoint Online with Office 365

If you are using SharePoint Online you need to check the feature set that you have purchased. If you have access to the enterprise features within SharePoint, you can use the solution as outlined in the chapter. If you do not have access to these features, you should refer to the following section for information about how to modify the solution to work in an environment using SharePoint Server Standard.

Using SharePoint Server Standard

If you do not have access to the enterprise features in SharePoint, you need to look at an alternative solution for developing the custom list forms in InfoPath. You would likely do this through custom list forms in SharePoint Designer.

Additional Customizations

We covered quite a few customizations in this chapter, but there are still many things that can be added to this solution. Here are some of the additional customizations that you might want to incorporate into your solution.

Additional Customization	Benefits
Customizing list forms in InfoPath	Provides a way to give users a rich, easy-to-use interface for working with list data.
Content types	Creating additional content types based on specific document templates would provide a way to easily promote the use of common templates within the environment.
Creation of a search center	Creating a search center provides a way for users to quickly and easily find common data. The search center would be created at the Project Central site and then customized for the audience. To create a search center, you must have SharePoint Server or SharePoint Enterprise Server.
Process automation	Our current solution requires the manual creation of new sites and inclusion in the Project Status list. This is one area that could be automated to simplify the process. This automation would require a custom code solution because no tools exist out of the box to create new sites.
Workflows	This solution does not include any custom workflows. This is an area that can easily be included with the creation of custom workflows in SharePoint Designer. When building workflows, be sure to follow the process outlined in this chapter so that you fully understand the needs of the users prior to designing the solution.

Summary

In this chapter you have looked at the process of creating a solution for managing projects from start to finish. You started by working through the business problem and then developed a solution using the technology available. Throughout the entire process you worked with the users to gather feedback and obtain approval before any solution was developed. Using this approach helps ensure that the users are comfortable with the solutions presented to them. This chapter should serve as a guideline for you as you work through the process of building a similar solution within your organization. While it is possible for you to build your solution to match the one within this chapter, it is also very likely that you will need to take some additional time to customize the solution to match your specific scenarios.

CHAPTER 2

Building a Training Registration Management System

In this chapter you will work through the process of creating a solution that enables users to register for training courses. The solution displays a list of the courses that are being offered, and then users can register for the courses they want to take. This solution addresses a common scenario across many organizations, and the techniques and methods that you learn in this chapter will apply to many other common scenarios in which user registration is required. The solution in this chapter relies heavily on the enterprise features in SharePoint, particularly those for Microsoft InfoPath Form services.

Identifying the Business Problem

To solve any problem using SharePoint, you must first look at and work through the business problem. When it comes to registering for training classes, every organization will likely take a slightly different approach. In this section we are going to identify the key business problems that this chapter addresses. You will want to review these items and then adjust them as needed to fit your specific scenario. The scenario in this chapter has three major areas of concern, which are discussed in detail in the following sections.

Low Registration

Currently, information about classes is being sent by email whenever a new class is scheduled. In many cases this means that users who do not immediately register for the class forget about it, and this results in poor attendance in many classes.

Trainer Overhead

Class registrations are processed by the Human Resources office and recorded in an attendee's file. Attendance is currently managed by the trainers as a manual process. In many cases a sign-in sheet is passed around the class, and the teacher uses it to compile a report that is sent to the HR office.

Report on Training Data

Once a class has been completed, attendance is recorded manually by HR based on the reports generated by the trainers. If a trainer needs to access attendance reports from a previous course, he is required to contact HR, which has access to the data. Because the reports have to be generated in HR, creating reports often takes several days once they are requested.

Summarizing the Business Problem

We have briefly covered three different problems that impact the success of the training program within the organization:

- Ability to find and register for classes

- Ability to record class attendance

- Ability to generate reports on past classes

Using SharePoint, we can build a solution that addresses each of these issues and provides an automated approach for the given problems. The first step in building the solution is to understand the key issues that we have identified. The next step is to gather information that is required to build the solution.

Gathering Information

With the business problem defined, it is time to turn our attention to gathering the specific requirements. This includes a look at the different users of the solution and their specific needs.

System Users

Our solution is going to be built to address the needs of three different user groups. For us to fully understand the requirements of the solution, each type of user needs to provide information about the specific tasks they need to complete within the system. This information will then be used to design and develop the solution.

All Employees

Employees will access the solution to manage their classes. This includes the following actions:

- Browse available courses

- Filter courses based on specified criteria

- Register for available classes

- Cancel existing class registrations

Human Resources

Human Resources is responsible for creating and managing the courses. Specifically in this scenario, the department is responsible for the following tasks:

* Create new courses

* Update existing course descriptions

* Generate reports for previous courses

* Generate student reports

Trainers

Trainers access the solution to record information about their assigned classes, which includes the following:

* Report class attendance

* Generate reports for previous courses

* Generate student reports

Solution Data

There are two key data elements within this solution: course information and student registrations. For each course, the following data will be provided:

* Course name

* Course ID number

* Course description

* Trainer

* Location

* Cost

* Maximum number of students

* Suggested audience

* Start and end dates

For student registration, the following data will be recorded:

* Student's name

* Course ID number

* Registration status

The registration status will be recorded by the trainers and will identify whether the student attended the course once registered. Any student who doesn't attend a course she registered for will be assigned the status Registered—Did Not Attend, and this status will remain part of the student's history.

Summarizing the Requirements Gathering Process

Now we have completed the process of looking at both the users of the solution and the types of data that will be included in our solution. It is time to start building out the solution's design. Before we do that, however, we should take a few minutes and summarize the process we just completed:

1. We identified business needs for providing a solution that lets users easily access and register for training courses, while also allowing trainers and the Human Resources department to track and report on course attendance.

2. All users were consulted and requirements were gathered based on their specific needs.

3. All data required for the solution was identified based on the needs of the users.

In the next section, we will examine how to translate these requirements into a working design.

Designing the Solution

With requirements gathered, it is now time to look at various decisions that need to be made before we build the solution. It is important to look at these items prior to completing any hands-on development. By following this process, you can be sure that you have completed the due diligence required to fully understand the business needs and requirements. In the following sections, two different areas will be described: design decisions and wireframes. The design decisions section examines the various tools that will be used to create this solution and explains why they were selected. The section about wireframes presents models of the required pages. Ideally, in a real-world scenario, the wireframes would be created and then reviewed and approved by the solution's stakeholders prior to any development being completed.

Design Decisions

In creating this solution, several key points need to be discussed about the tools that will be used and the methods for creating and managing the content. In this section, we will review each of these areas and look at the reason each approach was selected. The solution in this chapter is being built using the SharePoint enterprise features. If you do not have the enterprise features in your environment, refer to "Reviewing the Platform" at the end of the chapter to learn how to adapt the solution to different environments.

Important Your environment and scenario may differ from the one presented in the book. As you follow along in the chapter, be sure to make note of the things that differ and then adjust your solution development accordingly.

InfoPath Forms Services

This chapter's solution uses InfoPath Forms services to manage registration requests. We are using InfoPath Forms services for the following reasons:

- Users need the ability to interact with conditional data when they register for a class. If the class is full or if users have already registered, they need to see a notification message. If registration is still open, they need to see an option to complete registration.

- The registration form needs to be displayed along with class information. This can easily be done using the InfoPath web part on a standard list view page.

Since InfoPath provides features that satisfy both of these requirements, the choice to use it was an easy one.

Custom List to Store Class Information

At first glance, it might appear that we could use a SharePoint calendar to store the class schedule and information. However, a SharePoint calendar template has some special features that, while providing value, keep it from being able to be customized using InfoPath. For our solution, we want to make the list forms as easy to read as possible. This means that we are going to use a custom list to display our classes. Since all lists can have a calendar view, we will simply create a new view for the list and use that to create the training calendar.

Permissions

Our scenario has three primary groups of users. Two of the groups are responsible for managing the content, and one group is responsible for consuming the data. For simplicity, the users will be divided into two groups, and then site permissions will be granted to those groups. This means that all users within a group will have the same permissions.

Data Security!

Depending on your environment and its data security requirements, this solution may not meet your needs. If you have scenarios in which teachers can see only their own classes, you will want to update the solution structure to account for the added security requirements.

Data Thresholds

The solution in this chapter is being built within a single site collection. Two different lists will be created, one to store class information and one to store class registrations. It is assumed that the data loaded into these lists remains within the default list threshold limitations. It is also assumed that over time, previous class registrations can be archived to another location to make room for new registrations. While this chapter will not cover the archive process, it is still important for you to be aware of the constraints prior to building the solution. A SharePoint list can store millions of items, but the performance for viewing the list will be directly proportional to the methods used to query the data. If your particular scenario requires queries that are greater than the default limits, you will want to take the features described in this chapter and use them to create a custom solution that is aligned with your storage needs. This will likely mean spreading the data across multiple lists and libraries instead of the two that we are building within this solution.

Solution Wireframes

Our solution will use several different pages for viewing and managing data. Each of the wireframes will be created, and then they will be approved by the project's stakeholders before any development is completed.

Training Home

This is the home page for the entire solution. From this page users will be able to access the training calendar, and if they have permissions they will also be able to access the training admin pages.

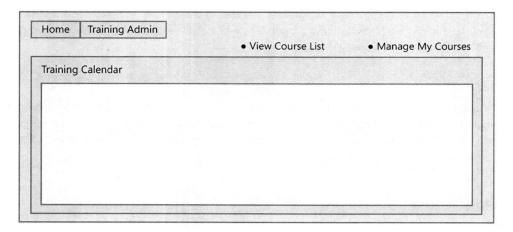

My Registration

On this page users will be able to see a list of all the classes that they are currently registered for.

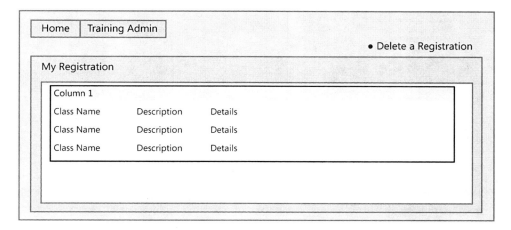

Class Information

This page provides a summary of all class information and allows training administrators to modify existing class information or create new classes.

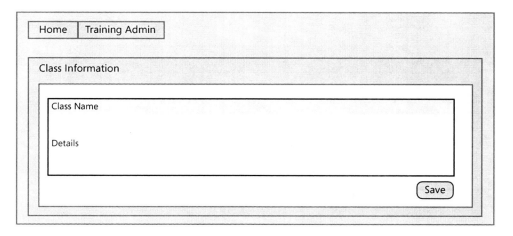

History

From this page, training administrators can generate reports for a selected course or user.

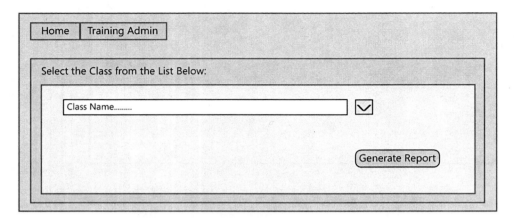

Manage Attendees

Training administrators will use this page to enter students' registration status after the course has been completed.

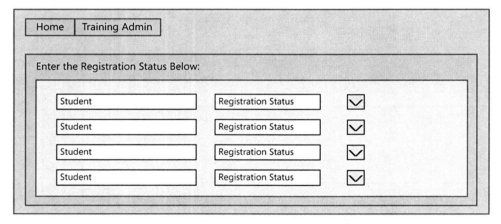

By identifying the site design early in the process, we are able to complete the solution with confidence that it will be aligned with the stakeholders' expectations. We will continue to work with the project team throughout the design phase, so these wireframes do not need to be in their final state for us to move on to building the solution. As long as the project team verifies that we are moving in the right direction, we are good to proceed.

Building the Solution

It is now time to start building our solution. The first step will be to create the training site collection. Once the site is created, we will create the lists and customize them using InfoPath. Finally, we will create and configure the pages.

Building the Training Site

The training site collection will be created from Central Administration and will use the settings listed in the following table. If you don't have access to your farm's Central Administration pages, you should request that a site be created using this information.

Field	Value
Title	Training Registration
Description	Central location for users to view the current training schedule and register for classes.
URL	.../sites/Training
Template Selection	Publishing Portal
Primary Site Collection Owner	Wallace, Anne
Secondary Site Collection Owner	Duncan, Bart
Quota Template	Application_40GB

This solution is using the Publishing Portal because this template is configured with many of the features that are used in a typical corporate intranet solution. By starting with this template, we can take advantage of the publishing features immediately, without having to activate any additional SharePoint features.

1. From the Central Admin home page, in the Application Management group, select Create Site Collections.

2. Enter the information provided in the preceding table, and then click OK to provision the site collection.

3. Once the site has been provisioned, follow the link provided to open the new site collection.

Replace the Site Logo

Notice the logo for Adventure Works in the top bar of the site collection. We will replace the existing logo with our Tailspin Toys logo. Since we want to take advantage of the master page that is provided on the site, we will rename our logo to use the same file name as the existing logo. By doing this we can upload our logo to the style library and not have to update the master page files.

1. Rename the site logo file to **Nd_logo.png**.

2. From the Site Actions menu, select View All Site Content.

3. Click the Style Library link in the Document Libraries section.

4. Navigate to the Images folder.

5. Using the ribbon, upload the logo that you renamed in step 1 to the document library and select the option to check in the logo.

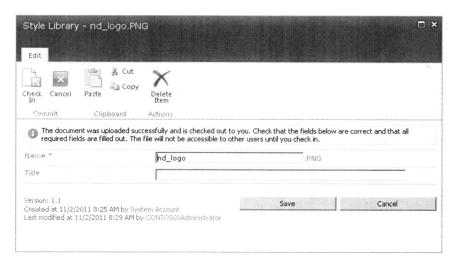

6. Select the check box next to the file, and click Publish on the ribbon.

7. Click OK when prompted for version comments.

8. Use the breadcrumbs to navigate to the home page. Your updated logo will now be displayed.

 Important If you do not publish your image, users who don't have permission to see draft items will not see the image. This might cause the page to load incorrectly or the image to not appear for a particular group of users. Since you have administrator rights to the site, the logo will work correctly for you. This is an example of when testing with a user who has only Read or Contribute permissions will help you quickly identify errors.

Delete the Press Releases Site

By default, when you use the Publishing Portal template, a site called Press Releases is created. Since we do not need this site, we can delete it from our site collection.

1. From the Site Actions menu, select Site Settings.

2. Click the Sites And Workspaces link in the Site Administration section.

3. Click the X next to the Press Releases site to delete the site collection.

4. Click the Delete button, and then click OK when prompted to confirm that you want to delete the site.

Creating a Class List

Now you need to create the two primary lists that will be used for this solution. You start by creating and customizing the Training Course list, including its columns, custom views, and InfoPath form customization. After you complete these steps, you will create the Registration forms library.

Create the List

Use the information provided in the following table to create the Training Course list.

List	Name	Template	Description	Navigation
Training Courses	Courses	Custom List	This list contains all the training courses that are available to employees. When you open a course, you will be able to see all the information pertaining to that course.	No

1. From the Site Actions menu, select More Options.

2. Locate the Custom List template, and click the More Options button.

3. Enter the information from the preceding table, and then click the Create button.

4. When the new list is displayed, select the List Settings option on the ribbon.

5. Click the Title, Description And Navigation link in the General Settings group.

6. Update the title to **Training Courses**, and then click OK.

Create the Columns

For the class list you need to create several custom columns. Each column is described in detail in the following table. The steps you take to create the columns are listed after the table.

Column Name	Field	Value
Description	Type	Multiple Lines of Text
	Description	(Leave blank since the column title is self-descriptive.)
	Specify Type of Text	Rich Text (bold, italics, text alignment, hyperlinks)
	Required	Yes
	Append Changes to Existing Text	No
	Add to Default View	Yes
Instructor	Type	Person or Group
	Description	(Leave blank since the column title is self-descriptive.)
	Required	Yes
	Allow Multiple Selections	No
	Allow Selection Of	People Only
	Choose From	All Users
	Show Field	Name (with presence)
	Add to Default View	Yes
Suggested Audience	Type	Choice
	Description	This class is recommended for the following audiences:
	Values	All Employees Managers New Hires (< 6 months) Team Leaders
	Display Choices Using	Drop-down
	Required	No
	Enforce Unique Values	No
	Default Value	All Employees
	Add to Default View	Yes
	Column Validation	NA

Column Name	Field	Value
Location	Type	Single Line of Text
	Description	(Leave blank since the column title is self-descriptive.)
	Required	Yes
	Append Changes to Existing Text	No
	Add to Default View	Yes
Training Dates	Type	Single Line of Text
	Description	(Leave blank since the column title is self-descriptive.)
	Required	Yes
	Add to Default View	Yes
Start	Type	Date and Time
	Description	(Leave blank since the column title is self-descriptive.)
	Required	Yes
	Date and Time Format	Date & Time
	Default Value	None
	Add to Default View	Yes
End	Type	Date and Time
	Description	(Leave blank since the column title is self-descriptive.)
	Required	Yes
	Date and Time Format	Date & Time
	Default Value	None
	Add to Default View	Yes
Max Number of Students	Type	Number
	Description	(Leave blank since the column title is self-descriptive.)
	Required	Yes
	Number of Decimal Places	0
	Default Value	None
	Add to Default View	Yes

Why Do We Have Multiple Date Columns?

The date columns are needed for the calendar configuration, but additional flexibility for how users can see dates and times is often desirable. By providing a single line of text field, you can offer this extra flexibility without having to worry about how it will affect the display if each person loading a class uses a slightly different format for dates. Some examples of how dates might be entered include Monday at 5pm EST or Tuesday–Thursday 5pm–7pm. Both of these formats are very user-friendly, but neither can be used in the calendar. Since creating new classes is a minimal task, requiring the extra column is not a burdensome task for contributors.

The final column that you will create is a calculated column. You will use this column later as a way to look up the various classes. Since instructors will think of the course in terms of title and start date, this column will be a user-friendly way for them to easily reference the course. This will also allow for the same course title to be used multiple times on different days.

Column Name	Field	Value
Course Reference	Type	Calculated Column
	Description	(Leave blank since the column title is self-descriptive.)
	Formula	=[Title]&" "&TEXT([Start],"mmm-dd-yyyy")
	The Data Type Returned from This Formula Is:	Single Line of Text
	Number of Decimal Places:	NA
	Add to Default View	Yes

To create each of the columns, follow these steps:

1. From the Site Actions menu, select View All Site Content.

2. Click the Training Course link to open the list.

3. Select the List tab on the ribbon.

4. Click Create Column in the Columns section.

Columns		
A column stores information about each item in the list. The following columns are currently available in this list:		
Column (click to edit)	**Type**	**Required**
Title	Single line of text	✔
Created By	Person or Group	
Modified By	Person or Group	
Create column		
Add from existing site columns		
Column ordering		
Indexed columns		

5. Enter the information based on the preceding tables.

6. Repeat the process for all the columns identified.

When you have completed the process, the Columns section on the List Settings page should appear as shown here.

Columns		
A column stores information about each item in the list. The following columns are currently available in this list:		
Column (click to edit)	**Type**	**Required**
Title	Single line of text	✔
Description	Multiple lines of text	✔
Instructor	Person or Group	✔
Suggested Audience	Choice	
Location	Single line of text	✔
Training Dates	Single line of text	✔
Start	Date and Time	
End	Date and Time	✔
Max Number of Students	Number	✔
Course Reference	Calculated (calculation based on other columns)	
Created By	Person or Group	
Modified By	Person or Group	
Create column		
Add from existing site columns		
Column ordering		
Indexed columns		

Create the Views

For this list you need to create two custom views. Each of the views is detailed in the table in this section. Following the specific details, the steps you follow to create the views are provided.

View Name	Field	Value
Course Summary	View Format	Standard View
	Default View	Yes
	View Type	Public
	Columns	Title Description Instructor Suggested Audience Location Training Dates
	Sort	Title
	Filter	Start Is Greater Than [Today]
	Inline Editing	No
	Tabular View	No
	Group By	None
	Totals	None
	Style	Newsletter
	Folders	Show Items in Folders
	Item Limit	30, Display in Batches
	Mobile	Enable, 3, Field = Name (linked to document with Edit menu)
Calendar	View Format	Calendar
	Default View	No
	View Type	Public
	Time Interval	Begin: Start, End: End
	Calendar Columns	Month View Title: Title Week View Title: Title Week View Subheading: Instructor Day View Title: Title Day View Subheading: Instructor
	Default Scope	Month
	Filter	None
	Mobile	Enable, 3

To create each of the views, follow these steps:

1. From the Site Actions menu, select View All Site Content.

2. Click the Training Course link to open the list.

3. Select the List tab on the ribbon.

4. Click Create View in the Views section.

5. Enter the information based on this section's table, repeating the process for both of the views identified.

When you have completed the process, the Views section on the List Settings page should appear as shown here.

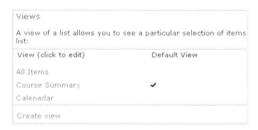

Now would be a good time to add some sample data to the list so that you can test the views. You can do this by using the ribbon to create new items. A sample of the default view with two test items is shown here.

Create the Custom View Form

The final piece of configuration required for this list is to customize the list form using Microsoft InfoPath 2010. The goal of these customizations is to provide a clear, user-friendly interface for viewing course data. Because we have two primary audiences that will use the form, we will create two views for the same form. This allows users to access the data in one format and the training administrators to access the data in a different format.

1. From the Site Actions menu, select View All Site Content.

2. Click the Training Course link to open the list.

3. Select Customize Form on the List tab.

4. Use the features in InfoPath to customize the list as needed.

5. Click the File tab, and then click Form Options on the Info page.

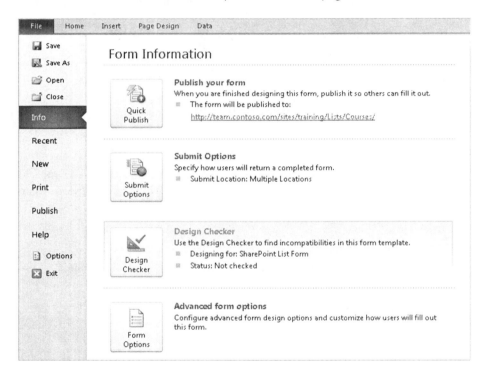

6. In the Web Browser category, clear the check box for Show InfoPath Commands In Ribbon Or Toolbar.

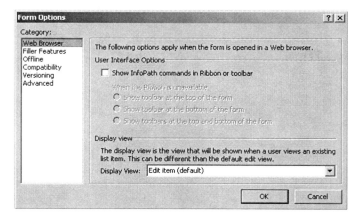

7. Click the Quick Publish button on the Info page to save the changes to the SharePoint list.

A sample of the custom form is shown in the following screenshot. Notice that not all the fields are displayed. Also notice that when the form is viewed, the ribbon is not displayed. We hid the ribbon so that users do not see information on the ribbon for this list. You might wonder how we would edit the list item. This is a great question! In the next section, you will create an additional view for this list that is used when items need to be edited. You will then use the Form web part to add that form to a web part page later in the chapter. Whenever an administrator needs to edit a class, she will access the page you create with the custom form view displayed.

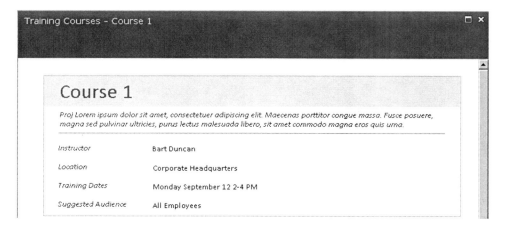

Create the Custom Edit Form

Next we will create another view of the same list within InfoPath. This view is used later in the chapter as a way for training administrators to update course information. Since this view is used to create and edit list items, you should be sure to include all fields. Remember that this view's functionality is more important than its look and feel. Since we have removed the ribbon from this form, you will need to add a custom submit operation for this form that provides users with a button that saves items back to the list.

1. From the Site Actions menu, select View All Site Content.

2. Click the Training Course link to open the list.

3. Select Customize Form on the List tab.

4. Select the Page Design tab in InfoPath.

5. In the Views group, select the New View option.

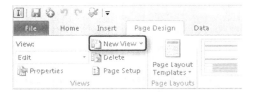

6. When prompted, call the view **Edit**, and then click OK.

7. Use the ribbon to create the layout for the new view.

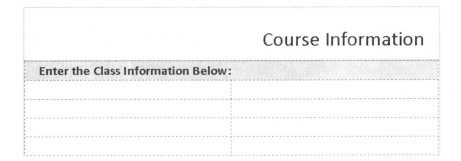

8. Use the Fields toolbar to add items to the new form layout. Note that if you select an item in the Fields toolbar and highlight and drag it over an entire row in the table, the item is formatted with the label in the first column and the value in the second.

Course Information

Enter the Class Information Below:

Title:	
Description:	
Instructor	*<e-mail addresses>*
Location:	
Start:	*End:*
Please also provide a friendly date for the course. (example - Monday Feb 12th 2-4 pm)	
Suggested Audience:	
Max Number of Students:	

9. Using the Home tab, insert a picture button control at the bottom of the form.

10. With the picture button control selected, use the Control Tools Properties tab to configure an image for the button.

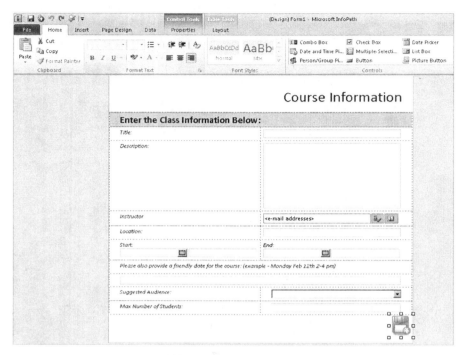

11. With the button selected, use the Control Tools Properties tab to add a rule that runs whenever the button is clicked to submit data.

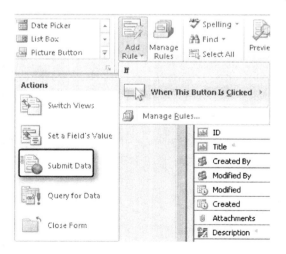

12. In the Rule Details menu, select Main Data Connection and click OK.

13. Click Quick Publish on the Info page to save the changes to the SharePoint list.

> ### Testing the Form
>
> We won't be using this form view until later in the chapter. If you want to take a few minutes to test your most recent changes, the best approach is to edit the form options to display the ribbon, which allows you to access this new view. You would open the list item, select the edit option, and then use the ribbon to switch to the Edit view we just created. Be sure to reset the form to hide the ribbon before moving to the next steps.

Creating the Registration Form Library

During this step in building the solution, you will create the registration form. Whenever this form is accessed, it checks the current registration of the student and the current class limits to determine what message should be displayed to the user. The following list represents the different messages that can be displayed:

- You are successfully registered

- This class is currently full

- Register for this class

- This class occurs in the past

The form will be added as a web part to the class list view that you customized earlier. This way, whenever a user opens a training course, he will see one of these messages based on his current registration status. To gather the data required for this calculation, you need to connect the form to several different data sources. Once those connections are configured, you can use a query operation to access the specific data that you need. For the option that allows for registration, a button will be provided that submits the form to the Registration library.

Create Form

In this step you will create the form library that stores information for a student's registration. You can create this library from InfoPath and then publish the form to the SharePoint library.

1. From the File tab in InfoPath, select the option to create a new SharePoint form library and then click Design Form.

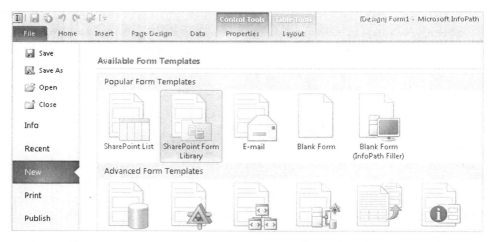

2. Update the formatting of the form so that it has one large section and a header. Update the header to read **Registration Status**.

3. Using the Home tab, add four section controls to the page, one for each of the message items identified at the beginning of this section.

Use Best Practices!

Remember as you build the form to use best practices when it comes to adding items to the InfoPath form. These include changing the properties for each field and giving them a name based on their function. This approach helps you in future steps because you have to use the fields to map to other properties or in calculations.

---

4. Within each section add the message that will be displayed to the user if that section is displayed.

5. Using the Home tab, add a button control to the section that will be displayed if the user can register for the class. A sample of the form is shown in the following screenshot. In later steps, you will apply conditional formatting so that only one of the sections is displayed when the form loads.

Add the CourseID Field

This form will be displayed whenever a course is accessed. When the page loads, the Form web part will need to access the current course ID. This can be accomplished through the use of an input parameter. To configure this parameter, you must add a new field to the list that will store the course ID. Since the field does not need to be displayed on the list, it can be configured from the Fields pane.

1. Open the drop-down menu for myFields in the Fields pane, and select the Add option.

2. Enter the following information when prompted, and then click OK to create the field:

- Name: CourseID

- Type: Field (element)

- Data Type: Text (string)

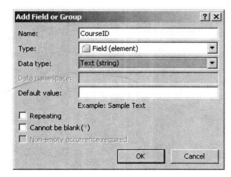

Add the User Field

You will also need to record the current user for registration purposes. This means that you need to create a field to store current user information. Using the same process as in the previous section, create a form field called User:

1. Open the drop-down menu for myFields in the Fields pane, and select the Add option.

2. Enter the following information when prompted, and then click OK to create the field:

   - Name: User

   - Type: Field (element)

   - Data Type: Text (string)

   - Default Value = userName()

Publish the Form to the Training Site

It is now time to publish the form to the server. This is the first of several times that we will publish the form. Because one of the fields you just created is needed in the next step, we are required to publish the form before going any further:

1. On the File tab, select Publish, and then select SharePoint Server.

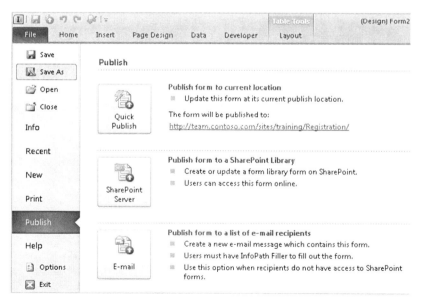

2. Save the form locally when prompted.

3. Enter **http://www.tailspintoys.com/sites/training** in the Publishing Wizard, and then click Next.

4. Select the option to create a new form library, and then click Next.

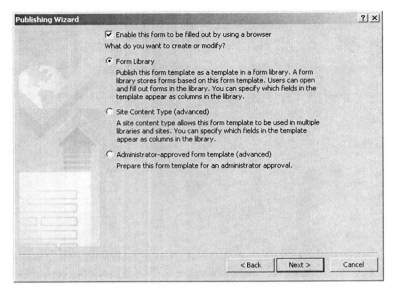

5. Enter the name **Registration**, leave the description blank, and click Next.

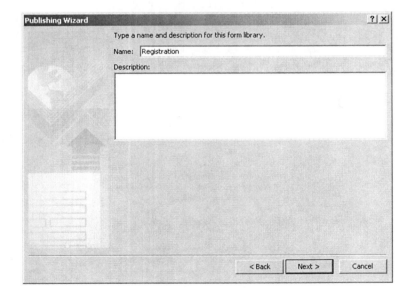

6. Click Add to add the Course ID field as a column in the SharePoint library. When prompted, select the option to create a new column in the library and call the column **Course ID**.

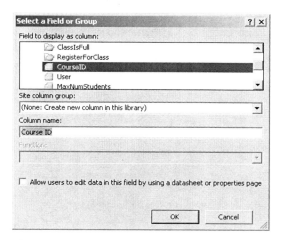

7. Click Add again, this time to add the User column to the SharePoint library. When prompted, select the option to create a new column in the library and call the column **User**.

8. Click Add to add the Course ID column as a parameter for web part connections. Name the parameter **Course ID,** and select Input And Output as the type for the connection.

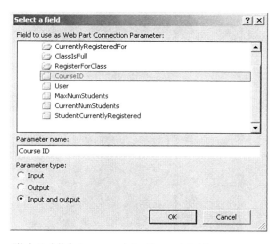

9. Click Publish to complete the publishing process.

Add the Data Connections

Now that the form is designed, you need to add some data connections that are used to provide the logic required to select the correct section to display. To display the correct section, the form needs to know if the user is currently registered for the course, if the course is currently full, or if the course occurs in the past. This means that the form needs to pull information from the class list to determine the maximum class size and from the registration list to determine the current user's registration status.

Several pieces of information are needed to configure the data connection. The following information identifies the properties for the two connections that are created in this step:

Data Connection	Property	Value
Registration	Create a Connection To:	Receive Data
	From Where Do You Want to Receive Your Data?	SharePoint Library or List
	Enter the Location of the SharePoint Site:	http://www.tailspintoys.com/sites/training
	Select a List or Library	Registration
	Select Fields	Title Course_ID (Course ID)
	Sort By	Course_ID, Ascending
	Store a Copy of the Data in the Form Template	No
	Name	Registration
	Automatically Retrieve Data When Form Is Opened	No
Training Courses	Create a Connection To:	Receive Data
	From Where Do You Want to Receive Your Data?	SharePoint Library or List
	Enter the Location of the SharePoint Site:	http://www.tailspintoys.com/sites/training
	Select a List or Library	Training Courses
	Select Fields	Title Start Max_Number_of_Students (Max Number of Students) User
	Sort By	ID, Ascending
	Store a Copy of the Data in the Form Template	No
	Name	Training Courses
	Automatically Retrieve Data When Form Is Opened	No

1. In the Fields pane, click Manage Data Connections.

2. Click Add to create a new data connection.

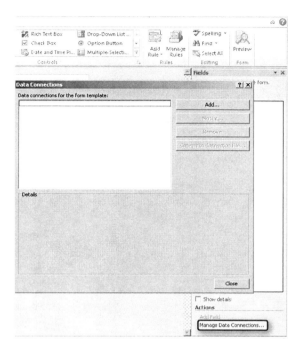

3. Using the information from the preceding table, enter the values required to create the data connections.

4. Once the data connections have been configured, open the drop-down menu for the Fields pane and switch from the Main data connection to the Registration and Training Courses data connections. As you expand the groups you should see the properties that you configured for the data connections.

Why Didn't I Want to Get the Data When the Form Loads?

InfoPath 2010 includes a feature that allows you to set a query value before you query for data. The form can be configured so that when it loads, it sets the value of the current course ID and then just queries the data sets for information that matches that ID. The data is filtered based on the query, and no additional filtering needs to be configured for the data. When you are working with large data sets, this feature is great because it allows for only the required data to be returned.

Configure the Conditional Formatting

The main components of our registration form are the sections that we configured in the previous steps that allow for a message to be passed to the user when she clicks on a training event. In the previous steps you created the four sections, and in this section you will configure the rules that are required to display the appropriate message to the user when she accesses the site. To do this you first need to create some additional fields for the form. Once these fields are created, you will add rules that run when the form parameters are entered. After the fields have been entered, we can apply the rules to the items that control the formatting of the sections.

1. Open the drop-down menu for myFields in the Fields pane and select the Add option.

2. Enter the following information when prompted, and then click OK to create the field:

   - Name: MaxNumStudents
   - Type: Field (element)
   - Data Type: Whole Number (integer)

3. Repeat steps 1 and 2 for the additional fields listed here:

   - Name: CurrentNumStudents
   - Type: Field (element)
   - Data Type: Whole Number (integer)
   - Name: StudentCurrentlyRegistered
   - Type: Field (element)
   - Data Type: Whole Number (integer)

Next you will add the rules that run when the form is loaded. These rules set the correct values for the fields you just created. Remember that this form will be added to the list view page for the training courses and that the Training Courses List web part will pass a parameter to this form, letting the form know the specific class that is being referenced. This means that you want the values to be configured only after the parameter is passed from the web part. The best way to do this is to add rules to the CourseID field so that whenever the item updates, the rules run and the data values are configured. The next table identifies the actions that will be completed when the course ID value changes. Included in the table is a description of the action.

Action	Syntax	Description / Purpose
Set a field's value	Registration (Secondary): Query Field: CourseID = Main: CourseID	Sets the query field so that only the registrations that match the current course ID are returned with the data query.
Set a field's value	Training Courses (Secondary): Query Field: ID = Main: CourseID	Sets the query field so that only the training course information for the current ID is returned with the query.
Query using a data connection	Registration	Queries the data set and adds the values to the form.
Query using a data connection	Training Courses	Queries the data set and adds the values to the form.
Set a field's value	MaxNumStudents=Training Courses (Secondary): Max Number of Students	Sets the maximum number of students to the value returned in the query. Since we filtered the data we were querying for, we don't need to filter the results set. We know the results set contains only the information we need for the current course.

Action	Syntax	Description / Purpose
Set a field's value	CurrentNumStudents=Count(Registration (Secondary) ID)	Counts the number of registrations returned by the query for the current course ID.
Set a field's value	StudentCurrentlyRegistered=Count(Registration (Secondary) ID, where Registration (UserName)=Main(UserName))	Counts the number of registrations where the UserName in the Registration data set is equal to the current user. If the value is greater than zero, we know that the current user is registered for the course.

InfoPath includes a Rule Manager pane that lets you easily create these rules:

1. Select the CourseID field in the Main data source in the Fields pane.

2. Select the Add Rule option on the Layout tab. Select the This Field Changes option, and then select the option to set a field's value.

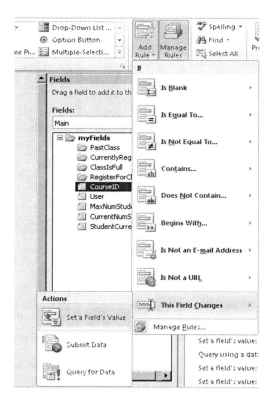

3. Navigate to the field whose value this rule will set:

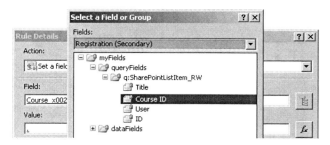

4. Navigate to the value that this field should be set to:

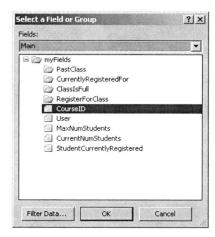

5. Once the rule is created, use the Add menu to add the remaining actions from the preceding table.

6. When you have added the remaining actions, your screen should look like the following:

With these values now configured, we can apply formatting rules to the various sections on the form that will hide the data based on the values captured. For the preceding rule, we used a single rule that generated all the actions we needed. For the next set of rules, each section will need multiple rules. This allows one rule to run and then the next rule until they are all completed. The rules must be separated into multiple rules because they cannot be joined with a logical operator (AND or OR). By separating them, we can run them in a sequence, each with a unique condition. All the rules will be formatting rules and will be used to hide a section if the condition supplied is true. The following information identifies each of the sections and the rules that need to be created for the section:

Section	Rule Name	Condition
PastClass	Hide if Registered	StudentCurrentlyRegistered > 0
	Hide if Future Class	Training Courses (Secondary): Start > now()
CurrentlyRegisteredFor	Hide if Not Registered	StudentCurrentlyRegistered < 1

Section	Rule Name	Condition
ClassIsFull	Hide if Registered	StudentCurrentlyRegistered > 0
	Hide if in Past	Training Courses (Secondary): Start < now()
	Hide if Not Full	MaxNumStudents > CurrentNumStudents
ClassNotFull	Hide if Registered	StudentCurrentlyRegistered > 0
	Hide if Full	CurrentNumStudents ≥ MaxNumStudents
	Hide if in Class	Training Courses (Secondary): Start ≤ now()

1. Select the section.

2. Select the Add Rule option on the Layout tab, and then select the Manage Rules option.

3. On the New menu, select the option to create a formatting rule.

4. Enter the rule name (in the Details For box) and condition from the preceding table and select the Hide This Control option.

5. Repeat this procedure until all the rules are created for each of the sections.

Configure the Register Button

Next we want to define the actions that will run when a user clicks the Register button. In our example, when the button is clicked, the form should be submitted for the current user. To do this, a new data connection needs to be created that allows for the form to be submitted. Because we want to clearly show that something is happening, we will also create a new view for the form. Whenever the button is clicked, the form will be submitted and then the view will switch to let the user know that his registration is being processed.

First we will add the data connection. The following table identifies the properties that will be needed for this configuration.

Data Connection	Field	Value
Registration	Create a Connection To:	Submit Data
	From Where Do You Want to Receive Your Data?	SharePoint Library or List
	Document Library	http://www.tailspintoys.com/sites/training/Registration
	File name	concat(CourseID,"_",User)
	Allow Overwrite	No
	Name	SharePoint Library Submit
	Set as Default Submit	No

1. In the Fields pane, click Manage Data Connections.

2. Click Add to create a new data connection.

3. Using the information from the table, enter the values required for creating the data connection.

Now you need to configure the new view that you want users to see when they click the Register button. The steps are similar to the ones provided earlier in the chapter when you created the Edit view for the course list.

1. Select the Page Design tab in InfoPath.

2. In the Views group, select the New View option.

3. When prompted, name the view **Processing**, and then click OK.

4. Use the ribbon to create the layout and add the text for the new view. A sample is shown here.

The final step in creating this form is to add the rules to the submit button. The process for adding the rules is the same as described for the other rules created in this chapter. The following table outlines the rules that we want to add to the submit button.

Action	Syntax	Description / Purpose
Submit data	Data Connection: SharePoint Library Submit	Uses the data connection created earlier in this chapter to save the items to the registration list.
Switch views	View: Processing	Changes the current view of the form to let users know that a request is being processed.

1. With the button selected, use the Properties tab to add a rule that runs whenever the button is clicked to submit data.

2. On the Rule Details menu, select the SharePoint Library Submit data connection, and then click OK.

3. Using the Add menu, add another action that switches the view to the Processing view.

4. Click Quick Publish on the Quick Access Toolbar to save and publish the changes to the SharePoint form library.

Add the Form Web Part to the List View

It is now time to add the form we just completed to the list view page for the training courses. This includes adding the web part and also adding the connections so that the Form web part can get the ID parameter from the current list item.

1. From the Site Actions menu, select View All Site Content.

2. Click the Training Course link to open the list.

3. Select the Modify Form Web Parts option on the List tab, and then select the (Item) Display Form option.

4. Click Add A Web Part.

5. In the Web Parts list, select InfoPath Form Web Part, and then click Add.

6. Move the web part below the existing web part. You do this by selecting the check box in the web part tool pane and dragging the web part to its new position.

7. Using the Web Part menu, select the Edit Web Part option to open the tool pane.

8. Enter the following information to configure the web part settings for the InfoPath form:

    - List or Library: Registration

    - Content Type: Form

    - Views: View 1 (default)

    - Submit Behavior: Leave Form Open

9. Click OK.

10. For Appearance, change Chrome Type to None.

11. Click OK.

12. Using the Web Part menu, select the Web Part Connections option.

13. Configure a connection to get data from InfoPath Form Web Part [1].

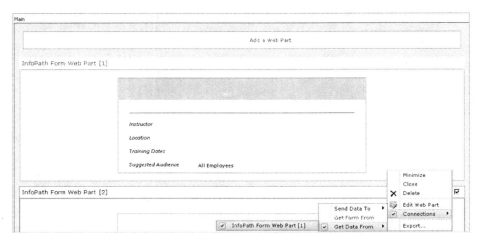

14. In the Connection wizard, set Provider Field Name to ID and Consumer Field Name to Course ID, and then click Finish.

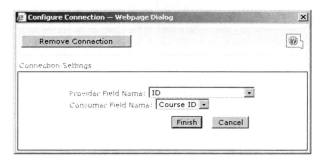

15. Click the Stop Editing option on the Page tab to close the Edit view of the page.

16. Click the Class Title link to open and test the form. The form will be displayed with the option to register.

17. Click the Register For This Class button. Notice that the view is changed.

18. Click the Close button in the form's top-right corner to close the form.

19. Click Class Title to open the same form again. This time you will see a message that you are registered for the course.

Creating and Configuring Pages

The final step in configuring the training site is to create the pages that users work with to navigate the site. Because access to pages will be restricted based on the user groups, users will see only the pages they have access to. Once the pages are created, you will update the navigation to show the pages using the default navigation options in SharePoint.

Create Additional Columns

Before the pages can be created, two additional columns need to be added to the registration list. The first column is a lookup column that refers to the training list. We're adding this column so that the additional training fields can be referenced in the list views. You might wonder why the initial list wasn't configured with the lookup column. We delayed this step because publishing the current course ID directly to the lookup column in InfoPath is not supported. So, to simplify options, the course ID is published from InfoPath to a text column, and then a workflow is generated that sets the lookup ID to the ID that was published. This workflow will be configured in the next section.

The second column we need is a choice field that stores registration status. This is the field that training administrators update after a course is complete.

The table that follows lists the specific characteristics of the columns that need to be created. Refer to the instructions earlier in the chapter if you need additional information about creating columns for the registration list:

Column Name	Field	Value
Course	Type	Lookup
	Description	(Leave blank)
	Required	No
	Enforce Unique Values	No
	Get Information From	Training Courses
	In This Column	ID
	Allow Multiple Values	No
	Allow Unlimited Length	No
	Add a Column to Show Additional Fields	Title Location Training Dates Course Reference
	Enforce Relationship Behavior	No
Registration Status	Type	Choice
	Description	(Leave blank)
	Values	Registered Attended Did Not Attend
	Display Choices Using	Drop-down
	Required	No
	Enforce Unique Values	No
	Default Value	Registered
	Add to Default View	Yes
	Column Validation	NA

Create the Custom Workflow

In this section you will create the workflow that adds the ID value to the lookup column that you just created.

1. From the registration list, click the option on the ribbon to create a SharePoint Designer workflow.

2. When prompted in SharePoint Designer, enter the name **Set Course ID** for the workflow, and then click OK.

3. Use the ribbon to insert an impersonation step and delete the default step 1.

4. Place your cursor inside the impersonation step and add an action to set a field in the current item.

5. Click the Field link, and select Course from the drop-down list. Click the Value link, and then select the fx control. Select Data Source: Current Item and Field From Source: Course ID, and then click OK.

6. Click Add Course ID in the breadcrumbs to open the workflow settings page.

7. Under Start Options, click the option Start The Workflow Automatically When An Item Is Created.

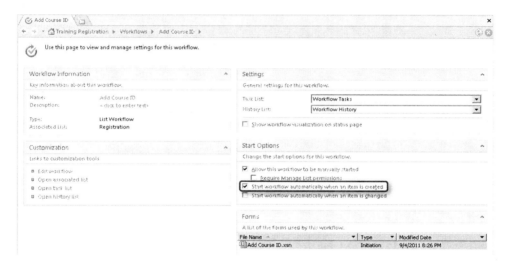

8. Click Publish on the ribbon to publish the workflow to the site.

Why Did I Need an Impersonation Step?

In the section "Managing the Solution" on page 117, I discuss the permission structure for this solution. Part of that structure includes a feature that allows users to create items but does not allow them to edit items. Because of this permission setting, the workflow needs to run under the identity of a workflow author and not the identity of the current user. When an impersonation step is used, the workflow uses the permissions of the workflow author for all the actions included in that step. This functionality allows users to start workflows that can complete actions that they wouldn't be able to complete in the browser. This ensures that users are making only approved changes because all changes are configured via the workflow.

My Registrations Page

The next step is to create the remaining pages for the site. Detailed instructions are provided for the first page. For the remaining pages, only the information needed for configuration is provided.

Page Property	Value
Title	My Registrations
Description	Leave Blank
URL Name	My-Registrations
Page Layout	(Welcome Page) Blank Web Part Page

1. Click Site Settings, and then click View All Site Content.

2. Open the Pages library from the ribbon, and select the option to create a new page.

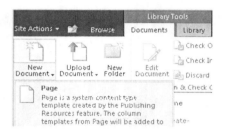

3. Enter the information for the page from the preceding table, and then click Create.

4. Click the title of the new page in the library view to open the page.

5. Click Site Actions, Edit Page to open the page in edit mode.

6. Click the Add Web Part link, and then add the Registration List web part to the page.

7. Open the Registration List web part tool pane, and edit the web part using the properties from the following table.

Property	Value
Selected View	Edit the Current View (see the following instructions)
Toolbar Type	No Toolbar
Title	My Registrations

8. To modify the web part's current view, select the Edit The Current View link directly below the Selected View list in the web part tool pane.

9. When the view is displayed, update the following settings:

Property	Value
Fields	Course: Title Course: Location Course: Training Dates
Sort	Course: Title
Filter	Created By Is Equal To [Me]
Tabular View	No
Style	Newsletter

10. Click Save & Close to stop editing the page. In a future step you will publish the pages and approve them. For now, you will see a status message on the top of the page.

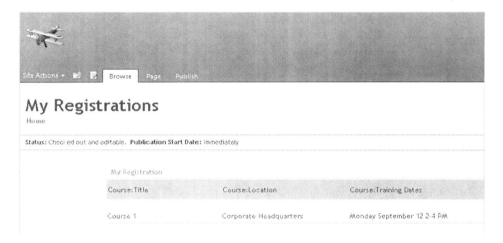

Manage the Registration Page

For the manage registration page, we need to add two web parts: the SharePoint List Filter web part and the Registration List web part. The filter web part is used by training administrators to select the course that they need to update registration for.

Page Property	Value
Title	Manage Registration
Description	(Leave blank)
URL Name	Manage-Registration
Page Layout	(Welcome Page) Blank Web Part Page

1. Create the page (refer to previous steps if necessary).

2. Add the Registration List web part to the page (refer to previous steps if necessary).

3. Open the Registration List web part tool pane and edit the web part using the following properties:

Property	Value
Selected View	Edit the Current View (see the following instructions)
Toolbar Type	No Toolbar
Title	Registrations

4. To modify the web part's current view, select Edit The Current View directly below the Selected View list in the web part tool pane.

5. When the view is displayed, update the following settings:

Property	Value
Fields	Created By Registration Status
Sort	Created By
Tabular View	No
Inline Editing	Yes
Style	Default

6. Click Apply.

7. Add the SharePoint List Filter web part to the page and make the following web part settings:

Property	Value
Filter Name	Select a Training Course
List	/sites/training/Registration
View	All Documents
Value Field	Course: Course Reference
Title	Select a Training Course

8. Click OK.

9. For the filter web part, select the web part connection Send Filter Value To, Registration.

10. Select Course: Course Reference for the consumer field, and then click Finish.

11. Click Save & Close to stop editing the page. In a future step you will publish the pages and approve them. For now you will see a status message at the top of the page.

Create the New Course Page

This page allows training administrators to create a new course.

Page Property	Value
Title	Create a New Course
Description	(Leave blank)
URL Name	New-Course
Page Layout	(Welcome Page) Blank Web Part Page

1. Create the page (refer to previous steps if necessary).

2. Add the InfoPath Form web part to the page (refer to previous steps if necessary).

3. Open the InfoPath Form web part tool pane and edit the web part using the following properties:

Property	Value
List or Library	Training Courses
Content Type	Item
Views	Edit
Submit Behavior	Open a New Form
Appearance: Chrome Type	None

4. Click Save & Close to stop editing the page. In a future step you will publish the pages and approve them. For now, you will see a status message at the top of the page.

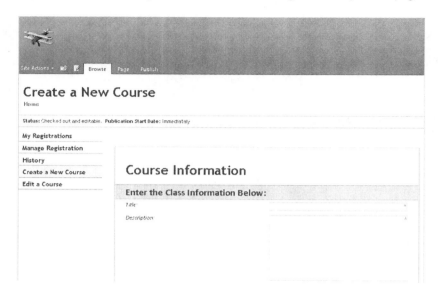

Edit a Course

This page allows training administrators to edit the information for an existing course.

Page Property	Value
Title	Edit a Course
Description	Leave blank
URL Name	Edit-Course
Page Layout	(Welcome Page) Blank Web Part Page

1. Create the page and add the InfoPath Form web part to the page (refer to previous steps if necessary) in the Right web part zone.

2. Add the Training Courses List web part in the Header web part zone.

3. Open the Training Courses List web part tool pane and edit the web part using the following properties:

Property	Value
Selected View	Edit the Current View (see the following instructions)
Toolbar Type	No Toolbar
Title	Training Courses

4. To modify the web part's current view, select Edit The Current View directly below the Selected View list in the web part tool pane.

5. When the view is displayed, update the following settings:

Property	Value
Fields	Course Reference
Sort	Start (Descending)
Tabular View	No
Inline Editing	No
Style	Shaded
Item Limit	Display in Groups of 30.

6. Open the InfoPath Form web part tool pane and edit the web part using the following properties:

Property	Value
List or Library	Training Courses
Content Type	Item
Views	Edit
Appearance: Chrome	None

7. For the InfoPath Form web part, select the web part connection Get Form From, Training Courses.

8. Click Save & Close to stop editing the page. In a future step you will publish the pages and approve them. For now you will see a status message at the top of the page.

History Page

The History page allows training administrators to quickly filter the registration list to see the registrations for a selected class or to see all the classes completed by a specific user.

Page Property	Value
Title	History
Description	(Leave blank)
URL Name	History
Page Layout	(Welcome Page) Blank Web Part Page

1. Create the page (refer to previous steps if necessary).

2. Add the Registration List web part to the page (refer to previous steps if necessary).

3. Open the Registration List web part tool pane and edit the web part using the following properties:

Property	Value
Selected View	Edit the Current View (see the following instructions)
Toolbar Type	No Toolbar
Title	Registrations

4. To modify the web part's current view, select Edit The Current View directly below the Selected View list in the web part tool pane.

5. When the view is displayed, update the following settings:

Property	Value
Fields	Created By Course: Reference Course: Location Course: Title Course: Training Dates Registration Status
Sort	Created By
Tabular View	No
Inline Editing	No
Style	Shaded

6. Click Apply.

7. Add the SharePoint List Filter web part to the page and make the following web part settings:

Property	Value
Filter Name	Select a Training Course
List	/sites/training/Registration
View	All Documents
Value Field	Course: Course Reference
Title	Select a Training Course

8. Click OK.

9. For the filter web part, select the web part connection Send Filter Value To, Registration.

10. Select Course: Course Reference for the consumer field, and then click Finish.

11. Click Save & Close to stop editing the page. In a future step you will publish the pages and approve them. For now you will see a status message at the top of the page.

Home Page

You now need to configure the Training Calendar web part (starting with the Training Courses List web part) to the home page.

1. Navigate to the home page and click Edit Page on the Site Actions menu.

2. Delete the default web parts and content from the page.

3. Change the page layout to the Blank Web Part Page layout.

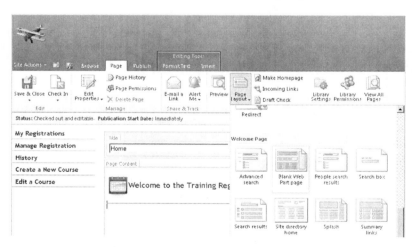

4. Add a welcome message and an image to the page.

5. Add the Training Courses List web part to the page (refer to previous steps if necessary).

6. Open the Training Courses List web part tool pane and edit the web part using the following properties:

Property	Value
Selected View	Calendar
Toolbar Type	No Toolbar
Title	Training Courses

7. Click Save & Close to stop editing the page. In a future step you will publish the pages and approve them. For now you will see a status message at the top of the page.

Check In, Publish, and Approve Pages

The last step in building the pages is to make sure that the final version of each of the pages you have been editing is checked in and approved. The quickest way to do this is to go directly to the Pages library and use the ribbon to publish and then approve each of the items in the library.

1. In the Pages library, select an item that needs to be approved and then click the Check In option on the ribbon.

2. When prompted, select Publish A Major Version And Start The Workflow.

3. Select the item check box, and then click the Approve/Reject button on the ribbon.

4. Select Approved, and then click OK. Click OK in the message about the workflow.

5. Repeat these steps for all pages in the library.

Site Navigation

The final configuration step you need to take in this chapter is to update the site navigation settings so that the pages are displayed in the Current Navigation area. Because these pages will be security-trimmed, they will be visible only if the user has access to the page. This means that only users in the training administrator's group will have access to the admin pages.

1. From the Site Actions menu, open the Site Settings page.

2. Click the Navigation link in the Look And Feel Section.

3. Set the Current Navigation area to display pages, and then click OK.

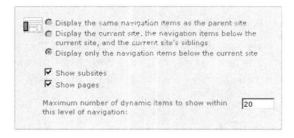

4. Navigate back to the home page to review the changes.

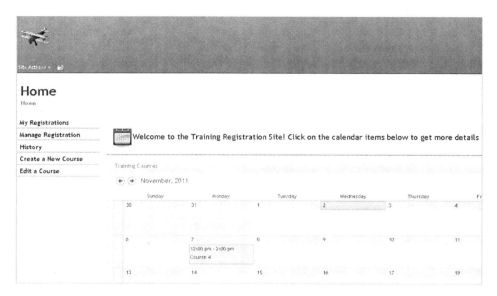

Managing the Solution

Managing this solution should be a relatively low-key task that doesn't require much interaction. By design, the solution is a simple one that requires configuration in the beginning but only minimum maintenance after it is being used.

Permissions Management

When the site is created, you need to create a custom role that allows only for the addition of items and two SharePoint groups. One group is created for the training administrators and one for trainees. The training administrators need to be given Member access to the site so that they can view and update content. Trainees need to be given only Add permissions so that they register for classes.

See Also *If you need additional information about creating custom roles and groups, refer to the TechNet article "Configure Custom Permissions (SharePoint Server 2010)" at* technet.microsoft.com/en-us/library/cc263239.aspx.

Delete Requirements

You may have noticed that if we give trainees only the ability to add items, they will not be able to cancel their registration for any classes. This is by design. This chapter does not go into detail about the delete process because it is assumed that each organization will have a custom process that should be followed. To create this process you will likely need to incorporate a custom workflow that ensures that the proper steps are followed.

Registration Notification

Another area that this solution does not cover in detail is the process of sending an email notification when a user registers for a class. I've assumed that readers will incorporate this feature into the solution based on their organization's specific needs. This feature can easily be incorporated by using a SharePoint Designer workflow that kicks off whenever a new item is added to the registration list.

Reviewing the Platform

The solution in this chapter was built using the features available in SharePoint Enterprise. In the remainder of this section, the different options that are available with the various other SharePoint licenses will be highlighted.

If You Are Using SharePoint Foundation

If you are using SharePoint Foundation you will be very limited when trying to implement this solution. Since you do not have access to InfoPath Forms services, much of the solution covered in this chapter will not work in your environment. The best approach for building a similar solution would be to use the same concepts but to replace the customized forms with out-of-the-box forms. This will likely have a huge impact on usability, and it is recommended that you develop a prototype that you review with your users for acceptance prior to implementation.

If You Are Using SharePoint Online with Office 365

If you are using SharePoint Online with Office 365 with access to the enterprise features, you can implement this solution as it is defined in the chapter. If you do not have access to the enterprise features, you should refer to the notes for SharePoint Foundation.

If You Are Using SharePoint Server Standard

If you are using the Standard version of SharePoint, you will have the same issues as those with SharePoint Foundation. Again, you are limited because this solution relies heavily on the features available within InfoPath Forms services, which are not part of the Standard version.

Additional Customizations

In this chapter, you learned about quite a few customizations; however, there are many other additions you can make to this solution. This information is provided so that you can see some of the additional customizations that you might want to incorporate into your solution.

Additional Customization	Benefits
Notification workflow	Notifies users via email that they have been successfully registered for the course.
Training request approval process	Would allow for an approval workflow to run before a student can register for a class.
Delete workflow	Would allow users to delete any of their current registrations.
Additional pages and views	Additional pages and views can be created that allow for users to easily sort and find relevant courses. An example would be a page that allows users to filter classes based on the suggested audience.

Summary

In this chapter you learned one way to build a training registration solution using InfoPath Forms services and SharePoint Enterprise server. This solution gives you a way to present class data to a collection of users and have them register for the classes based on their needs. This chapter should serve as a guideline for you to implement a similar solution within your environment. As you implement the solution, keep in mind that you can easily tweak and modify it to fit any specific needs within your organization.

CHAPTER 3

Building a Basic FAQ Solution

In this chapter you will step through the process of creating a basic FAQ solution using SharePoint Foundation. This solution relies on some of the basic features in SharePoint Foundation and will highlight simple things you can implement in any solution to provide large benefits. As in the other chapters in this book, you will start by reviewing the business problems. You'll then work through the solution's design and then build the solution.

Identifying the Business Problems

The business need driving an FAQ solution is common across many organizations and is focused on helping users quickly find the data they need when they run into questions. For example, the following sections describe the key areas of concern at Tailspin Toys.

Self-Service Access to Common Information

One of the biggest issues within the organization is that users do not know where to go to find information. Since the data within the organization is so spread out, it is a common occurrence for users to quickly become frustrated and open support tickets if their initial search fails. Since the help desk is available only during certain working hours, this means that users who work after hours or who try to gain assistance during peak working hours have a hard time getting access to the data that they need. If a self-service solution was implemented, users would be able to access the needed data and submit help desk claims only when they were unable to find the data they need in the solution.

Extended Time on Help Desk Calls

Currently, with the added volume of calls to the help desk, the completion time for many calls is above the average threshold. Users have become frustrated because it is difficult to reach the help desk. Help desk staff have become frustrated because they are answering the same questions over and over again and are not able to focus more on the higher-level support requests.

Support for Third-Party Vendors and Partners

Recently, Tailspin Toys has entered into a partnership with several small toy companies. The partnership requires that the companies work together on several initiatives. As a result, many internal users are now responsible for working with internal systems as well as with several external environments. In addition, a collection of vendors now has access to Tailspin Toys' systems. The vendors have requested that each environment include a standardized FAQ solution that allows users to quickly search for and find information that they need.

Summarizing the Business Problems

We have briefly covered three problems that are affecting the working environment for three user groups:

- Difficulty finding answers to common questions

- Lack of quick turnaround on support questions

- Desire to use similar systems in multiple environments

Looking at these issues, it is clear that a centralized FAQ solution would address them and would improve the general working environment for employees, vendors, and the help desk support team.

Gathering Information

With the business problems defined, we can turn our attention to gathering specific requirements. This step includes looking at the unique users of the solution as well as their specific needs.

System Users

Our solution is going to be built to focus on the needs of two groups of users. For us to fully understand the requirements of the solution, the users in each group need to provide information about the specific items that they would like to include in the solution. This information will then be used to design and develop the solution.

All Employees and Partners

Employees and partners who will be accessing the solution have requested that the following items be included:

- Quick access to the newest FAQs

- Ability to search existing FAQs

- Ability for the site to guide them in the process of looking for content

- Ability to request more information if they are unable to find what they need on the site

Help Desk Support Team

The help desk support team would like to have the following items included in the solution's site:

- Easy interface for adding new FAQs and content

- Ability to provide additional information for users, such as links to other content or other documentation

- Ability for users to submit requests for additional information directly on the site

Solution Data

The key piece of information within these requirements is the FAQ. For our solution, an FAQ includes the following data elements:

- Question

- Answer

- Additional links

- Additional documentation

- Keywords

- FAQ category

Summarizing the Requirements Gathering Process

Now we have completed the process of looking at the requirements of the users of the solution and the types of data that it will include. It is time to start defining the solution's design. Before we do that, however, we should take a few minutes and summarize the process we just completed:

- Users are requesting a central location that they can access to find the answers to common questions. This would reduce their need to contact the help desk directly and allow them anytime access to the data.

- The help desk is requesting that its staff have a central FAQ location that will reduce the number of calls made to the help desk about simple questions, allowing staff members to spend more time working on more complicated requests.

- Since users have started working closely with partners, they have expressed a need for a common solution so that they can use the same approach for finding content no matter what environment they are working in.

It is now time to start designing the FAQ solution. In the next section of the chapter we are going to look at how we can translate these requirements into a working design.

Designing the Solution

With the requirements gathered, it is time to look at the decisions that need to be made before the solution is built. It is important to look at these items prior to completing any hands-on development. By following this process you can be sure that you have completed the due diligence required to fully understand the business needs and requirements.

In the sections that follow, two areas will be described: design decisions and wireframes. The design decisions section reviews the tools that we will use to create this solution as well as details about why they were selected. The section about wireframes presents the required pages. Ideally, in a real-world scenario, the wireframes would be created and then reviewed and approved by the solution's stakeholders prior to any development being completed.

Design Decisions

Several key points need to be discussed about the tools that will be used to create this solution and the methods for creating and managing the content the solution will manage. The following sections review each of these areas and provide information about the reasons that the selections were made.

SharePoint Foundation

The most important design decision for this chapter's solution is the use of SharePoint Foundation as our platform. Because there are different organizations working together that want to build a common solution, this is the best tool to use to ensure that requirements are satisfied.

Single Site Collection

Based on the projected amount of data, it was determined that our solution will remain within the quota (40 gigabytes) that has been set up for our environment. This means that a single site collection can be created for our FAQ solution, which will provide users a single location to search for and access common FAQs.

Permissions

All users will be given read access to all FAQs. Each FAQ will be assigned to a category and some keywords will be defined for the FAQs so that the questions remain easy to find and access. Help desk staff will be given permission to add FAQs, but any new FAQs will require approval before they are visible to the organization. This will allow for help desk managers to review and approve content before it goes live to a large audience.

Solution Wireframes

Three pages will be created for the solution in this chapter. Each of the wireframes will be created and then approved by the project's stakeholders before any development is completed.

FAQ Home Page

This page will be the landing page for the FAQ solution. It will highlight the newest FAQs as well as provide links to the remaining FAQs based on category.

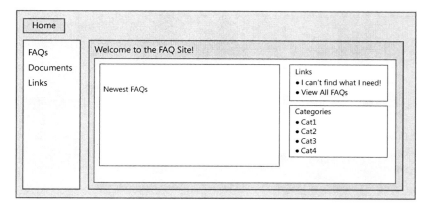

FAQ Item View Page

This page will be displayed when a user clicks on an FAQ item. It will be a customized version of the default list view and will be created simply by adding related web parts to the existing page.

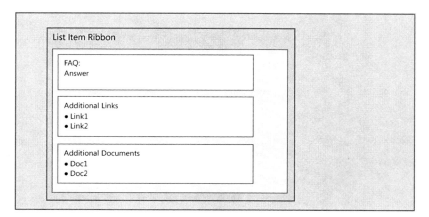

Help Me Page

This page will provide users with additional information about using the site. When users go to this page, they will be able to access additional help and guidance for finding the content they are looking for. If they are still unable to find the content, they will be able to quickly contact the help desk.

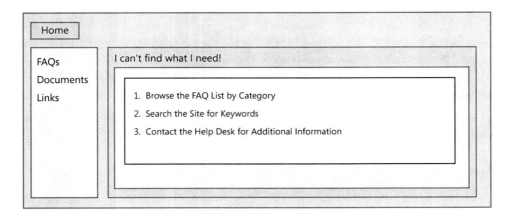

Building the Solution

It is now time to start building the simple FAQ solution. You start by building the FAQ site and then you configure the various lists. Once the lists are configured, the final step is to add the web parts to the different pages in our solution.

Build the FAQ Site

The FAQ site collection will be created from Central Administration using the settings in the following table. If you don't have access to the farm's Central Administration pages, you should request that a site be created using this information.

Field	Value
Web Application	http://www.tailspintoys.com
Title	FAQ
Description	Central repository for common Tailspin FAQs.
URL	.../sites/FAQ
Template Selection	Team Site
Primary Site Collection Owner	Wallace, Anne
Secondary Site Collection Owner	Duncan, Bart
Quota Template	Application_40GB

1. On the Central Admin home page, click Create Site Collections in the Application Management group.

2. Enter the information provided in the preceding table, and click OK to provision the site collection.

3. Once the site is provisioned, follow the link that's provided to open the new site collection.

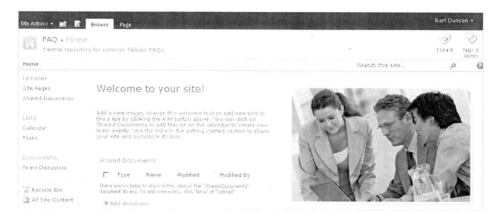

Change the Site Logo and Theme

To provide some additional styling to the site, you can update the site logo and theme. You first need to upload the logo to the site and copy the URL. You then specify that URL on the Title, Description And Logo page:

1. On the Site Actions menu, click the Site Settings link.

2. Click Title, Description, And Icon in the Look And Feel section.

3. Enter the URL for the company logo in the URL text box, and then click OK.

4. Click Site Theme in the Look And Feel section.

5. Select the Construct theme, and then click Apply.

The home page will now reflect your corporate logo and the updated theme.

Create and Customize the FAQs List

Use the information provided in the following procedure to create the FAQs list:

1. From the Site Actions menu, select the More Options link.

2. Locate the Custom List template, and then click the More Options button.

3. Enter the information from the following table, and then click the Create button.

List	Name	Template	Description	Navigation
FAQs	FAQs	Custom List	(Leave blank)	No

Create the Columns

For this list you need to create several custom columns. Each column is described in detail in the following table. After the table, the steps you need to complete to create each of the columns are provided.

Column Name	Field	Value
Answer	Type	Multiple Lines of Text
	Description	(Leave blank since the column title is self-descriptive.)
	Specify Type of Text	Rich text (bold, italics, text alignment, hyperlinks)
	Required	Yes
	Append Changes to Existing Text	No
	Add to Default View	Yes
Keywords	Type	Multiple Lines of Text
	Description	(Leave blank since the column title is self-descriptive.)
	Specify Type of Text	Rich text (bold, italics, text alignment, hyperlinks)
	Required	No
	Append Changes to Existing Text	No
	Add to Default View	Yes

Column Name	Field	Value
Category	Type	Choice
	Description	This FAQ falls into the following category:
	Values	General FAQ Human Resources Benefits IT / Technology
	Display Choices Using	Drop-down
	Required	Yes
	Enforce Unique Values	No
	Default Value	General
	Add to Default View	Yes
	Column Validation	NA

To create each of the columns, follow these steps:

1. From the Site Actions menu, select the View All Site Content link.

2. Click the FAQs link to open the list.

3. Under List Tools on the ribbon, click the List tab.

4. Click Create Column.

5. Enter the information for each column from the preceding table.

When you have completed the process, the Columns section on the List Settings page should appear like the following screenshot.

Customize the Shared Documents List

One of the solution requirements is that each FAQ item can be linked to additional documents. To manage this, we can use the default document library that is created as part of the Team Site template. The only item you need to configure is a column that provides a way to associate the documents with an FAQ. You can do this is by adding a lookup column using the information from the following table.

Field	Value
Column Name	FAQ
Type	Lookup
Description	(Leave blank)
Required	No
Enforce Unique Values	No
Get Information From	FAQs
In This Column	Title (linked to item)
Allow Multiple Values	No
Allow Unlimited Length	No
Add a Column to Show Additional Fields	None
Enforce Relationship Behavior	Yes, Restrict Delete

When you have created the column, your List Settings page should look like the following. If you need step-by-step instructions for creating the column, see the preceding section.

Customize the Links List

In addition to referencing documents related to various FAQs, the solution includes a requirement to be able to easily link to additional content. You can do this by adding a column to the Links list that is included in the Team Site template. The information for the column is found in the following table.

Field	Property
Column Name	FAQ
Type	Lookup
Description	(Leave blank)
Required	No
Enforce Unique Values	No
Get Information From	FAQ
In This Column	Title (linked to Item)
Allow Multiple Values	No
Allow Unlimited Length	No
Add a Column to Show Additional Fields	None
Enforce Relationship Behavior	Yes, Restrict Delete

When you have created this column, your List Settings page should look like the following. If you need step-by-step instructions for creating the column, see "Create the Columns" earlier in this chapter.

Columns

A column stores information about each item in the list. The following columns are currently available in this list:

Column (click to edit)	Type	Required
URL	Hyperlink or Picture	✓
Notes	Multiple lines of text	
FAQ	Lookup	
Created By	Person or Group	
Modified By	Person or Group	

Create and Customize the Help Me List

Within the solution, users need to send a request for additional information to the help desk. We will implement this requirement by creating a list to manage these requests. The list will be secured so that users see only the items they have submitted. Once a user submits an item, a workflow will start that notifies the help desk that a new request has been submitted. The help desk will review the request and provide a response to the user who submitted it.

The first step in configuring this feature is to create the list. After the list is in place, you will use SharePoint Designer to build the workflow.

1. From the Site Actions menu, select the More Options link.

2. Locate the Custom List template, and then click the More Options button.

3. Enter the information from the following table, and then click the Create button.

List	Name	Template	Description	Navigation
Help Me	HelpMe	Custom List	(Leave blank)	No

4. When the list is displayed, select the List Settings option on the ribbon.

5. Click the Title, Description And Navigation link in the General Settings group.

6. Update the title to **Help Me**, and then click OK.

7. Click the Advanced Settings option in the General Settings group.

8. Change the settings under Item-Level Permissions so that users can read only items that were created by the current user and create and edit only items that were created by the current user. Click OK.

Create the Columns

For the Help Me list, you need to create several custom columns. Each column is described in detail in the following table.

Column Name	Field	Value
Question	Type	Multiple Lines of Text
	Description	(Leave blank since the column title is self-descriptive.)
	Specify Type of Text	Rich text (bold, italics, text alignment, hyperlinks)
	Required	Yes
	Append Changes to Existing Text	No
	Add to Default View	Yes
Response	Type	Multiple Lines of Text
	Description	(Leave blank since the column title is self-descriptive.)
	Specify Type of Text	Rich text (bold, italics, text alignment, hyperlinks)
	Required	Yes
	Append Changes to Existing Text	No
	Add to Default View	Yes

Column Name	Field	Value
FAQ	Type	Lookup
	Description	If this question prompted the creation of a new FAQ, the link will be provided here.
	Required	No
	Enforce Unique Values	No
	Get Information From	FAQs
	In This Column	Title (linked to item)
	Allow Multiple Values	No
	Allow Unlimited Length	No
	Add a Column to Show Additional Fields	None
	Enforce Relationship Behavior	Yes, Restrict Delete

When you have created the columns, your List Settings page should look like the following screenshot. If you need step-by-step instructions for creating the columns, see the section "Create the Columns" on page 128.

Columns

A column stores information about each item in the list. The following columns are currently available in this list:

Column (click to edit)	Type	Required
Title	Single line of text	✓
Question	Multiple lines of text	
Response	Multiple lines of text	
FAQ	Lookup	
Created By	Person or Group	
Modified By	Person or Group	

Configure the Workflow

You will use SharePoint Designer to configure the workflow for this list. Later in the chapter you will create a page with a custom view for users to add items to this list, but for now we will focus on the workflow. The workflow will follow the process shown here:

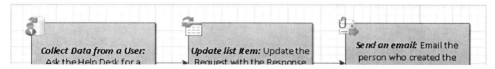

The purpose of the workflow is to notify the help desk that a new request has been submitted. The workflow notifies all users in the Help Desk Site Owners group. Everyone in that group will receive an email message that a new task has been assigned. Once a help desk staff member accesses the task, she can respond and complete the task, or she can claim the task to let others in the group know she is working on a response. After the task is completed, the item's creator will receive an email with the response and the workflow will be marked as completed.

Here are the steps to create the workflow using SharePoint Designer:

1. Navigate to the List tab for the Help Me list that you created earlier.

2. Click the Workflow Settings option, and select Create A Workflow In SharePoint Designer.

3. When prompted, enter the following information, and then click OK:

   - Title: New Request

   - Description: Workflow that is started when a user requests additional information from the FAQ site.

4. In the Workflow editor, use the ribbon to add the following actions within Step 1:

   - Collect Data From This User (Output To Variable: Collect)

   - Update Item In This list

   - Email These Users

5. Click *data* in the first action, and enter the following information when prompted:

   - Next

   - Name: Please Provide Feedback

   - Description: A new FAQ has been submitted to the site. Please review and provide a response.

   - Next

6. Click the Add button on the screen, and then enter the following information:

   - Field Name: Help Desk Response

   - Description: Please provide a response to the user. This response will be sent to the user via email after you complete the task.

   - Information Type: Multiple Lines of Text

   - Next

7. Click the check box next to all options and click Finish.

8. Click *this user* in the first action. When prompted, add the FAQs Owners group to the Selected Users column, and then click OK.

9. Click *this list* in the next action.

10. Select Current Item from the list drop-down menu.

11. Click Add.

12. Select Response from the Set This field list.

13. Click the *fx* button to open the lookup configuration.

14. Enter the following values, and then click OK:

   - Data Source: Association: Task List

   - Field From Source: Help Desk Response

   - Field: ID

   - Value: Variable: Collect

15. Click OK.

16. Click *these users* in the final action. When prompted, complete the email as follows:

- To: Current Item: Created By

- Subject: A New Response Is Available!

- Body: Recently you submitted the following question to the help desk on the FAQ site: [%Current Item: Question%]. The Help Desk has reviewed your request and has provided the following response: [%Current Item: Response%].

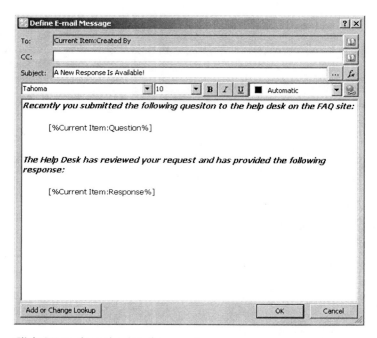

17. Click OK to close the email generator.

The final workflow should look like the screenshot shown here:

18. Click New Request in the breadcrumbs to open the workflow details page.

19. Select the check box for Start The Workflow Automatically When An Item Is Created in the Start Options.

20. Click the Publish option on the ribbon to publish the workflow to the Help Me list.

Workflow in Action

To test the workflow, create an item in the list. Assuming you are a member of the Owners group for the site, you will receive an email that informs you that a new task has been created.

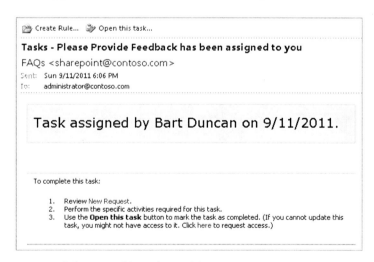

1. Click Open This Task to add your response.

2. Close the task.

Notice that you are presented with an option to claim the task, as shown in the following screenshot. If you select this option, the task is assigned to you individually instead of to the group. Others in the group who open the task will see that you have claimed the task.

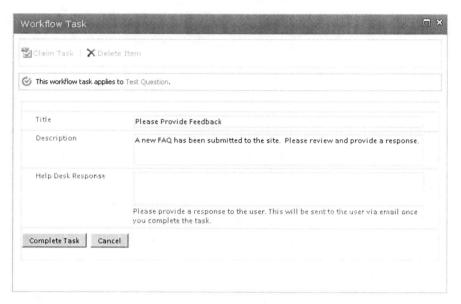

Once the task has been completed, the person who created the item will receive an email such as this:

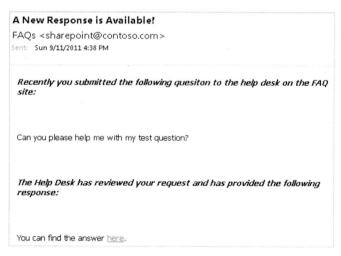

This workflow provides a simple way for users to communicate directly with the help desk if they have any questions that they can't find an answer to within the site. Since the help desk can respond via email, the workflow helps reduce the amount of time help desk staff spend on the phone answering requests.

Design the List View Page

Now that the content has been built, it is time to work on a few of the design elements. The first area that you will focus on is the customizations that need to be made to the FAQs list view. Because you are using SharePoint Foundation you do not have access to InfoPath Forms services to customize the list form. However, this doesn't mean that you can't make any customizations. In this section you will make several simple web part customizations that help improve the value of the FAQs list view.

1. From the Site Actions menu, select the View All Site Content link.

2. Click the FAQs link to open the list.

3. Click the Customize Form item on the Lists tab, and then select the Default Display Form option.

4. Click Add A Web Part.

5. From the Web Parts menu, add the FAQs web part to the page twice.

6. Select Modify Web Part for the FAQs [3] web part, and then edit the web part by changing the following properties:

Property	Value
Selected View	Edit the Current View (see the followinginstructions)
Toolbar Type	No Toolbar
Chrome	None

7. To modify the web part's current view, select Edit The Current View directly below the Selected View list in the web part tool pane.

8. When the view is displayed, update the following settings:

Property	Value
Fields	Title
Style	Newsletter

9. Select Modify Web Part for the FAQs [2] web part, and then edit the web part by changing the following properties:

Property	Value
Selected View	Edit the Current View (see the following instructions)
Toolbar Type	No Toolbar
Chrome	None

10. To modify the web part's current view, select Edit The Current View directly below the Selected View list in the web part tool pane.

11. When the view is displayed, update the following settings:

Property	Value
Fields	Answer Keywords Category
Style	Newsletter

12. Select Modify Web Part for the FAQs [1] web part, and then edit the web part by changing the following property:

Property	Value
Layout	Hidden

13. In the FAQs [1] Web Part menu, click Web Part Connections, and then add a connection to FAQs [2] that passes the ID filter by using the Get Filters Value From connection type.

14. Configure the connection so that the Provider and Consumer fields are both set to ID, and then click Finish.

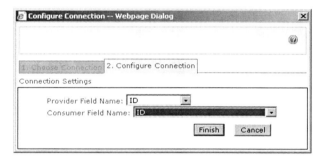

15. Add the same connection from FAQs [1] to FAQs [3].

16. On the ribbon's Page Tools Insert tab, open the Related List drop-down menu.

17. Click the Links option to add the related web part to the page.

18. Select the Modify Web Part menu for Related Items in the Links web part, and then edit the web part by changing the following properties:

Property	Value
Selected View	Summary View
Toolbar Type	No Toolbar
Title	Related Links (if applicable)

19. On the Related List menu, click the Shared Documents option to add the related web part to the page.

20. Select the Modify Web Part menu for Related Items in the Shared Documents web part, and then edit the web part by changing the following properties:

Property	Value
Selected View	Edit the Current View (see the following instructions)
Toolbar Type	No Toolbar
Title	Related Documents (if applicable)

21. To modify the web part's current view, select Edit The Current View directly below the Selected View list in the web part tool pane.

22. When the view is displayed, update the following settings:

Property	Value
Fields	Type (icon linked to document) Name (linked to document)
Style	Newsletter

You have just replaced the default list view with a collection of custom-configured web parts. The results can be seen in the following screenshot. This is a quick way to make the default views more user-friendly by using only browser-based changes.

Design the Help Me Page

One of the requirements for this solution is that users be able to quickly submit a request to the help desk when they can't find what they are looking for. To address this requirement, you created the Help Me list and its associated workflow. In this step you will create a page that users can access when they want to submit a request. After you create the page, you'll use SharePoint Designer to add a custom form web part.

1. From the Site Actions menu, select the More Options link.

2. Locate the Web Part Page template, and then click the Create button.

3. For the page's name, type **HelpMe.aspx**.

4. For the layout template, select Header, Footer, 3 columns.

5. For the document library, enter **Site Assets**.

6. Click Create.

7. In the Header section, click Add A Web Part.

8. Locate the Content Editor web part, and then click Add.

9. For the web part that was just added, click the Modify Web Part menu.

10. Choose Chrome as the property.

11. Select None as the value for Chrome.

12. Click in the web part to add new content.

13. Type a welcome message for the Help Me page.

14. Click Stop Editing.

    Your page should look similar to the screenshot shown here:

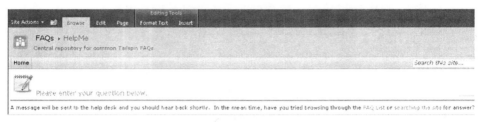

15. From the Site Actions menu, select the Edit In SharePoint Designer link.

16. Use the Navigation menu to open the HelpMe.aspx page in the Site Assets library.

17. Click Edit File on the summary page.

18. With your cursor in the left column, use the ribbon to insert a custom list form.

19. Select the Help Me list, the Item content type, and the Edit Item form, and then click OK.

20. Customize the form so that only the Question field is displayed with the Save and Cancel buttons at the bottom of the page.

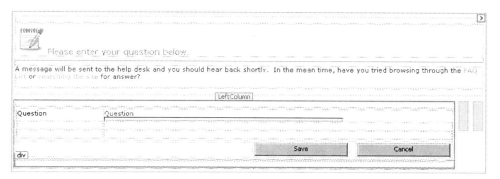

21. Click the Save icon in the top menu bar.

22. Use the Navigation menu to open the Help Me list.

23. Click Edit List Columns.

24. Click Title.

25. For the default value, enter **New Request**.

26. Click OK.

If you navigate back to the HelpMe.aspx page in the browser, your screen should look similar to the screenshot shown here.

Design the Home Page

The final step in configuring this solution is to create the home page. You'll do this simply by adding a few web parts and links to the home page.

1. Navigate to the site's home page.

2. Click Edit Page on the Site Actions menu.

3. Delete the existing default content.

4. Add a welcome message to the right column.

5. Add the FAQs List web part below the welcome message.

6. Select the Modify Web Part menu for the FAQs web part, and then edit the web part by changing the following properties:

Property	Value
Selected View	Edit the Current View (see the following instructions)
Toolbar Type	No Toolbar
Title	Most Recently Created FAQs

7. To modify the web part's current view, select Edit The Current View directly below the Selected View list in the web part tool pane.

8. When the view is displayed, update the following settings:

Property	Value
Fields	Title Answer Category Keywords
Sort	Modified
Style	Newsletter
Item Limit	5, Display items in batches of specified size.

9. Using the ribbon and the rich text tools, add links to the right column for the following items:

Link	URL
View All FAQs	http://tailspintoys.com/sites/FAQ/Lists/FAQs/AllItems.aspx
I can't find what I need!	http:// tailspintoys.com /sites/FAQ/Lists/FAQs/AllItems.aspx

10. From the Site Actions menu, select the View All Site Content link.

11. Open each of the list settings pages and check that only the Shared Documents, Links, and FAQs lists are displayed on the Quick Launch.

12. From the Site Actions menu, select the Site Settings link.

13. Click Quick Launch in the Look And Feel section.

14. Click the edit icon next to the Discussions heading.

15. Delete the heading.

The final home page should look similar to the following screenshot. Depending on how you created your links, you may have some differences. The links in the screenshot were created by inserting an image and a hyperlink followed by the horizontal rule markup style. This provides a styled look and feel to the site. Examples of the different styles and items used are provided for your reference in the following screenshots.

Managing the Solution

The management of this solution will be performed by the help desk team. This team will be responsible for creating FAQs and replying to the new requests that are generated by users.

Permissions for this site are relatively simple to manage. The help desk staff responsible for the site will be added to the Owners group. All other staff will be given read access to the site and contributor access to the Help Me list. This means that you need to break inheritance on the Help Me list.

Reviewing the Platform

The solution in this chapter was built using the features in SharePoint Foundation. The remainder of this section discusses the design options available to you if you are using a different version of SharePoint.

If You Are Using SharePoint Online with Office 365

This solution can be implemented as is on the Office 365 platform. If you are running a version of Office 365 that includes the enterprise features, refer to the following sections to learn about additional customizations you can make to this solution.

If You Are Using SharePoint Server Standard

If you are using the SharePoint Server Standard version, you can implement this solution as is. Because you have access to additional search capabilities, you could consider adding those to your solution by providing search links for your users that help them quickly locate various FAQs.

If You Are Using SharePoint Server Enterprise

If you have access to the features in SharePoint Server Enterprise, you can use InfoPath Forms services to further customize and style the list views. In this chapter, we added multiple web parts to the pages to accomplish some simple styling. With the enterprise features, you can easily do the same by using InfoPath Forms services.

Additional Customizations

This chapter covers several customizations, but there are still many features that can be added to this solution. The following information is provided so that you can consider some of the additional customizations you might want to incorporate into your solution.

Additional Customization	Benefits
Filtered views	One way to help users quickly find content is to provide filtered views of the FAQs. You could create views based on the assigned categories and then provide links to those views on the home page of the site.
Specific FAQ sites	This solution creates a single repository of FAQs, but this might not meet your needs if you have a large list of categories or subcategories. An alternative solution or customization would be to create this solution as is and then save it as a template. Then, for each area or application that you need to generate FAQs for, you could create a site based on this template. This would give you a collection of FAQ sites for users to search through.

Summary

In this chapter we looked at ways to implement a simple FAQ solution using SharePoint Foundation. This solution provides a one-stop experience for users who are looking for answers to common questions they have about the organization. This chapter should serve as a guideline for you as you address similar needs within your organization. While it is likely that you will need to customize this solution to meet your specific needs, the basic solution should get you started in addressing the needs of a centralized internal FAQ solution.

CHAPTER 4

Building a Learning Center

In this chapter you will work through the process of building a learning center. This learning center aggregates not only available classes but also class-associated documents, discussion lists, and links to external resources. This chapter's solution will be built using the functionality in SharePoint Foundation, but the chapter also describes some of the enterprise features that may be available in your environment. In addition, you will explore implementing SharePoint Designer workflows to automate certain tasks.

Identifying the Business Problems

Before you begin designing any solution, you must understand the business problems being faced. After you identify and understand the problems, you can architect a solution to properly address them. The following sections review some of the business problems associated with the sample learning center.

Linking Content to Classes

There is a saying that "context is king." When it comes to classroom learning, this is especially true. Many times, learning classes have associated documents, group discussions, and external links to give further context to the content in the class.

In the current system, each class has a folder on a file share with its own copy of class documents. Many times this content is identical across multiple classes, which consumes additional disk space on servers.

The discussion boards and links are maintained in separate systems. The discussion boards are hosted on a third-party system that the organization does not own, and the links are hosted on a website that the development team built.

Users need one unified location where associated content can be viewed. Administrators would also like to reduce the duplication of documents that currently exist.

Unable to Find New Classes in Real Time

In the current system, classes are maintained on a spreadsheet shared monthly by the learning administrators. End users read through the spreadsheet and then reply as to which classes they want to attend. In this model, there can be a delay of days to weeks before users receive updated information on class offerings. In addition to the delay in sending out information, dozens of classes are added to the calendar each month. This means not only that users do not have a real-time view of the classes, but they also have difficulty identifying newly added classes. Users need the ability to find newly added classes quickly and easily.

Provisioning Class-Related Infrastructure

When learning administrators add new classes, there are a number of repetitive, manual implementation steps required for each class. In the existing system these steps include creating a document repository, a discussion board, and an external links list. These steps are common to all classes and could be automated given a suitable framework.

Summarizing the Business Problems

You have covered three different problems that are affecting the success of the learning center. In summary, they are as follows:

- Associate documents, links, and discussion forums to classes in a unified location

- Find recently added classes in real time

- Provision classes with class-related infrastructure

Gathering Information

Now that the business problems have been defined, you can look to the specific requirements that need to be gathered. The first thing to do is identify the user roles that will be involved. This solution has three primary user roles: class presenter, attendee, and learning center administrator.

Class Presenter

The class presenter is the subject matter expert (SME) who will be leading the class and delivering the content. They need to be able to modify classes, add associated documents, and initiate and moderate discussions.

Attendee

As the name implies, these users will be attending the classes. Before they attend a class, they need to find their class online. They also need to view class-related materials and contribute to discussion threads posted by the class presenter. Attendees should not be able to add or edit classes.

Learning Center Administrator

The learning center administrator is tasked with maintaining the learning center site. The primary tasks for the administrator are provisioning infrastructure and removing old content from the site.

Designing the Solution

Planning is paramount when it comes to designing a solution. In the case of the learning center, there are a number of interconnected pieces, so the order of implementation is important. There are also multiple ways to fulfill the same goal.

Content Infrastructure

In this solution you need to store classes, documents, discussion threads, and links. SharePoint provides a number of out-of-the-box features that map to these components. Classes, for example, can be stored on a calendar.

Storing documents deserves a little additional consideration. Most SharePoint list items can have a column for attachments, which could fulfill the need for associated documents. However, as described in the business problems, the existing system has duplicates of documents, which has led to a waste of server disk space. To avoid this duplication, it is best to split documents into a separate document library that can be shared across multiple classes.

Initialization Workflow

Because of the number of connected pieces that are required, it is helpful to remove user error from as much of the process as possible. To facilitate this goal, the solution will implement a few simple workflows to automate many rote tasks. These include creating an announcement for new classes.

Document Sets (SharePoint Server Feature)

If you happen to be using SharePoint Server (Standard or Enterprise) you will have access to a new feature called *document sets*. Document sets allow you to group multiple related documents into a single entity for easier usage and management. If your class documents consist of a standard template (for example, a syllabus, survey, homework, and so on), you might want to look into using document sets. Since this chapter is focused on SharePoint Foundation, document sets will not be covered in detail.

See Also *Read the following TechNet article for additional information on document sets:* technet.microsoft.com/en-us/library/ff603637.aspx.

Solution Data

Users make up one portion of the solution. Another portion relates to the data that is to be captured. Here are the data types that will be required:

- Class calendars

- Class documents

- Class links

- Class discussions

- Class announcements

Your organization might require additional data to be captured. These data types should serve as a basis to build upon if necessary. You will be building these data types into a SharePoint site infrastructure using out-of-the-box components.

Association Design Decisions

Associating classes to their related components can be done in one of two ways: with a class as the parent in a relationship or with a class as a child in a relationship. The first of the following illustrations shows the logical architecture of class as parent, and the second chart shows the logical architecture of class as child.

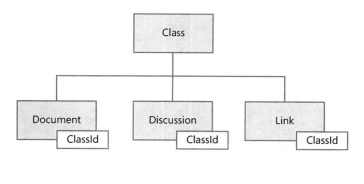

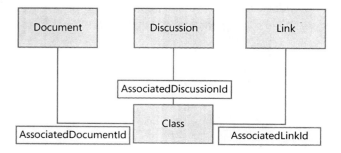

Class as Parent

If the class is the parent in the relationship, the class can have zero to many child components (documents, links, and so on). This may be ideal if child components are always unique (if each class has a separate set of documents, discussions, links, and so on that are not shared with any other classes.) This model is implemented by lookup columns pointing from the child entities to the parent class.

One benefit of this approach is that you can relate content to a single class and enforce a cascading deletion (more on this shortly.) This means that when you delete a class item, any associated items are also deleted. This could be useful in speeding up the process of removing content.

There is, however, a significant downside to this approach that needs to be considered. The user who is adding or editing content has to define the relationship from each child item to its parent. In SharePoint, this means navigating to each document, discussion, or other item and assigning the associated class ID. This can be a *very* time-consuming process. In addition, when you view a class, you won't have a clear view of which content is associated with the class.

Class as Child

If the class is the child in the relationship, the class can have zero to many parent components. This may be favorable if associated components are reused among multiple classes (in other words, if multiple classes use a single document, discussion, link, or so on). This model is implemented by lookup columns pointing from the class to the parent entities. You might notice that this model involves a class having multiple types of parent entities.

There are two major benefits of this approach. First, when you view a class you can instantly see the associated content because the lookup columns are located on one item. This is helpful in addressing the first business issue: unifying content in one location. The second benefit is that multiple classes can be associated with the same content. This fulfills the desire to reduce disk usage.

The downsides to this approach are mostly conditional. If a class presenter modifies the content of an associated document, those changes are also applied to any other classes that are associated with that document. This could cause issues unintentionally if the changes are not meant for the other classes.

See Also *To read additional information about lookup column software boundaries and limits, go to* technet. microsoft.com/en-us/library/cc262787.aspx#Column.

Association Decision

Now that you have read about the advantages and disadvantages of both relationship patterns, it is time to make a decision. In this scenario, content is reused frequently and ease of administration is important. Based on these priorities, you should implement your associations using the class as child pattern.

Cascading and Restricted Deletion

At this point it will be good to cover a feature new to SharePoint 2010: lookup columns with enforced relationships. Linked lists are not a new concept. In previous versions of SharePoint (and still with SharePoint 2010) you are able to use lookup columns that allow you to relate records from one list to a record in another list. In SharePoint 2010, a Relationship attribute has been added with an option to enforce relationship behavior.

The two options for the Relationship attribute are restrict delete and cascade delete. In simplified terms, restrict delete means a parent record cannot be deleted if a child record exists. Cascade delete means deleting the parent record will also delete any child records. The following screenshot illustrates an example of creating a new lookup column with cascading deletion configured. After providing a column name and selecting the column type Lookup (Information Already On This Site), look to the bottom of the form and select Enforce Relationship Behavior. Then select the Cascade Delete option.

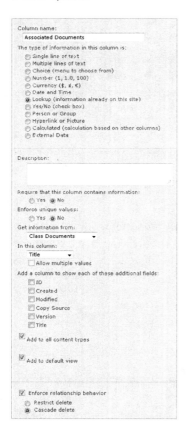

The one exception to this relationship behavior is if you select Allow Multiple Values under In This Column. If this option is selected, the current item can have multiple parent records in the target list. In that scenario, the Enforce Relationship Behavior check box is disabled so that you cannot have cascading or restricted deletion. Logically this makes sense because it is impossible to enforce a relationship when multiple dependencies are involved.

See Also *Read the following MSDN article for additional information about list relationships in SharePoint 2010:* msdn.microsoft.com/en-us/library/ff798514.aspx.

Building the Solution

Now that you have laid out the design, it is time to begin building the solution. For this scenario you need to use the SharePoint 2010 web UI as well as SharePoint Designer 2010. The following sections will guide you through the implementation process of creating the site, infrastructure, workflows, and other supporting components that are required. After the implementation is completed, you'll find a list of steps you can use to verify that the site is functional.

Build the Learning Center Site

The learning center will be built in its own site collection. Use the information in the following table as input to the corresponding fields during site collection creation.

Field	Value
Web Application	http://www.tailspintoys.com
Title	Learning Center
Description	Central site for users to view the current classes and their associated documents, discussion groups, and external links.
URL	.../LearningCenter
Template Selection	Blank Site
Primary Site Collection Owner	Davis, Sara
Secondary Site Collection Owner	Albrecht, Brian T.
Quota Template	Application_40GB

Create Class Calendar

As you may have guessed, the calendar is going to be the focal point of the learning center. You will start out creating the calendar with a basic set of columns. Later in this chapter, after you have created all of the supporting infrastructure for additional lists and libraries, you will add lookup columns to the calendar to enable associations to be created for those entities.

Create the Calendar

Start by creating a new calendar on your learning center site. Use the information in the following table to create the Classes calendar.

Name	Template	Description	Navigation
Classes	Calendar	This calendar contains all the classes available to users.	Yes

Create the Columns

Many of the columns that you require are provided out of the box on a standard calendar list: start date, end date, location, attendees, and so on. However, some additional columns are necessary to create a fully functioning and useful solution. Reference the information in the following tables to implement two new columns on the calendar.

Note When creating columns with column names that are multiple words, it is advisable to create the column first without using spaces between the words. After the column is created, go back and add the spaces. For example, Class Id should be entered as ClassId and then changed to Class Id. The reason ties into the underlying structure of how the column name is stored and the ease of use for developers or power users who may work with the column in the future.

Field	Value
Column Name	Presenter
Type	Person or Group
Description	(Leave blank since the column title is self-descriptive.)
Required	Yes
Allow Multiple Selections	No
Allow Selection Of	People Only
Choose From	All Users
Show Field	Name (with presence)
Add to Default View	Yes

This example assumes that your organization allows only a single presenter for a given class. If that is not the case, select Yes for Allow Multiple Selections. However, this setting might have side effects outside what is intended with this example.

Field	Value
Column Name	ClassId
Type	Single Line of Text
Description	Unique identifier for the class, which will be used in creating associations to other lists and libraries.
Required	Yes
Enforce Unique	Yes

Field	Value
Maximum Number of Characters	255
Add to Default View	Yes
Indexed Column	Yes (prompt appears after click OK)

Why are you creating a separate column for ClassId when you already have the default ID?

In some organizations or companies, classes are identified by a specific combination of numbers or letters (for example, HR-302). To be more closely aligned with these considerations, you can use a Single Line of Text column instead of the default ID integer column to handle this data.

These are all the columns you will be adding at this time. You will revisit this list once you have created additional infrastructure for documents, discussion boards, and links.

Create the Views

Next you will create a view to address one of the business problems: the inability of users to find recently added classes. This view displays all classes that were created within the last 7 days. You can adjust the number of days as you see fit for your organization. Use the information in the following table to create the new view.

Field	Value
View Name	New Classes
Start From an Existing View	All Events
Default View	No
Audience	Public
Columns	Title (linked to item) Description Presenter Location Start Time End Time
Sort	Start Time
Filter	Created is greater than [Today] - 7
Inline Editing	No
Tabular View	No
Group By	None
Totals	None
Style	Newsletter
Folders	Show items inside folders
Item Limit	30, Display in Batches
Mobile	Enable, 3

Create Announcements List

Now that you have created the Classes calendar, you can begin implementing the rest of the supporting infrastructure. The next list, for announcements, also helps address the issue of finding classes. You will use this list along with a workflow on the Classes calendar to automatically post classes as they are added.

Create the List

Create a new announcements list on your learning center site. Use the values in the following table to fill in the metadata during list creation.

Name	Template	Description	Navigation
Class Announcements	Announcements	This list contains all the announcements able to be viewed by users.	Yes

Create the Columns

Out-of-the-box announcement lists are very simplistic with primary fields of Title, Body, and Expiration. As it turns out, these fields satisfy most of the needs you have for class announcements. One additional column that will help in linking directly to the class is a lookup column. The following table contains the metadata you will use to create this column.

Field	Value
Column Name	AssociatedClassId
Type	Lookup
Description	(Leave blank)
Required	No
Enforce Unique	No
Get Information From	Classes
In This Column	ClassId
Add a Column to Show Each of These Additional Fields	Title
Add to Default View	Yes
Enforce Relationship Behavior	Yes, cascade delete
Indexed Column	Yes (prompt appears after click OK)

Create the Alerts (Optional)

An announcements list is a good way to alert users of recently added classes. If you want to take the solution one step further you can optionally configure alerts on the Class Announcements list or Classes calendar to send notifications to users. You will not be creating an alert in this scenario, but it is important to be aware of some of the advantages and disadvantages with alerts in case you do explore this path.

See Also *For more information about creating alerts, go to* msdn.microsoft.com/en-us/library/bb802949.aspx.

In terms of advantages, you can specify the delivery schedule (immediate, daily, or weekly), the action conditions (item added, item modified, and so on), and additional criteria that is list-specific. Also, you have additional delivery methods (sending the alert as an email or as an SMS text message), provided that you have properly configured your farm to send alerts via these methods.

See Also *To read more about configuring SMS text messages, go to* technet.microsoft.com/en-us/sharepoint/ ff679921.aspx.

As for the disadvantages, if you create an alert for another user, that user might not be aware that you have configured the alert. In addition, you lose the ability to modify the alert after it has been created. You can delete the alert if you have permissions to do so, but you cannot modify it.

Add List View Web Part to Page

To make the most out of the Class Announcements list, you will want to add a list view web part for the list to the root page of the learning center site. Browse to the root page by clicking Learning Center on the breadcrumb link near the top of the page. Follow these steps to add the web part to the page:

1. Click the Page tab at the top of the page, and then click Edit Page on the ribbon.

2. After the page refreshes, click the Insert tab.

3. Click Web Part.

4. Select the Lists And Libraries category and the Class Announcements web part. Select Left from the Add Web Part To list. Click Add.

The following screenshot shows an example of adding the Class Announcements web part to the page.

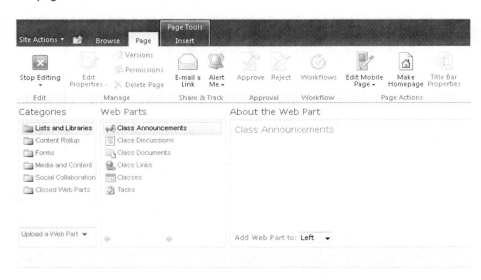

5. After the page refreshes, click the Page tab and then click Stop Editing.

After you have added the web part to the page, your screen should look similar to the following screenshot.

Create Announcement Workflow

Presenters want other users to know about upcoming classes as soon as a presenter adds a class. Adding an announcement to the Class Announcements list can fulfill this need. To automate the process you will create a workflow on the Classes calendar. The workflow process will be as follows:

1. Log that workflow has initiated.

2. Define the expiration date as 7 days from today (store output in variable).

3. Create a list item in the Class Announcements list (store output in variable).

4. Log that workflow has concluded.

The workflow will be triggered when items are added to the Classes calendar. The expected outcome is to automatically add an item to the Class Announcements list with a link back to the new class item so that users can find more information about the class. You will also be performing simple logging should you need to troubleshoot the workflow in the future.

Create the Workflow

Open SharePoint Designer 2010 and open the URL of your site. Click Workflows in the bar at the left. Use the information in the following table to fill in the metadata for the workflow. To create the workflow, first click the List Workflow button in the upper-left corner and choose Classes. The screenshot shown here displays an example of the list workflow options. Note that the image includes some of the additional infrastructure that you will be adding throughout this chapter. Disregard those items for now.

Type	Target List	Name	Description
List Workflow	Classes	Create New Class Announcement	Creates an announcement when new classes are added to the Classes calendar.

If you are familiar with the design surface for workflows in SharePoint Designer 2007, you may be in for a bit of a surprise, because the design surface in SharePoint Designer 2010 went through quite an overhaul from the previous version. Refer to the following screenshot for an example of using the SharePoint Designer 2010 workflow interface. To add workflow actions, you can begin typing the name of the action you want to use.

Start out by creating three steps for the workflow. Use the values in the following table for the steps and types of actions to create.

Step Name	Action Type
Initialization	Log to History List Add Time to Date
Create Announcement	Create List Item
Conclusion	Log to History List

As listed in the explanation of the workflow process, two variables need to be defined: Announcement Expiration Date and New Announcement Reference. You will need to define these variables when you fill out the associated action steps. Use the information in the following table to define the necessary variables.

Variable Name	Type
Announcement Expiration Date	Date/Time
New Announcement Reference	List Item ID

With the variables created, you can now fill out the action steps. Use the information in the following table to fill out the Initialization step.

Action Type	Value
Log to History List	New announcement workflow initiated from item "[%Current Item:Title%]" with ID "[%Current Item:ID%]" being added.
Add Time to Date	Add 7 days to Today (Output to Variable: Announcement Expiration Date)

In the preceding table, you might notice seemingly peculiar syntax for "[%Current Item:...%]" in the value column. This is SharePoint Designer's syntax for specifying a lookup to a column in the Current Item object. In this scenario, Current Item equates to the class list item that the workflow is firing on. Refer to the following screenshots when selecting the "[%Current Item:Title%]" and "[%Current Item:ID%]" lookups.

 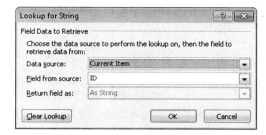

Next you will implement the Create Announcement step. Use the information in the following table for the metadata to use.

Action Type	Value
Create List Item	Create item in Class Announcements (Output to Variable: New Announcement Reference) ■ Title = New class [%Current Item:Title%] added ■ Expires = Variable: Announcement Expiration Date ■ AssociatedClassId = CurrentItem:ClassId

Next, fill out the Conclusion step's actions with the values in the following table.

Action Type	Value
Log to History List	New announcement workflow concluding from item "[%Current Item:Title%]" with ID "[%Current Item:ID%]" being added.

At this point your workflow steps should look like the example in the following screenshot.

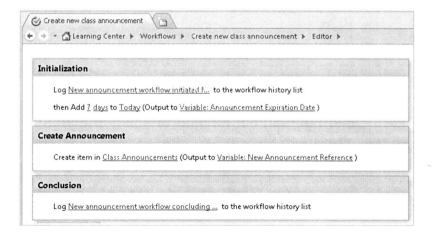

The last step is to define the workflow start options. Click Workflow Settings (see the following icon) on the ribbon.

You will be taken to the Workflow Settings page, which gives an overview of the workflow metadata, links to customize the workflow, and other useful information. To change the start options, look at the Start Options panel on the right side. By default your workflow will be set to Allow This Workflow To Be Manually Started only. Clear this check box, and then select the option Start Workflow Automatically When An Item Is Created.

After you have made your selections, the Start Options screen should look similar to the following:

If everything was configured successfully, you should be able to click Check For Errors on the ribbon and see the following dialog box. At this point you can save and publish the workflow back to the site.

See Also *To read more about how accounts affect the starting of workflows, go to* blogs.technet.com/b/victorbutuza/archive/2009/03/14/workflows-do-not-start.aspx.

Create Class Documents Library

The next major business problem that needs to be addressed is linking content to classes. To do this, you need additional infrastructure. The first component will be a document library in which to store class-related documents such as a syllabus or an agenda, prereading materials, and the like.

Create the Document Library

Create a new document library on the learning center site. Use the information in the following table as metadata for the new document library.

Name	Template	Description	Navigation
Class Documents	Document Library	This document library contains all the documents able to be associated with classes.	Yes

The Class Documents document library contains all the columns that are required, so there is no need to add other columns at this time.

Create Class Discussions Board

Many times, classes or homework generate a number of questions, comments, or discussions between attendees and presenters. Discussion boards are a great tool to capture these elements so that multiple users can contribute to them and view them in a threaded manner. You will be creating a discussion board to help facilitate these needs.

Create the Discussion Board

Create a new discussion board on the learning center site. Use the information in the following table as input during the creation process.

Name	Template	Description	Navigation
Class Discussions	Discussion Board	This discussion board contains all the discussions able to be associated with classes.	Yes

The Class Discussions discussion board contains all the columns that will be required, so there is no need to add any additional columns at this time.

Create Class Links List

When a presenter delivers a class, the presenter will typically provide a number of links to websites, articles, or other web references. Even if attendees have enough time to write down these URLs, they might not navigate to them right away. To facilitate attendees being able to visit these URLs, you will be creating a Class Links list that can be linked back to classes.

Create the List

Create a new links list on the learning center site. Use the information in the following table to create the Class Links list.

Name	Template	Description	Navigation
Class Links	Links	This list contains all the links able to be associated with classes.	Yes

Create the Columns

When it comes to using the Links list template, you will run into an issue (which will become apparent in the next section) when you try to link to this list. The problem is that hyperlink columns cannot be the target of a lookup column. By default the Links list template uses a hyperlink (rather than a Title string) to represent the list item. Since you need a column to reference against, you'll be adding a new Single Line of Text column and a workflow to work around this issue. Use the information in the following table to create a new column.

Field	Value
Column Name	URLAsText
Type	Single Line of Text
Description	Copy of the URL column value in string/text format.
Required	No
Enforce Unique	No
Maximum Number of Characters	255
Add to Default View	No

Implement the Workflow

As mentioned in the previous section, "Create the Columns," the workaround for referencing a link column from a lookup requires a workflow. This custom workflow may be one of the simplest you will ever create. The workflow will set the value of the URLAsText column to the value of the URL column formatted as a string. Use the information in the following table to create a new list workflow.

Type	Target List	Name	Description
List Workflow	Class Links	Copy URL to URLAsText	Copies the value of the URL column formatted as a string into the URLAsText column on Class Links list.

Since this workflow will have only one action step, you can omit additional logging steps and actions. Use the values in the following table to define the single step and action for this workflow.

Step Name	Action Type
Copy URL value	Set Field in Current Item

Next, fill out the action step using the following information:

Action Type	Value
Set Field in Current Item	Set URLAsText to Current Item:URL

Lastly, you need to define the starting options. Since the value of URLAsText must always be kept in sync with the URL value, you need to trigger the workflow whenever an item is created or edited. As you did with the workflow you created for class announcements, clear any default values and use the values Start Workflow Automatically When An Item Is Created and Start Workflow Automatically When An Item Is Changed.

Click the Check For Errors button on the ribbon. If no errors are returned, save and publish the workflow back to the site.

Finish Classes Calendar

Now that you have implemented the additional infrastructure for class documents, class discussions, and class links, you can define the columns on the Classes calendar to associate them together.

Create the Columns

You need three additional columns on the Classes calendar that correspond to the lists you just created. Use the following table to implement these additional columns.

Column Name	Field	Value
AssociatedDocuments	Type	Lookup
	Description	(Leave blank)
	Required	No
	Enforce Unique	No
	Get Information From	Class Documents
	In This Column	Title
	Allow Multiple Values	Yes
	Add to Default View	Yes

Column Name	Field	Value
AssociatedDiscussions	Type	Lookup
	Description	(Leave blank)
	Required	No
	Enforce Unique	No
	Get Information From	Class Discussions
	In This Column	Subject
	Allow Multiple Values	Yes
	Add to Default View	Yes
AssociatedLinks	Type	Lookup
	Description	(Leave blank)
	Required	No
	Enforce Unique	No
	Get Information From	Class Links
	In This Column	URLAsText
	Allow Multiple Values	Yes
	Add to Default View	Yes

With these columns in place, you can now associate classes to documents, discussions, and links that have been added. Because you implemented the relationship in a class-as-child model, the associations will all be visible in a centralized location when users view the class.

Add List Web Part to Page

With the Classes calendar completed you can now add it to the root page of the site. This provides users with a quick glance of the classes when they visit the site. Follow the same process you did when you added the Class Announcements web part to the root page, only this time select the Classes calendar for the left web part zone. Once the web part is added, drag it below the Class Announcements web part. After you have completed these steps, your root page should look similar to the following screenshot.

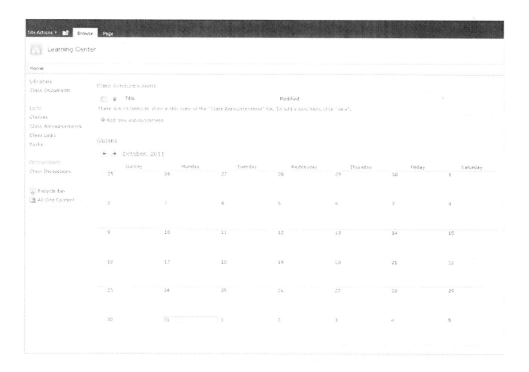

Implement Class-Initialization Workflow

The last business issue to address is automating some of the manual steps during the initialization process. Since the creation of a class triggers the creation of other elements (discussion board, document repository, and so on), you will use class creation to initiate a workflow. This workflow will be separate from the Create New Class Announcement workflow that you created earlier in this solution.

You may be asking yourself "Why am I creating a new workflow? Why don't I add new logic and actions to the announcement workflow?" The reasons are maintainability and separation of concerns. You want your solution to be modular, meaning that each component addresses a single concern and doesn't perform more actions than are necessary. By implementing a separate workflow for processes that are not directly related, you reduce the risk of breaking existing functionality.

The goal of this workflow is to add a new discussion thread to the Class Discussions list. The discussion thread subject line will be dynamically built from the name and ID of the class that is being created. After the discussion thread is created, you will go one step further and link the class (via the AssociatedClassDiscussions column) to the newly created discussion thread.

Implement the Workflow

If you still have SharePoint Designer 2010 open, bring it back into focus. If not, launch it again and open the URL of the learning center site. Click Workflows in the left bar and create a new list workflow associated with the Classes list. Use the information in the following table to define the workflow.

Type	Target List	Name	Description
List Workflow	Classes	Create New Class Initialization	Creates a discussion thread and links to current item when new classes are added to the Classes calendar.

This workflow will have four steps. Use the information in the following table to define the steps and types of actions needed.

Step Name	Action Type
Initialization	Log to History List Set Workflow Variable
Create Discussion	Create List Item
Link Discussion to Class	Update List Item
Conclusion	Log to History List

As you can see, the Link Discussion to Class step is a new step. This step is where you create the association between the class and the discussion thread. To do that, you need to define workflow variables. Use the values in the following table to define variables for use later in this workflow.

Variable Name	Type
Discussion Subject	String
New Discussion Reference	List Item ID

You will begin by filling out the Initialization step. Use the information in the following table for the values to use for each action.

Action Type	Value
Log to History List	New class initialization workflow initiated from item "[%Current Item:Title%]" with ID "[%Current Item:ID%]" being added.
Set Workflow Variable	Welcome discussion for class "[%Current Item:Title%]" with class ID "[%Current Item:ClassId%]".

Refer to the following screenshot when selecting the "[%Current Item:ClassId%]" lookup.

Next you will implement the Create Discussion step. Use the information in the following table for the metadata to use.

Action Type	Value
Create List Item	Create item in Class Discussions (Output to Variable: New Discussion Reference) ■ Content Type ID = Discussion ■ Subject (*) = Variable: Discussion Subject ■ Body = Post here any generic questions or comments you have regarding this class.

The Link Discussion to Class step is different from what you created in the Create Announcement workflow. In this step you link the discussion just created to the current item. By doing so you replace two manual processes with one automated process, which helps out the learning center administrators. Use the following information to fill out actions in this step:

Action Type	Value
Update List Item	Update item in Current Item ■ AssociatedDiscussions = Variable: New Discussion Reference (Return field as: Item Key)

Note in the preceding table that you are setting the value of AssociatedDiscussions equal to Variable: New Discussion Reference (Return field as: Item Key). The last section about returning a field as an item key (the actual reference to the list item) is important and different from returning a value as a string (just the text of the list item property). See the following screenshot for an example of how to configure the lookup.

Next fill out the Conclusion step's action using the following information:

Action Type	Value
Log to History List	New discussion workflow concluding from item "[%Current Item:Title%]" with ID "[%Current Item:ID%]" being added.

The following screenshot shows what your workflow should look like at this point.

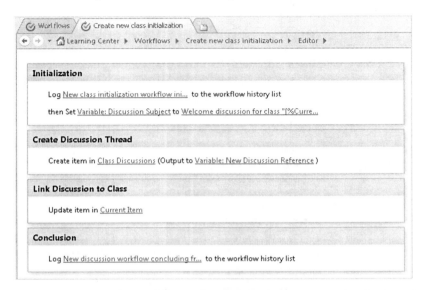

Since you want this workflow to be triggered when a new class is created, you need to change the workflow start options. Click Workflow Settings on the ribbon. Clear the option Allow This Workflow To Be Manually Started, and then select Start Workflow Automatically When An Item Is Created.

Again, you should be able to click the Check For Errors button and receive the dialog box stating there are no errors. Save and publish the workflow to the site to finish up your work.

Implement Security and Permissions (Optional)

Security considerations vary greatly by organization. Some organizations must adhere to laws or regulations for implementing security. Other organizations freely allow end users to assign permissions. Based on these variances, you might or might not decide to restrict the out-of-the-box permissions. The security changes in this step will be optional for you to implement.

One of the primary security concerns will be that attendees have contributor access in order to view and add to discussion threads. Contributor access also grants permissions to delete list items (classes, documents, and so on). It is possible to remove the permission to delete items while retaining add and edit permissions through the use of custom permission levels.

Create the Permission Level

Since you are interested in making modifications to the Contributor permission level, you will make a copy of that permission level and save modifications to a new one. Navigate to the root of the site collection and open Site Permissions from the Site Actions menu in the upper-left corner. Click Permission Levels (see the following screenshot.)

On the list of permission levels, click Contribute. You want to copy these permissions to a new permission level, so scroll to the bottom of the page, and then click the Copy Permission Level button. Once the page refreshes, use the following information to define the new permission level:

Name	Description	Permissions to Remove
Attendee	Copied permissions from Contribute permission level but remove Delete Items and Delete Versions list permissions.	■ Delete Items ■ Delete Versions

Assign the Permission Level

With the custom Attendee permission level created, you can now assign it to a SharePoint group. Navigate back to the Site Permissions screen. Click the Create Group button on the ribbon. Define the group metadata as you see fit, with the exception of the Give Group Permissions To This Site section. You will see that the new Attendee permission level is available. Select the check box for the Attendee permission level before saving. Now you can place attendee users into this group to ensure that they won't be able to delete content from the site.

End Result

At this point you should have a fully functioning learning center—congratulations! Now take a quick review of your solution from the perspective of each user type to ensure that everything is working properly. Use the following information to perform the activities per user role to ensure that your site is working properly. Note that this is not a full test of functionality or compatibility.

User Role	Activity to Test
Learning Center Administrator	■ Add a class ■ Check if announcement is created ■ Check if discussion thread is created and linked to class
Presenter	■ Add associated content for class ■ Link content to class
Attendee	■ Navigate to class via Class Announcements web part ■ Navigate to class discussion thread via link in class ■ Add to class-specific discussion thread

Reviewing the Platform

The solution in this chapter was built using SharePoint Foundation. Since the other SharePoint licenses build upon what is in Foundation, let's take a minute to discuss some of the additional options available if you are using a different SharePoint platform.

Using SharePoint Online with Office 365

If you are using SharePoint Online, the implementation of this solution should be nearly identical. You will have access to the same lists and libraries used in SharePoint Foundation as well as the ability to create SharePoint Designer 2010 workflows.

Using SharePoint Server Standard

If you are using SharePoint Server Standard you will have access to more advanced Enterprise Content Management (ECM) features. One example that relates to this solution is document sets, which are mentioned earlier in the chapter. Other potentially useful features in Server Standard include Federated Search (search external to a SharePoint farm), managed metadata to classify content, or tagging and rating to allow users to provide opinions about content. Federated Search uses an external search index outside the current farm. Enterprise search can search content external to SharePoint just by crawling it. This can also be done in SharePoint Foundation by using Search Server or Search Server Express.

Using SharePoint Server Enterprise

If you are using SharePoint Server Enterprise you will have access to all the features mentioned in SharePoint Server Standard and more. For the purposes of this solution, there are no clear advantages to using Enterprise over Standard.

Summary

In this chapter you looked at business problems that could be addressed by implementing a learning center solution. These problems included associating class content together in a unified location, finding recently added classes in real time, and provisioning class-related infrastructure. Using a combination of out-of-the-box SharePoint Foundation lists and libraries and lookup columns, you addressed associating content together in one location. Using SharePoint Designer 2010 workflows and the list view web part, you addressed the issue of finding recently added classes. Finally, another SharePoint Designer workflow reduced the manual steps in provisioning infrastructure.

CHAPTER 5

Building a Help Desk Solution

I n this chapter you will work through the process of building a help desk application. This solution allows users to enter and view service requests, identify root causes, and track solutions to common issues. This chapter's solution will be built using the functionality in SharePoint Server Standard. In addition, you will explore using Microsoft Visio and Microsoft SharePoint Designer 2010 to build workflows.

One of the primary reasons for building a help desk solution is to transform an IT organization's outlook from reactive to proactive. A few years ago, Microsoft released a paper that scoped out the maturity level of an IT organization. The paper identified four levels, going from reactive to proactive. Toward the reactive side, there is little or no planning, little or no automation, and no strategic goal looking forward. As an IT organization moves toward the proactive side, each of these practices is implemented to a greater degree. A help desk solution is a way of furthering progress toward the proactive side.

For those readers familiar with the Fab 40 solutions that were released with SharePoint 2007, this solution draws inspiration from the Help Desk template. Since the Fab 40 templates are not supported in SharePoint 2010, this is a good opportunity to replace the functionality that template provided and build upon it where it makes sense. One portion that you will not be building into this solution is the frequently asked questions (FAQs), as a similar solution is covered in Chapter 3 of this book.

Identifying the Business Problems

Before you begin designing any solution, you must understand the business problems being faced. After you identify and understand the problems, you can architect a solution to properly address them. The following sections describe some of the business problems associated with the sample help desk application.

Track Service Requests

George Santayana famously said that "[t]hose who cannot remember the past are condemned to repeat it." IT organizations can receive end user issues and service requests every day of every week throughout the year. No matter if you are in a 50-person organization or a 50,000-person organization, you should be tracking these requests from creation to resolution. By recording service requests you can collect metrics that can later be used for analysis and input for strategic decision making.

Service Requests Not Worked On in a Timely Manner

When requests are not worked on in a timely manner, there is a breakdown on many fronts, from communication to trust to productivity. There are a number of reasons for requests not being worked on in a timely manner, including the interface used for tracking requests, no metrics being captured about the status of a request, and no mechanism to distinguish urgent from nonurgent requests.

End Users Aren't Updated on Status

One factor of end users' satisfaction with a help desk solution is the visibility they have into the current status of their requests. Visibility can come in many forms: emails, a request dashboard, or weekly reports. This feedback can give requestors confidence that they are being heard and kept informed. Hence, some form of feedback should occur when a request is initiated, when it enters active status, and when it is closed.

Summarizing the Business Problems

We have briefly covered three different problems that are affecting the success of the help desk:

- Tracking service requests

- Service requests not being worked on in a timely manner

- End users aren't updated on request status

Gathering Information

The help desk solution will be used by a number of user roles, each with its own goals and requirements. The following brief descriptions detail the roles that you will be taking into consideration when designing this solution.

End User

End users will be entering information into the help desk solution to create a service request. End users will also periodically check back for status updates on their requests. Ideally, some form of communication about request status will be automated.

Help Desk User

The help desk user will be reviewing incoming requests, assigning them to the correct user for resolution, and updating service requests throughout their life cycle. If a service request has been entered but not worked on for a specified number of days, the help desk user should receive a notification.

IT Manager

The IT manager is primarily concerned with ensuring that service requests are being processed and resolved in a timely manner. This includes monitoring requests, reviewing status reports, and determining when additional attention is required on specific requests.

Designing the Solution

Since the help desk solution will be used by a variety of groups, you should plan the interactions of those users, determine what process service requests will follow, and design mechanisms for request status to be communicated between groups. In this section you will explore these elements of the solution.

Designing Workflows

Resolving service requests is very process oriented and follows a specific flow of actions. This defined process allows for consistency, ease of reporting, and follow-up activities when necessary. The following list is a high-level overview of the preferred flow of activities:

1. Workflow start

2. Determine if request is an emergency

3. Email requestor that request received

4. Set current status on service request

5. Wait for predetermined number of days and send follow-up email to help desk if request not yet worked on

6. Email requestor when work on service request has begun

7. Email requestor that request completed

8. Workflow end

Visio to SharePoint Designer

Many times when you are designing a workflow it helps to visualize the actions, logic, and overall structure. One way to draw out that visualization is by designing UML (Unified Modeling Language) diagrams. Microsoft Visio can be used to create just such a diagram. If you were to model the service request workflow steps in Visio and flesh out additional actions, you would see a diagram similar to the following:

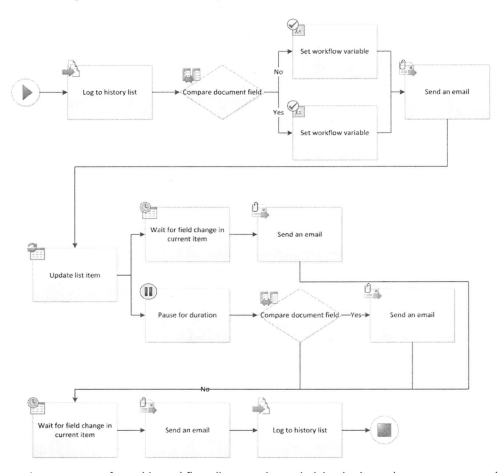

As you can see from this workflow diagram, the underlying logic can become very complex as the number of steps and actions increases. One powerful new feature in SharePoint 2010 is the ability to design and transfer workflow diagrams between Visio Premium 2010 and SharePoint Designer 2010. It is important to note that this capability is available only in Visio Premium 2010; the SharePoint Workflow template is not included in the Standard or Professional editions of Visio 2010.

Transferring a workflow between Visio and SharePoint Designer is powerful because it allows a nondeveloper user to mock up the workflow structure in Visio and export it to a .VWI file. This .VWI file can then be imported by a developer or power user into SharePoint Designer 2010 for additional work. The process of designing, exporting, and importing can occur as many times as necessary. It is also possible to perform a one-way export of a workflow from SharePoint Designer 2010 to Microsoft Visual Studio 2010 when you need to have access to more APIs and workflow options. This is a one-way export, however; you cannot export from Visual Studio to SharePoint Designer.

Note The preceding diagram was created by importing into Visio the exported SharePoint Designer 2010 workflow that you will be designing later in this chapter. You will be shown how to perform this process after you implement the workflow.

Targeting Content

You have already identified that the help desk solution is going to have a diverse set of users accessing similar data. Even though the data is similar, each group of users is concerned about different interpretations or views of the data. In this light, SharePoint audience targeting may make sense to implement. Audience targeting is not a security feature, so you should not rely on it for limiting access to specific user groups. Instead, audience targeting is a way to direct specific users to a defined view of the data.

In a high-level overview of your scenario, end users want to enter service requests and check the status of their requests. Help desk users are interested in detailed information about all service requests that are not yet resolved. IT managers are interested in process metrics and finding trends in those metrics.

To serve the various user types, you could go one of two ways. The first is to define multiple pages with individualized content and configurations. The other is to define one common page that has audience-targeted content. Because of the complexity and additional work required to configure audiences, this chapter will not make use of this approach, but it will describe aspects of it should you want to implement it.

Solution Data

Users make up one portion of the solution. Another portion relates to the data that is to be captured. The following list contains a number of the data types that will be required:

- Service Requests

- Service Request Tasks

- Site Pages (contains wiki pages)

  - End Users

  - Help Desk Users

  - IT Managers

Your organization might require additional data to be captured. These data types should serve as a basis to build upon if necessary. You will be building these data types into the SharePoint site infrastructure by using out-of-the-box components.

Building the Solution

Now that you have laid out the design, it is time to begin building the solution. For this scenario you will use the SharePoint 2010 web UI as well as SharePoint Designer 2010. The following sections guide you through the implementation process of creating the site, infrastructure, workflows, and other supporting components. After the implementation steps, you'll find a wrap-up with steps you can follow to verify that the site is functional.

Build Help Desk Site

The help desk will be built in its own site collection to prevent any conflicts with other solutions you may be building. You can create the site collection through Central Administration or the SharePoint PowerShell commandlet New-SPSite. If you do not have access to either of these, contact your administrator for assistance. Use the information in the following table as input for the corresponding fields during site collection creation.

Field	Value
Web Application	http://www.tailspintoys.com
Title	Help Desk
Description	Site used to enter and track service requests for a departmental organization.
URL	.../HelpDesk
Template Selection	Blank Site
Primary Site Collection Owner	Herriman, Annie
Secondary Site Collection Owner	Price, Jeff
Quota Template	Application_40GB

Create Pages Document Library

One aspect of the help desk solution is that it will be used by a variety of user types. To provide more targeted content to each user type, you will be creating multiple pages to host the content specific to each group. By default, the Blank Site template does not contain a document library to contain these pages, so you will have to create one.

Create the Document Library

You will be adding a new document library through a different method than you may be used to. The purpose of this is to highlight that you cannot add a new page to the Blank Site template without the supporting infrastructure—a document library—to support it. Click Site Settings and then click More Options. Choose Page in the Pages And Sites section. You should see the window shown in the following screenshot, stating that you need to have a wiki page library and site assets library in order to create a new wiki page. Click the Create button to create the document libraries.

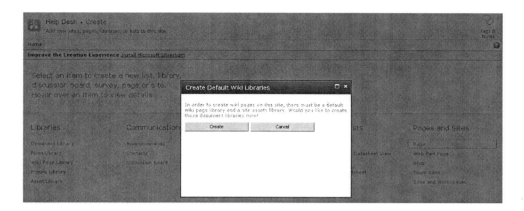

Note The preceding screenshot assumes that you have not installed the Silverlight runtime or are using the non-Silverlight interface for creating items. If you are not using this interface, your screen and steps will look slightly different, but the concept is the same.

After the document libraries are created, you will be asked to enter the name of the page to create. Enter **Help Desk Users** as shown here:

Create the User Pages

After the wiki page and site assets libraries are created, you are taken to the Help Desk Users wiki page. For the time being, leave this page alone. You need to define the wiki pages for the other user groups, and it will be easiest to complete this work from the home wiki page. You can get to the home wiki page from a number of locations, but two readily available ones are the Site Pages link under Libraries or the Home link under Recently Modified on the left hand navigation bar. Note that the Home link at the top of the navigation list will take you to the root of the site, not the home page of the wiki. See the following screenshot for an example.

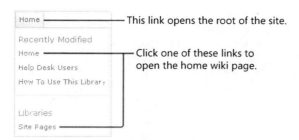

This link opens the root of the site.

Click one of these links to open the home wiki page.

Wiki pages use a special markup language that allows users to quickly and easily link to (or add) other pages. The process involves putting the page name you want to use in a set of double square brackets, such as [[Help Desk Users]]. You will be adding links to the three user pages from the Home page.

Once you are on the Home wiki page, click the Page tab on the ribbon and click Edit to edit the page. Clear all content from the page. Next you will enter links to the pages that you want to define and link to. Enter the following links on separate lines on the page:

- [[End Users]]

- [[Help Desk Users]]

- [[IT Managers]]

When you have entered the links on the page, click Save & Close on the ribbon. The following screenshot shows the results.

Notice that the links for End Users and IT Managers have dotted lines beneath them. The dotted line signifies that you have linked to a page that does not currently exist. Click the link for End Users. You will then see the following dialog box. Click Create.

You will be taken to a blank page, which is the End Users page. You still need to create the IT Managers page, so return to the Home page using one of the two methods described earlier. Once on the Home page, click the link for IT Managers. You will be presented with a dialog box that asks you to create the IT Managers page. Click Create.

Modify the Quick Launch

To make it easier for users to access these pages, you can modify the Quick Launch bar. You will create a new heading for Site Pages with direct links to the pages. Then you will clean up the default links that were created.

Start by navigating to the Site Settings page and clicking Quick Launch under Look And Feel. Click the New Heading button. Use the information in the following table to create the new heading. This will be a relative address to the current site because it does not begin with http:// or a slash (/).

Web Address	Description
SitePages	Site Pages

You will then be returned to the Quick Launch settings page. Next you will create the three links below the Site Pages heading you just created. Use the information in the following table to create the links. You need to click New Navigation Link once for each link to enter the information.

Web Address	Description	Heading
SitePages/End Users.aspx	End Users	Site Pages
SitePages/Help Desk Users.aspx	Help Desk Users	Site Pages
SitePages/IT Managers.aspx	IT Managers	Site Pages

The next step is to remove the default Site Pages link to reduce confusion for all groups of users. Click the edit icon next to Site Pages under the Libraries heading. On the Edit Navigation Link screen, click the Delete button. After you finish this step, your Quick Launch will now contain links directly to each user page, as seen in the following screenshot. Try clicking the links to be sure they work properly.

Home

Site Pages
End Users
Help Desk Users
IT Managers

You will revisit these pages later in the solution to add and configure web parts. Next up is creating lists.

Create Service Requests List

The Service Requests list is going to be the heart of this help desk solution. End users will enter new requests, help desk users will act on service requests, and IT managers will review requests throughout their life cycle.

Create the List

Start by creating a new custom list on your help desk site. Use the information in the following table to create the Service Requests list.

Name	Template	Description	Navigation
Service Requests	Custom List	This list contains service requests entered by users.	Yes

Create the Columns

A default custom list is created with ID and Title fields. You will change the name of the Title column to a more meaningful name. Use the information in the following table to edit the Title column.

Field	Value
Column Name	Service Request
Type	Single Line of Text
Description	(Leave blank since the column title is self-descriptive.)
Required	Yes
Enforce Unique	No
Maximum Number of Characters	People Only
Choose From	255
Default Value	Text, [blank]

Next you will create a number of new columns to be used for tracking requests. Use the information in the following table to create these columns.

 Note When creating columns with column names that are multiple words it is advisable to define the column name without spaces first. After the column is created, go back and add in the spaces. For example, Assigned To should be entered as AssignedTo and then changed to Assigned To. The reason ties into the underlying structure of how the column name is stored and the ease of use for developers or power users who may work with the column in the future.

Column Name	Field	Value
AssignedTo	Type	Person or Group
	Description	User who is assigned to the request and is responsible for ensuring it is resolved.
	Required	Yes
	Allow Multiple Selections	No
	Allow Selection Of	People Only
	Choose From	All Users
	Show Field	Name (with presence)
	Add to Default View	Yes
Details	Type	Multiple Lines of Text
	Description	(Leave blank since the column title is self-descriptive.)
	Required	No
	Number of Lines for Editing	6
	Type of Text	Plain text
	Append Changes	No
	Add to Default View	No
IsEmergency	Type	Yes/No
	Description	Check this box if this request requires immediate attention, otherwise you will receive an action response within 48 hours.
	Default Value	No
	Add to Default View	Yes

Column Name	Field	Value
Status	Type	Choice
	Description	Current status of the service request.
	Required	Yes
	Enforce Unique	No
	Choices	Entered Active Resolved Closed
	Display Choices Using	Drop-Down Menu
	Allow Fill-in	No
	Default Value	Entered
	Add to Default View	Yes
Comments	Type	Multiple Lines of Text
	Description	Comments for actions taken by help desk user towards resolution of request.
	Required	No
	Number of Lines for Editing	6
	Type of Text	Plain text
	Append Changes	Yes
	Add to Default View	No
Resolution Date	Type	Date and Time
	Description	(Leave blank since the column title is self-descriptive.)
	Required	No
	Enforce Unique	No
	Date and Time Format	Date Only
	Default Value	None
	Add to Default View	No

In the description for IsEmergency, you specify that a nonemergency request will receive a response in 48 hours. This is only a sample value. Your organization might have a different value or none defined. Update the value or reword the description to suit your organization's needs. Note that there are additional references to this 48 hour/2 day wait period that you would also need to update.

Create the Views

There are a number of views that can be created for the Service Requests list. Many of these can be drawn from the Fab 40 Help Desk template. For the sake of brevity, you will define three commonly used views: My Service Requests, Entered and Active Service Requests, and Service Requests Needing Action.

Each of these views will be used primarily by a specific user group. My Service Requests will be used by end users to track the progress of their service requests. Entered and Active Service Requests will be used by help desk users to find incoming service requests to be worked on. Service Requests Needing Action will be used by IT managers to find emergency requests, as well as requests that have been entered but not moved from the entered status after two days.

Use the information in the following table as input to define the My Service Requests view.

Field	Value
View Name	My Service Requests
Start From an Existing View	All Items
Default View	No
Audience	Public
Columns	Service Request IsEmergency Status
Sort	ID
Filter	Created By = [Me]
Inline Editing	No
Tabular View	No
Group By	None
Totals	None
Style	Default
Folders	Show items inside folders
Item Limit	10, Display items in batches
Mobile	Enable, 3

Next you will define the Entered and Active Service Requests view. Use the information in the following table as input to define this view.

Field	Value
View Name	Entered and Active Service Requests
Start From an Existing View	All Items
Default View	No
Audience	Public
Columns	Service Request IsEmergency Status
Sort	Start Time
Filter	Status = Entered or Status = Active
Inline Editing	No
Tabular View	No
Group By	None
Totals	None
Style	Default
Folders	Show items inside folders
Item Limit	30, Display items in batches
Mobile	Enable, 3

The last view is Service Requests Needing Action. This view will have additional sorting and grouping because it captures two different classifications of requests: emergency and nonemergency requests that are inactive for more than two days. Use the information in the following table to create the new view.

Field	Value
View Name	Service Requests Needing Action
Start From an Existing View	All Items
Default View	No
Audience	Public
Columns	Service Request IsEmergency Status Created
Sort	IsEmergency, then Created
Filter	IsEmergency = Yes or Created is less than [Today] − 2 and Status = Entered
Inline Editing	No

Field	Value
Tabular View	No
Group By	None
Totals	None
Style	Default
Folders	Show items inside folders
Item Limit	30, Display items in batches
Mobile	Enable, 3

This concludes the creation and configuration of the Service Requests list. Next up is the Service Request Tasks list that will be associated with the Service Requests list.

Create Service Request Tasks List

The Service Requests list will be used for tracking individual service requests. Service requests can have a number of subtasks that may need to be completed to fulfill a given service request. You will be creating a customized task list to track these service request tasks.

Create the List

The Service Request Tasks list will be based on the out-of-the-box Tasks list template. Use the information in the following table to fill out the metadata when creating the list.

Name	Template	Description	Navigation
Service Request Tasks	Tasks	This list contains all the tasks associated with service requests.	Yes

Create the Columns

Tasks created in the Service Requests Tasks list will have a parent service request in the Service Requests list. This hierarchical relationship can be represented in a lookup column relating the task to the Service Requests list. Use the following information to create a new column for the Service Request Tasks list.

Field	Value
Column Name	ParentServiceRequest
Type	Lookup
Description	(Leave blank)
Required	Yes
Enforce Unique	No
Get Information From	Service Requests

Field	Value
In This Column	Service Request
Allow Multiple Values	No
Add to Default View	Yes
Enforce Relationship Behavior	Yes, cascade delete
Indexed Column	Yes (prompt appears after click OK)

Create the Views

The list of service request tasks could potentially grow very large. It's helpful to create a view that will filter the tasks to only the ones that the logged-in user owns. Ownership in this scenario is defined by the user who created the service request. Note that this is separate from the out-of-the-box My Tasks view included with a list based on the Tasks template. Use the information in the following table as input for creating a new view.

Field	Value
View Name	My Service Request Tasks
Start From an Existing View	All Events
Default View	No
Audience	Public
Columns	Service Request IsEmergency Status
Sort	ID
Filter	Created By = [Me]
Inline Editing	No
Tabular View	No
Group By	None
Totals	None
Style	Default
Folders	Show items inside folders
Item Limit	10, Display items in batches
Mobile	Enable, 3

Create Service Request Workflow

As mentioned earlier in this chapter, the management of service requests is very process oriented and follows a defined set of paths. You will be implementing a SharePoint list workflow to follow this path. At a high level, the workflow process will take the following steps (refer to the logical workflow diagram earlier in chapter for more details):

- Log initialization and check if request is an emergency
- Send confirmation email to requestor
- Update item metadata
- Send follow-up email to requestor and help desk users
- Send resolved email when request completed
- Log conclusion

 Note If you have not already done so, please read the section "Create the Workflow" on page 163 in Chapter 4 for an example of creating a list workflow with SharePoint Designer 2010. It contains many screenshots and instructions that will be helpful if this is your first time using SharePoint Designer 2010 for implementing a workflow.

Create the Workflow

Launch SharePoint Designer 2010 and open the URL of the help desk site. Click Workflows in the bar at the left. Use the information in the following table as input for the workflow metadata.

Type	Target List	Name	Description
List Workflow	Service Requests	New Service Request Created	This workflow sends notifications throughout life cycle and checks if service request is active after specific time period.

Next, create the workflow steps. Use the information in the following table to define the step name and action types to insert inside the associated step.

Step Name	Action Type

Initialization	Log to History List
	If current item field equals value
	   ■ Set Workflow Variable
	Else
	   ■ Set Workflow Variable

Send Confirmation Email	Send an Email
Set Status	Update List Item

Step Name	Action Type
Send Follow-Up Email	Parallel block (will contain two substeps)
Send Resolved Email	Wait for Field Change in Current Item Send an Email
Conclusion	Log to History List

Notice in the Send Follow-Up Email step that you added a parallel block. Practically speaking, a parallel block is not an action type but is more similar to a workflow execution pattern. In a standard SharePoint Designer 2010 workflow, all actions are executed sequentially, meaning that each action follows after the completion of the previous action. A parallel block executes actions (or steps) at the same time and doesn't wait for the others to finish. The following illustrations show the difference between sequential (first illustration) and parallel (second illustration) actions.

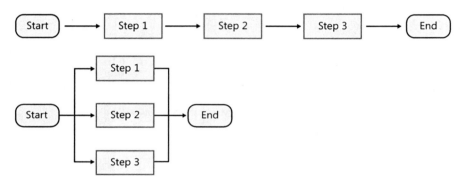

In your scenario, you want to send emails to two different groups of users. Because there are different conditions and configurations, it is best to group these actions into substeps that will run in parallel. Use the information in the following table to create two substeps and associated actions for the parallel block inside the Send Follow-Up Email step.

Step Name	Action Type
Send Follow-Up Email—To Help Desk	Pause for Duration If current item field equals value ■ Send an Email
Send Follow-Up Email—To Requestor	Wait for Field Change in Current Item ■ Send an Email

There is one workflow variable that you need to create for the workflow. This variable will keep track of the number of days the workflow might need to pause before sending a reminder to defined groups. Use the information in the following table to create the workflow variable.

Variable Name	Type
Number Days Pause Before Reminder	Integer

The next step will be to fill in the values of the actions that you have added. Start with the Initialization step. Use the information in the following table to fill in the values for the actions.

Action Type	Value
Log to History List	New service request workflow initiated from item "[%Current Item:Service Request%]" with ID "[%Current Item:ID%]" being added.
If Current Item Field Equals Value	If Current Item:IsEmergency equals Yes
Set Workflow Variable	Set Variable: Number Days Pause Before Reminder to 0
Else	NA
Set Workflow Variable	Set Variable: Number Days Pause Before Reminder to 2

Move on to the Send Confirmation Email step. Use the following information to fill out the Send An Email action.

Action Type	Value
Send An Email	Email ■ To = Current Item: Created By ■ Subject = Your service request [%Current Item:ID%]: "[%Current Item:Service Request%]" has been received

Note To properly send emails from SharePoint, you need to be sure that your farm has been configured for outgoing mail via the settings in Central Administration. The steps to configure this feature are outside the scope of our solution, but refer your farm administrator to the following article if necessary: *technet.microsoft.com/en-us/library/cc263462.aspx.*

The next step to complete is Set Status. Use the following information to fill in the values for the Update List Item action.

Action Type	Value
Update List Item	Update item in Current Item ■ Status = Entered

As mentioned previously, the Send Follow-Up Email step has two substeps. You will configure the Send Follow-Up Email—To Help Desk step first. Use the information in the following table to fill in the actions for this step. Note that the Help Desk Users and Help Desk Managers groups are generic names. The groups that you use will be unique to your environment.

Action Type	Value
Pause for Duration	Pause for Variable: Number Days Pause Before Reminder days, 0 hours, 0 minutes
If Current Item Field Equals Value	If Current Item: Status equals Entered
Send an Email	Email ■ To = Help Desk Users ■ CC = Help Desk Managers ■ Subject = Service Request [%Current Item:ID%]: "[%Current Item:Service Request%]" has not been worked on

Next you will complete the Send Follow-Up Email—To Requestor step. Use the following information to fill in the actions for this step.

Action Type	Value
Wait for Field Change in Current Item	Wait for Status to not equal Entered
Send an Email	Email ■ To = Current Item: Created By ■ Subject = Your service request [%Current Item:ID%]: "[%Current Item:Service Request%]" has moved to an active state

The next step is Send Resolved Email. Use the following information to fill in the actions for this step.

Action Type	Value
Wait for Field Change in Current Item	Wait for Status to equal Resolved
Send an Email	Email ■ To = Current Item: Created By ■ Subject = Your service request [%Current Item:ID%]: "[%Current Item:Service Request%]" has moved to a resolved state

The last step to configure is the Conclusion step. Use the information in the following table to fill in the logging message.

Action Type	Value
Log to History List	New discussion workflow concluding from item "[%Current Item:Service Request%]" with ID "[%Current Item:ID%]" being added.

After you complete all of the configuration steps, your workflow should look similar to the following screenshot.

Integrate with External Workflow (Informational)

One new feature of SharePoint 2010 is its ability to use external, or pluggable, workflows. External workflows were available in the Workflow Foundation APIs that SharePoint leveraged since SharePoint 2007, but the SharePoint implementation of the workflow engine locked down these APIs until SharePoint 2010. Now it is possible to have a SharePoint workflow make calls to external systems, workflows, or processes and receive data back that is then acted on.

The implementation and configuration of external workflows can be fairly complex. External workflows are available only by building them in Visual Studio 2010. You also need to define an external event receiver for the external process to call into. You can get more information and examples at *msdn.microsoft.com/en-us/magazine/ee335710.aspx*.

The purpose of mentioning external workflows in this chapter is to provide options for integration with other systems you might use. These could be anything from third-party task-management systems to time-entry workflows to resource-scheduling processes and beyond. Work with your developers and managers to decide if there are integration points that make sense for your scenario and environment.

Export Workflow: SharePoint Designer to Visio (Optional)

When the workflow diagram was introduced earlier in this chapter, it was mentioned that you would walk through the process of exporting and importing the workflow in Visio Premium and SharePoint Designer. In this section you can walk through those steps so that you are aware of the process.

First, open the New Service Request Created workflow that you just completed in SharePoint Designer 2010. On the ribbon, look for the Export To Visio button, as shown here:

You will be prompted to save the file with a .VWI (Visio Workflow Interchange) extension. Choose a folder location, type a file name, and click Save. You are now ready to import this file into a Visio diagram.

Launch Visio Premium 2010 if you have not done so yet. You cannot import a .VWI file directly to Visio. Instead, you must create a blank workflow diagram that you then overwrite with your imported .VWI file. Create a new diagram by selecting the Flowchart category Microsoft SharePoint Workflow. Next, click the Process tab on the ribbon and click Import in the SharePoint Workflow group. Refer to the following screenshot for the appearance of the Import and Export buttons you use in Visio.

Select the .VWI file that you exported from SharePoint Designer. Visio will convert the SharePoint Designer workflow steps, actions, and interactions into Visio components. The resulting diagram may not look the same as the workflow diagram earlier in this chapter. You can move elements and process flow arrows to match that diagram if you want to.

Export Workflow: Visio to SharePoint Designer (Optional)

The process to export a drawing from Visio Premium 2010 to SharePoint Designer 2010 is similar to the process you just went through. Open the Visio diagram if you closed it. Click the Process tab on the ribbon, and then click Export. Again you will be presented with a dialog box to save the file with a .VWI extension. Choose a folder location, type a file name, and click Save.

Now switch back to SharePoint Designer 2010 or launch it if you closed it. Open the help desk site you are implementing. Click Workflows on the menu at the left. You will notice that the Import From Visio button is enabled on the ribbon. The following screenshot shows this button.

Click the Import From Visio button and specify the .VWI file that you exported from Visio. If you are importing into the same site that you originally exported from, you will receive a warning dialog box stating that you will replace the existing workflow. The following screenshot shows an example of that warning dialog box. As the message states, this operation cannot be undone, so be sure that you are overwriting the correct workflow.

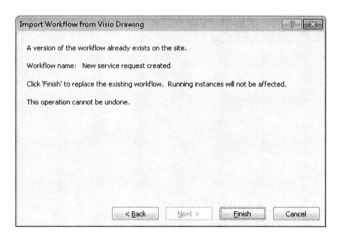

Click Finish to continue. If you have not made any changes to the workflow in Visio, the imported workflow should look just as it did when you exported it from SharePoint Designer. This concludes the process of exporting and importing in SharePoint Designer 2010 and Visio Premium 2010.

Configure Wiki Pages

Earlier in the chapter, you created three wiki pages to be used by the different user groups. Now that you have created the site infrastructure with lists and views, it is time to add and configure useful web parts on those pages.

Add List Web Part to Page

Each of the three pages needs a list view web part for the Service Requests list, but they will be configured with different views. Use the information in the following table to add an instance of the specified web part and view to the associated page. Since there are no web part zones on these wiki pages, you will add them all to the Rich Content area.

Page	Web Part	View
End Users	Service Requests	My Service Requests
Help Desk Users	Service Requests	Entered and Active Service Requests
IT Managers	Service Requests	Service Requests Needing Action

On the Help Desk Users page, it would be helpful to display any associated service request tasks filtered by a selected service request. You can do this by creating what is called a *web part connection*. You can add the Service Request Tasks web part and create the web part connection in one action by using the Insert Related List button on the ribbon. With the Help Desk Users page in edit mode, click the upper-right box of the Service Requests web part. Next click Options on the Web Part Tools tab. Click Insert Related List and select Service Request Tasks from the list of options. See the following screenshot for an example.

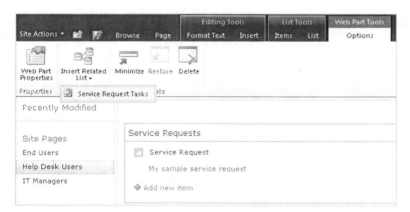

After you have inserted the related list, you can rearrange the web parts to put Service Requests above Service Request Tasks. The following screenshot illustrates this configuration along with a sample service request and associated task.

Configure Audiences on Web Part (Optional)

As mentioned in the section "Designing the Solution" on page 181, you will not be implementing audience targeting in this solution. The following, however, is a quick overview of the process and components that are required. Some of these items might require the assistance of your farm administrator because they involve farmwide configurations.

Audiences are based on user profiles. Thus, the first component that you need is a running instance of the User Profile Service service application. From the User Profile Service settings page you will define an audience. Audiences are composed of one to many filters. Once the filters are defined, you must compile the membership for the audience. At this point, you have a usable audience to which you can target content. When you edit an applicable web part, you will see a new option for target audience. Assign the target audience, and now they will begin to see the targeted content.

End Result

You should now have a fully functioning help desk application. As with any application, you should review and test all functionality from the perspective of each user type. Use the following information to perform the activities per user role to ensure that your site is working properly. Note that this is not a full test of functionality or compatibility.

User Role	Activity to Test
End User	■ Enter an emergency service request ■ Enter a nonemergency service request ■ Navigate to the End Users wiki page ■ Check mailbox for confirmation emails
Help Desk User	■ Navigate to the Help Desk Users wiki page ■ Add a service request task for each request ■ Update status of service requests to Resolved
IT Managers	■ Navigate to the IT Managers wiki page

Reviewing the Platform

The solution in this chapter was focused on using SharePoint Server Standard. Since you may not be using this version of SharePoint, take a minute to review what the other versions have to offer.

Using SharePoint Foundation

If you are using SharePoint Foundation, you will have access to the majority of features used to build the solution presented in this chapter. There are a few SharePoint Server specific elements that will not be usable, such as audiences that target content (web parts in this solution) to specific end user groups.

Using SharePoint Online with Office 365

If you are using SharePoint Online, the implementation of this solution will be very similar to that of SharePoint Foundation. There are a few optional components, such as external workflows, that will not be available to you, however, because they require farm solutions, and SharePoint Online supports only sandbox solutions. As with SharePoint Foundation, you will not have access to audiences.

Using SharePoint Server Enterprise

If you are using SharePoint Server Enterprise, you will have access to additional business intelligence (BI) and reporting service applications such as Excel Services and PerformancePoint Services. These could be used to analyze the metrics from the service requests, create dashboards with KPIs (key performance indicators), and visualize trending patterns.

Summary

In this chapter you solved business problems associated with an IT department setting up a help desk application. The problems included tracking service requests, ensuring that service requests are worked on in a timely manner, and keeping end users updated on request status. The solution was based on SharePoint Server Standard and included lists, wiki pages, workflows, and list view web parts.

CHAPTER 6

Building a Remote Teams Activity Site

In this chapter, you will work through the process of creating an activity site for geographically dispersed teams. The site enables remote teams to better collaborate and track both deliverables and tasks. This solution demonstrates a method for aggregating documents, tasks, and calendars, with events color-coded by region in a top-level site that provides individual team views into the same data. The need for aggregating documents, tasks, and events is common in organizations seeking to better connect their remote teams and still provide a filtered view for each team. The chapter is built around functionality in SharePoint Enterprise, although most functionality is available in other versions.

Identifying the Business Problems

In most matrix organizations, it can be easy to lose perspective on projects and priorities across the broader organization. Teams need the ability to centrally track and manage important project documents, assign and track tasks, and manage events at a team level, but they also might need to view these team artifacts at a higher organizational level to better assess overlaps and scheduling conflicts. In this chapter, we outline a simple team-based activity site and then create an aggregated view at the business unit or organizational level. While your own business or team might require a more detailed solution, with additional metadata components or custom workflows, this scenario should resolve some of the basic areas of concern discussed in the sections that follow.

Calendar Review

Currently, schedules are being coordinated by email and shared Exchange calendars rather than in a transparent way on a central SharePoint site. What tends to happen is that many end users are left out of the loop, not all calendars are open to others, the free-busy functionality in email calendars is sometimes unreliable, and the complexity of viewing so many calendars in Outlook makes planning and organizing at a large scale difficult. This chapter's solution provides the ability for each team to control its own calendar, but it also provides a single, centralized calendar that combines all team calendars for improved planning.

Permissions Controls

Each team wants to maintain control over its events and artifacts, sharing only that data that is relevant to a broader audience. While all employees might have access to the top-level site and shared calendar, individual teams may want the ability to lock down access to their team sites, calendars, and any document or task repositories.

Different organizations might have varying security needs, but in the proposed model, teams can make the decision on what to open to the broader organization or lock down to only those team members that require access.

Team Site Individuality

The top-level organizational calendar and site should follow corporate standards for look and feel and use any core content and web parts that make this site consistent with any internal SharePoint standards and organizational guidelines. However, teams should be allowed to design their team sites to meet their individual tastes and collaborative needs. While the team calendar will roll up to the organizational level, team document libraries, task lists, link lists, and any other web parts should, for the most part, remain unique to the team site.

One of the most compelling stories around SharePoint is the ability it provides for individual teams to design and build SharePoint environments that allow them to collaborate and work in the way that best suits that team—but to do so within a common framework and with a series of shared services that allow for centralized governance and management of the platform.

Summarizing the Business Problems

We have briefly covered three problems that are affecting the widespread support and use of a shared calendar within the organization:

- Ability to centralize a shared calendar while maintaining team-level visibility and control

- Ability to customize permissions by team

- Ability to individualize team sites

Using SharePoint, you will build a site that addresses each of these issues and provides an automated solution for the given problems. The first step in the process of building this solution is to understand the key issues identified in this section. The next step is to gather the information that is required to build the solution.

Gathering Information

With the business problems defined, we can now turn our attention to gathering the specific requirements. This step includes a look at the unique users of the solution as well as their specific needs.

All Employees

Our solution will focus on the needs of three user types—all end users, members of individual teams, and content authors, who have the ability to post documents and tasks on the top-level site. (Most end users can only post within their defined team site.) To fully understand the needs of the solution, each user group needs to provide information about the specific tasks its members need to complete within the system. This information will then be used to design and develop the solution.

Team Members

Employees will access the top-level activity site to compare schedules with sister teams and to create or edit document and task details at the organizational level. They will also be accessing calendar information, adding events, and adding and reviewing content and tasks (and using other web parts and artifacts) at the team level. This will include the following actions:

- Review team calendar
- Review team calendar against other team calendars
- Add new team event
- Add new content
- Add new tasks

Management Content Authors

Content authors are responsible for posting content at the top-level site—content and tasks that require visibility across all teams, not just an individual team site. Specifically, these content authors are responsible for the following tasks:

- Add new content to the top-level site
- Add new tasks to the top-level site

Solution Data

Users make up one portion of the solution. Another portion relates to the data that is to be captured. Here are a number of the data types that the solution requires:

- Event title
- Description

- Event type

- Start date

- Complete date

- Team

In your organization, you might require additional data to be captured depending on how much detail and content is centralized. In this scenario, three remote teams seek only to share their schedules (events), but in other scenarios, teams may want to also share documents and tasks across the broader organization.

Summarizing the Requirements Gathering Process

Now that we have completed the process of looking at the users of the solution and the types of data that will be included, it is time to start building the solution design. Before we do that, however, we should take a few minutes and summarize the process we just completed:

1. We defined the business needs for providing multiple remotely located teams with the means to share their team-related event information with the broader organization.

2. All users were consulted and requirements were gathered based on their specific team needs.

3. All data required for the solution was identified based on the needs of the end users.

In the next section of the chapter, we will look at how to translate these requirements into a working design.

Designing the Solution

It is now time to look at some of the important decisions that may affect the time it takes to make the solution available to your organization. It is important to review your options and develop a plan before moving forward. This ensures that you have completed the due diligence required to fully understand the business needs and requirements.

The sections that follow discuss design decisions and wireframes. The design decisions section reviews the various tools that will be used to create this solution and provides details about why they were selected. The wireframes section shows the pages to be created, which helps you visualize the solution. Ideally, these mock-ups are created, reviewed, and approved by the solution stakeholders prior to any development being completed.

Design Decisions

In this solution, several key points need to be discussed about the tools that will be used and the methods that will be implemented for creating and managing the content. This section reviews each of the key areas and provides information about the reason the selection was made.

> **Important** Your environment and scenario might differ from the one presented in the book. As you follow along in the chapter, be sure to make note of the things that differ and then adjust your solution development accordingly.

Setting Permissions

This solution includes five primary groups of users. The first group contains all end users across the organization, including three remote teams. This group might not include all authorized users in your system. It could be a subset of your company with read-only access to the top-level site. Three of the groups correspond to the three remote teams. The fifth group consists of team leads, managers, or other authorized content authors who can post content to the top-level site that is pertinent to all three remote teams. Unique site permissions will be granted to each of these groups, which means that every user within a group will have the same permissions and that each remote team will be able to manage who can access their team site and what level of permissions they receive.

It is important to understand the top-level site permissions and how your activity site solution might differ. Given the creation of the new user groups, we recommend that you break the permissions inheritance from the parent site and modify the permissions to meet your security goals. Separating classes of end users allows for greater control over any content authoring and approval process, which ensures that only defined users can add content or events to the activity site.

Clarifying Event Activities

The solution will walk through the creation of a top-level site and three separate team sites, each with a calendar and each with the potential to include unique lists and tools based on the specific collaborative needs of its associated team. Some teams might require an approval workflow for their event creation, an example of which is covered in Chapter 7.

Content Security

Depending on your environment and its content security requirements, this solution might not meet your needs. This solution assumes that all employees will have access to the published calendar on the top-level site. If you have scenarios that include additional subsets of employees and want to publish content to different groups based on category, for example, you should update the solution structure to account for the added security requirements.

A single team calendar can provide a feed (through the calendar overlay feature) to multiple aggregated calendars, each with unique permissions, but each aggregated calendar is limited to 10 calendar overlays.

Solution Wireframes

The solution in this chapter uses the out-of-the-box Group Work Site template, but it can also be created from the basic Team Site template. The out-of-the-box views in these two templates are different, but they function the same way. The wireframes shown in this section will help project stakeholders better understand the scope of the project and the implications of permissions configurations before any development has been completed.

Group Activity Site

This is the home page for the entire solution. From this page, users will be able to access aggregated calendar items, color-coded based on team, and review any tasks or content added at the organizational level. Permissions are view-only for the majority of end users, with calendar items accessed through the individual team sites. Tasks and shared content at this level are maintained by a select group of administrators.

For the sake of this example, the template is being kept very simple, but more solutions and complexity can be added to automate aggregation of content, tasks, and other important activities from this top-level site.

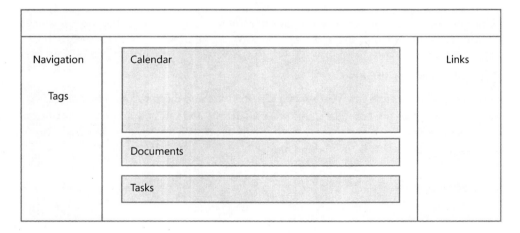

Team Activity Site

On this page, each team is able to manage and control its own calendar items, project tasks, and shared documents. In addition, although this template is being kept simple for the sake of this solution, real-world teams could add additional web parts and solutions that are relevant to their team.

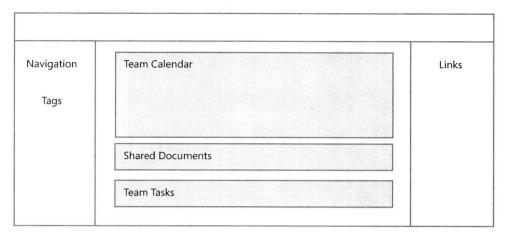

These wireframes should provide you with the basic outline of how to set up your environment for this solution. Your organization will likely want to include branding, additional web parts and solutions, and custom navigation to help your final site fit with the flow and functionality of your portal, but the designs shown here should serve as a good starting point. As for any web project, you should ensure that the entire team verifies that you are moving in the right direction before you move forward with building the solution.

Building the Solution

It is now time to start building the solution. The first step is to create the top-level site collection. Once the site is created, the primary calendar list will be created and customized and the subsites created and modified. Finally, we will configure permissions across all sites and discuss additional options.

Build the Team Activity Site

The team activity site collection will be created from Central Administration. It will use the settings listed in the following table and be based on the Group Work Site template. If you don't have access to your farm's Central Administration pages, you should request a site be created using the information listed.

You can also create this solution by using the Team Site template, which contains some of the same out-of-the-box web parts, depending on your future plans to add to the template. While the default calendar view might look different in these two templates, the functionality is the same.

Create your team activity site with the following parameters:

Field	Value
Web Application	http://www.tailspintoys.com/
Title	ActivitySite
Description	Centralized activity site for remote teams
URL	.../sites/activitysite
Template Selection	Group Work Site or Team Site
Primary Site Collection Owner	Wallace, Anne
Secondary Site Collection Owner	Duncan, Bart
Quota Template	Application_40GB

The activity site will probably be considered part of the corporate intranet and should be named appropriately to remain consistent with company branding and navigation standards.

1. On the Central Admin home page, select Create Site Collections in the Application Management group.

2. Select the Group Work Site template, and enter the information as provided in the preceding table. Click OK to provision the site collection.

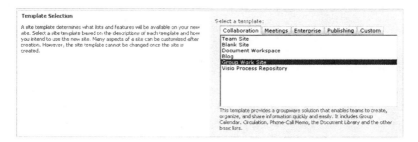

3. After the site is provisioned, follow the link provided to open the new site collection and bookmark the location in your browser for easy reference while building out the solution.

Create Team Subsites

Once you have established your top-level team activity site, you can create subsites for each individual team within the organization. Only approved team members will have the ability to publish content and calendar items within their team's subsite, which will help enforce document security and also ensure that only authorized team members are able to modify team calendar activities that roll up to the broader organization through the top-level team activity site.

Creating Subsites

From the top-level team activity site, you will create a new site based on the Team Site template and then add the appropriate web parts and content.

1. Go to Site Actions, New Site.

2. In the Create dialog box, select the Team Site template. On the right, enter the following parameters:

Field	Value
Team Site Name	Team 1 Site
Team Site URL	Team1

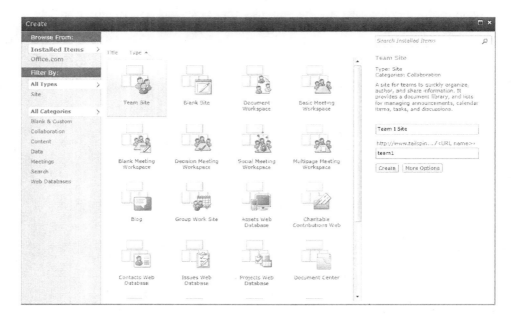

3. Click Create.

4. Navigate back to the top-level team activity site, and then repeat the process two more times, adding Team 2 Site and Team 3 Site. You should have one top-level team activity site, with subsites for Team 1, Team 2, and Team 3.

5. After the subsites are completed, navigate back to the top-level team activity site.

With the default settings configured when you add these subsites, your top-level navigation should appear as follows, which allows individual team members to quickly navigate to their appropriate team sites.

Add Calendar to Team Site Page

When building out your individual team site pages, you need to deploy the Calendar web part to your team site and change the default view. The calendar is part of the template, but it does not, by default, appear on the front page. To add the calendar to your team site, do the following:

1. On Team 1 Site, go to Site Actions, and then select Edit Page.

2. Click the center web part zone on the page, and then on the Editing Tools Insert tab, click Web Part.

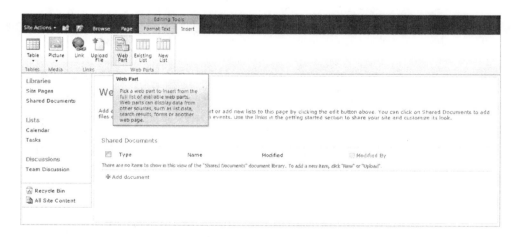

3. In the Lists And Libraries category, select Calendar, and then click Add.

The calendar should be added to the center zone and is now ready for adding events.

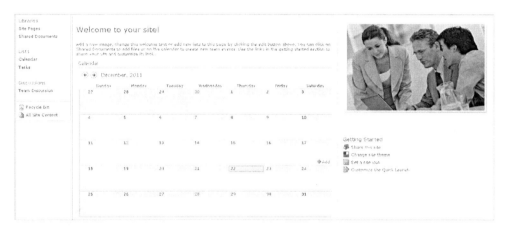

Cleaning Up Unused Web Parts

For the purpose of this solution, we are going to remove most components from the standard Team Site template. Each individual team might have its own standards for look and feel and will decide which components it wants to leave in place. This solution will focus on the Calendar web part, with suggestions for managing the Shared Documents library and the Links and Tasks lists at the team level.

To remove unwanted web parts and text, continue using edit mode by going to Site Actions, Edit Page. Then follow these steps:

1. Highlight unwanted text and delete.

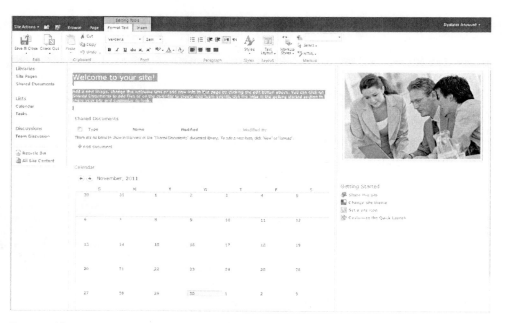

2. Repeat this step to remove any unwanted images or any other items within the rich text workspace, such as the Getting Started section.

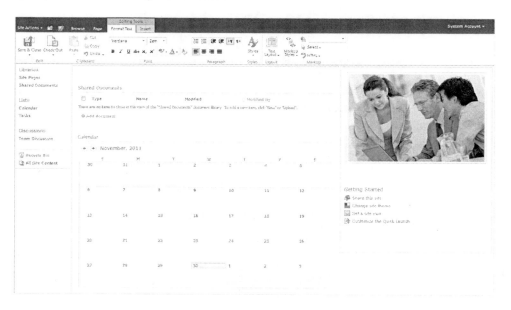

3. To move a web part to another section, simply drag it to the appropriate location. In this example, drag the Shared Documents web part to the right column. Also, add a new Tasks web part to the center column underneath your team calendar. When you're done modifying the look and feel of your page, exit out of edit mode.

Adding Calendar Items

Because it can be difficult to test some functionality without data, at this stage you should add some temporary events to each team calendar. Add two or three events per calendar, with one event occurring at the same time as one of the events on each of the other sites. This will allow you to see the overlapping schedules and ensure that everything is working as designed.

As you create each event, provide the necessary data from the following table.

Field	Value
Title	Meeting Name
Location	Room/Building
Start Time	Select start time
End Time	Select end time
Description	Enter a brief meeting description
Category	Meeting
All Day Event	No
Recurrence	No
Workspace	No

For this exercise, keep the temporary events simple. To create your test events, go to Team 1 Site, select the Calendar web part, and follow these steps:

1. On the Calendar Tools Events tab, click New Event.

2. Complete the new event form using the information from the preceding table.

3. After the form is complete, click Save. Your new event should now appear in the calendar view.

4. Repeat the process, adding several calendar items for testing purposes. Once the events are added, your calendar should appear something like the following:

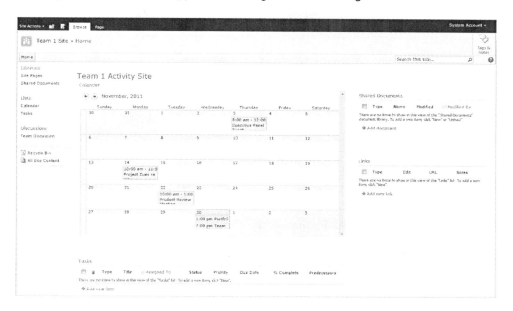

Edit Activity Site Calendar View

The default calendar view for the top-level activity site template is the weekly view. To give site visitors a more comprehensive view of the shared calendar, we will change the view to the monthly view.

1. Open the context menu on the far right of the Calendar web part, and select Edit Web Part.

2. The Group Calendar configuration menu will appear on the far right. Select Edit The Current View.

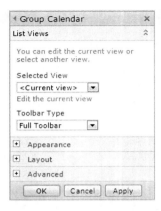

3. The Edit Calendar View page will open. In the Default Scope section, change from the Week Group option to the Month option, and then click OK.

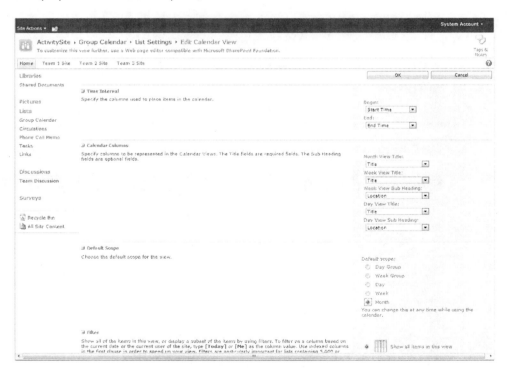

4. Your default view will be updated to the month view.

You could repeat these steps to modify the calendar view on the group calendar page as well, to keep your views consistent across all calendars.

Now that you have set your default view, you can clean up (remove) any content or web parts on the team activity site that will not be part of your final design. We will add the Shared Documents and Links web parts to the right column and the Tasks web part beneath the calendar (even though these components are not relevant to the overall solution).

Note To move the Tasks list below the Calendar web part, edit the page, and then edit the web part. In the Tasks edit controls on the right, go to Layout, Zone Index, then type **2**, and then apply your change. This will move the web part to the correct position.

Once your functional layout is done, you are ready to add calendar overlays to link the three team site calendars to your top-level team activity site.

Create a Calendar Overlay

Calendar overlays are an out-of-the-box feature in SharePoint 2010 and are fairly simple to set up. The major limitation is that only 10 overlays can be performed on a calendar. Each calendar overlay can be color-coded, making identification of overlapping team activities easier to decipher.

Note You must go through the steps of creating calendar overlays for each page on which you wish to see these overlays. In other words, the overlays will only be viewable on the page (the calendar) in which you create them. If you were to add a view into your calendar on a separate page, you would need to recreate the overlays for that view.

To add calendar overlays, do the following:

1. On your top-level team activity site, click the Group Calendar title to go to the calendar page.

2. On the Calendar Tools Calendar tab, click Calendars Overlay.

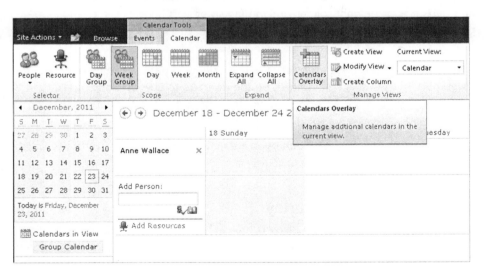

3. The Calendar Overlay Settings window opens. Select New Calendar.

4. The New Calendar dialog box opens. Create and point to the new calendar overlay by adding the following information.

Field	Value
Calendar Name	Team 1
Type	SharePoint
Description	Team 1 Calendar
Color	Select color from drop-down menu
Web URL	http://www.tailspintoys.com/sites/Activity/Team1
List	Calendar
List View	Calendar
Always Show	Selected

5. As you complete the form, the web URL should point to the team site and not include the calendar itself. SharePoint will locate the calendar on its own. Click Resolve to confirm that the URL has been entered correctly, which will automatically populate the List and List View options.

6. Select a unique color for each team site, select Always Show, and then click OK to complete the calendar overlay.

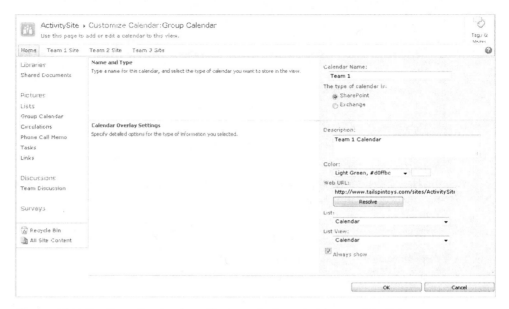

Once added, the Team 1 calendar will appear in the calendar overlays list.

7. Add the calendars for Team 2 and Team 3 following the same steps. Use a unique color to identify each. Once you complete the steps, the calendar overlays list should appear as follows:

8. Go back to the group calendar. All three team site calendar overlays should now appear on the site.

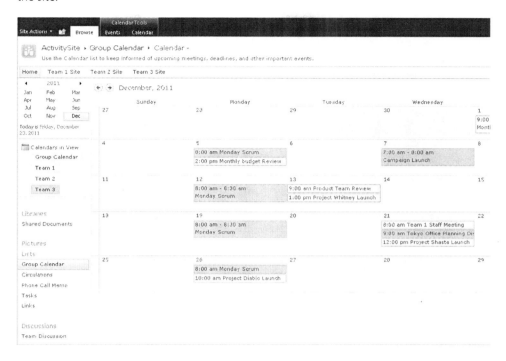

Establish Site Permissions

There are a number of ways that you can protect your content and calendars, including automating workflow and using document-level permissions. Additionally, you can manage permissions using either Active Directory groups or SharePoint groups. Active Directory groups should be more static and are generally less flexible for the proactive changes necessary inside SharePoint, so for this solution we will focus on creating SharePoint groups and assigning their permissions within our scope.

Breaking Inheritance for the Team Sites

By default, permissions for the team activity sites will be inherited from the parent site unless they are created with custom permissions. Because we will be specifying unique permissions for the top-level team activity site and its underlying team sites, you need to break the permissions inheritance from the parent site and change the permissions settings. When you break inheritance, you are simply creating a copy of the existing permissions, which allows you to customize them to meet your specific needs.

1. On the Site Actions menu, select Site Settings.

2. Select Users And Permissions, and click Site Permissions. This displays the Permission Tools tab and a list of all individuals and groups with current permissions.

3. If the site is inheriting permissions, select Stop Inheriting Permissions on the ribbon, and then click OK to continue.

Creating New Groups and Setting Site Permissions for Team Sites

Now that you have established unique permissions for your top-level team activity site, you can set up permissions for the team members within each of your team sites. The standard templates used come with several groups already in place, which you can modify or remove. Because the differences between the various standard groups can be confusing, for this solution we will walk through the creation of five new groups with distinct functions and permissions.

To set up your new groups, follow these steps:

1. Go to Site Actions, Site Permissions to see a list of all current SharePoint groups and individuals that were part of the previously inherited site permissions.

2. Select Create Group on the ribbon.

The Create Group page opens.

3. Create the Team 1 group, completing the form with the following information, and then click Create. The purpose of this group is to give all members of Team 1 write access for their site. You may also decide to restrict access to the site for all other users, or possibly give other users read-only access. If this is the case, it may be easier to create an Active Directory group for each team site and manage these user subsets in Active Directory instead of through SharePoint groups.

Field	Value
Name	Team 1
Description	All Team 1 Members
Owner	Your name and the names of other group owners
Group Settings	Group members should be able to view membership of the group. Group owners should be able to edit membership to the group.
Membership Requests	Allow requests to join or leave this group. By default, auto-accept requests are not allowed, and no e-mail is required for membership requests. Add email for join and leave requests.
Give Group Permission to This Site	Contribute access

The new group is created, and the group membership page is displayed.

4. Add users to this group by selecting New, Add Users.

5. The Grant Permissions dialog box opens, in which you can enter individual names or select from the directory. Search for the appropriate corporate or NT Authorized (authorized corporate users) group to allow all authorized employees to view the activity site.

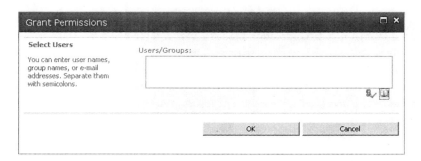

The new Team 1 group now appears on the page shown here:

6. Repeat this step to create the Team 2 and Team 3 groups.

7. Once you complete these steps, navigate up to the top-level team activity site, and repeat this process to create a permissions group for content authors. This role is for adding content and tasks to the top-level activity site. These may be leaders, project managers, or trusted content authors. They will be able to assign tasks across all three teams and add content that will be visible to all authorized users.

Field	Value
Name	Content Authors
Description	Content Authors from Tailspin Toys
Owner	Your name and the names of other group owners
Group Settings	Group members should be able to view membership of the group. Group owners should be able to edit membership to the group.
Membership Requests	Allow requests to join or leave this group. Do not allow auto-accept requests to join this group. Provide an e-mail to receive membership requests.
Give Group Permission to This Site	Contribute access

When adding content authors to this new group, select those individuals who will regularly and consistently post content to the site.

8. Finally, follow the same steps as described previously and create one more permissions group at the top-level activity site, giving view-only access to all NT Authorized users. This will give all authorized users the ability to view but not to modify the calendar, content, and tasks published on the team activity site.

Field	Value
Name	All Users
Description	Authorized Employees of Tailspin Toys
Owner	Your name and the names of other group owners
Group Settings	Group members should be able to view membership of the group. Group owners should be able to edit membership to the group.
Membership Requests	Allow requests to join or leave this group. Do not allow auto-accept requests to join this group. Provide an e-mail to receive membership requests.
Give Group Permission to This Site	View-only

Note Name your groups appropriately. At any time, you can use the Group Settings dialog box to delete a group if it is no longer relevant. You can access this dialog box by going to Site Actions, Site Permissions, and clicking on the relevant group name to gain access to the group profile. Then, under Settings, select Group Settings.

From here, you can delete a group by clicking Delete at the bottom of the dialog box.

Managing the Solution

Because the management of the top-level shared calendar has been distributed, with each individual team controlling its own events and content, managing the overall solution will be fairly simple. By design, the solution is set up around roles that will help the process run smoothly and restrict access to those who should have access.

This solution has not touched on look and feel. There are many options for design and further configuration based on the level of activity on your activity site and the need to closely mirror the look and feel of your corporate environment. But from a management standpoint, this solution should give you what you need to build a centralized calendar, with minimal management needed on an ongoing basis.

Reviewing the Platform

The solution in this chapter was built using the features available within SharePoint Enterprise. In the remainder of this section, the different options available with the various other SharePoint licenses will be highlighted.

If You Are Using SharePoint Foundation or SharePoint Server Standard

All features demonstrated in this chapter are available in both Foundation and Standard.

If You Are Using SharePoint Online with Office 365

If you are using SharePoint Online with Office 365, your environment includes the enterprise features, allowing you to re-create everything demonstrated here.

Additional Customizations

In this chapter you learned about a few customizations. However, there are still many things that can be added to this solution. This information is being provided so that you can see some of the additional customizations that you might want to incorporate into your solution.

Additional Customization	Benefits
Personal views	SharePoint allows you to create personal views into calendars, lists, and libraries. By including personal views in your design, end users will be able to focus on content relevant to them. While the purpose of this solution is to provide shared calendar data, you might consider adding a second copy of each relevant web part and then modifying the views of these duplicates to allow visitors to see group and personal views of this data.
Filter content by team	When aggregating content, it may be easier to sort content by adding a custom column. In this example, we have shared documents and tasks on the top-level team activity site. By including a column for Team Name, this data can be better sorted and tracked.
Aggregate data using the Content Query or Data View web part	Another option for filtering content is to aggregate data from each of the team sites rather than duplicate content (and effort) at the top-level site. You can use either the Content Query web part or the Data View web part to accomplish this task. Both involve modifying XML, and may require some administrative or development help to configure and deploy. If your goal is to simplify management at the top level and let the individual teams drive content creation and task assignment, you may want to investigate one of these options.
Event approval workflow	Some teams may require an approval process for any events. Because this solution places control of calendar items at the team level, each team can individually decide how it wants to manage this process. An out-of-the-box approval workflow can easily be added to the calendar list, as with any other SharePoint list, allowing teams to monitor and approve new items.

Summary

In this chapter, you learned how to create a centralized team calendar using the out-of-the-box Group Work Activity and Team Site templates and the calendar overlay feature. This solution allows teams to manage individual team and broader organizational events in a structured manner to ensure security and consistency of content. This chapter should serve as a guideline for you to implement a similar solution within your environment. Keep in mind that as you implement that solution, you can easily tweak and modify the solution described here to fit any specific needs within your organization.

CHAPTER 7

Building a Team Blog Platform

I n this chapter you will work through the process of creating a functional internal blog. Although the default blog template is functional, it lacks some key features that allow teams to manage blog content. This chapter's solution demonstrates one method for submitting new content, flagging content for peer review, and submitting content for approval. This is a common scenario for organizations seeking to provide some degree of editorial control over the content on their intranet. The chapter's example is built using functionality in SharePoint Enterprise.

Identifying the Business Problems

Blogs have been a fairly common tool for many organizations, but asserting some degree of control over the content they contain is often needed. Many teams look at blogging as an all-or-nothing activity: either you allow it, or you don't. Either authors can say what they want, or you lock the blog down (sometimes by pushing it through the legal team—in other words, no blogging). In this section, we will identify the key business problems associated with internal blogging and provide solutions for addressing these concerns. Not every issue may apply to your own business or team, but raising these issues might help resolve concerns by introducing processes and best practices for content approval. The scenario you will work through has four major areas of concern, which are discussed in the following sections.

Peer Review

Currently, content is being discussed by email rather than in a shared, transparent way that is available to the entire team. What tends to happen is that some people are missed in the distribution, while others shut out the "noise" of constant back and forth and miss important ideas and dialog. In addition, other ideas are not properly vetted with the team before being made public. The solution should provide an option to flag content for peer review by a defined group of users.

Content Approval

Management prefers to have some level of review and approval for any content being made available to the entire company. This level of control lets managers address any legal concerns, policy issues, or timeliness of the content shared about team or corporate strategy, among other topics. Depending on the volume of content being produced, there might also be a need to throttle (control) the volume of content being published, and a formal content-approval process will provide management with the ability to release content at a more measured rate.

By default, the blog template in SharePoint is set up for direct content approval—meaning that content authors with the ability to post content have the ability to publish content—unless permissions are modified. This solution will expand the approval process by creating a workflow-driven notification process for both peer review and content approval.

Personal View of Content

Most authors would like the ability to review their draft content, see which articles are awaiting peer review or final approval, and know which content has been approved and published. This solution will include a personalized view of the blog, showing a history of all personal content.

Tagging Through Categories

Many organizations increasingly recognize the importance of a planned metadata strategy, which impacts the quality of search, the accurate application of metadata to content, and the use of a taxonomy to put artifacts (documents, primarily) into the proper context. As with a content-approval process, many organizations also require the flexibility to add metadata to and remove it from their blog content to improve the overall usability of the content being published. While SharePoint does not yet provide a true out-of-the-box tag-cloud feature (compared with those on consumer-based blog platforms), this solution will walk through the easy steps of managing the category list, which provides quick tagging navigation to posted content.

Ratings

Another important feedback mechanism to help content authors and readers measure the value and effectiveness of content is a ratings system. Additionally, ratings extend the search experience—for example, locating all content with five out of five stars. The solution in this chapter demonstrates how to add this feature to the blog template.

Content Syndication (RSS)

Once content has been published, it is important to provide multiple methods for consuming the information. An RSS (Really Simple Syndication) feed is one way that users can quickly and easily subscribe to the data they want so that they don't have to go to a given site to find new content. Instead, any new content is provided to them through their RSS aggregator or email application (such as the Outlook web client). This solution will walk through the configuration steps.

Summarizing the Business Problems

We have briefly covered six different problems that are affecting the widespread support and use of blogs within the organization:

- Ability to request peer reviews

- Ability to queue content for approval

- Ability to view personally authored content

- Ability to apply tagging and metadata for easier search

- Ability to apply ratings to each blog post

- Ability to subscribe using RSS

Using SharePoint, we will build a blog site that addresses each of these issues and provides an automated solution for the given problems. The first step in the process of building this solution is to understand the key issues identified earlier in this section. The next step is to gather the information that is required to build the solution.

Gathering Information

With the business problems defined, it is now time to turn our attention to gathering the specific requirements. This step includes a look at the unique users of the solution as well as their specific needs.

System Users

Our solution will focus on the needs of four user types. To fully understand the needs of the solution, each type of user needs to provide information about the specific tasks those users need to complete within the system. This information will then be used to design and develop the solution.

All Employees

Employees access the blog to read the content and provide feedback (comments) as appropriate. This includes the following actions:

- Review most-recently published content

- Filter content based on categories

- Filter content based on tag cloud (metadata)

- Filter content based on author

- Apply content ratings

- Subscribe via RSS feed

Content Authors

Content authors are responsible for posting content and for initiating the review process. Specifically, they are responsible for the following tasks:

- Add new content
- Apply appropriate metadata (tags)
- Request peer review
- Submit post for content approval

Peer Reviewers

Peer reviewers might be content authors or other individuals in the system with peer review (write) capability. Specifically in this scenario, these users are responsible for the following tasks:

- Review pending content
- Edit pending content
- Reject content and send it back to author for further edits
- Approve content and forward it to content approver to publish

Content Approvers

Content approvers will likely be a manager or an editor who is authorized to publish content following team or organizational content guidelines. After reviewing and providing any edits, content approvers will push the edits back to the author, send them to a peer reviewer for additional feedback, or approve the content to be immediately published. Their actions include the following:

- Review pending content
- Edit pending content
- Reject content and send it back to author for further edits
- Approve content and publish

Solution Data

Users make up one portion of the solution. Another portion relates to the data that needs to be captured. Here are a number of the data types that are required:

- Blog title
- Blog body
- Categories (tags)

- Publish date (proposed publish date)

- Status

In your organization, you might need to capture additional data. The publish date will be set by the content author, although it can be modified by the approver, based on their feedback.

Summarizing the Requirements Gathering Process

Now that we have completed the process of looking at the users of the solution and the types of data that will be included in our solution, it is time to start building the solution's design. Before we do that, however, we should take a few minutes and summarize the process we just completed:

- We defined the business needs for providing a method for content authors to submit blog content for peer review and content approval, while giving the business a way to appropriately track content being authored and review it prior to publishing to ensure that all corporate standards are met.

- All users were consulted and requirements were gathered based on their specific needs.

- All data required for the solution was identified based on the needs of the users.

Designing the Solution

With the requirements gathered, it is now time to look at some of the important issues that might affect the time it takes to make the solution available to your organization. It is important to review your options and develop a plan before moving forward to ensure that you have completed the due diligence required to fully understand the business needs and requirements.

The following sections discuss design decisions and wireframes. The design decisions section will review the various tools that will be used to create this solution and provide details about why they were selected. The section about wireframes helps you visualize the solution by outlining the pages to be created. Ideally, these mock-ups are created, reviewed, and approved by the solution's stakeholders prior to any development being completed.

Design Decisions

In this solution, several key points need to be discussed about the tools that will be used and the methods that will be implemented for creating and managing the content. This section reviews each of the key areas and provides information about the reason the selection was made.

 Important Your environment and scenario might differ from the one presented here. As you follow along in the chapter, be sure to make note of the things that differ and then adjust your solution development accordingly.

Setting Permissions

This solution includes four primary groups of users. One is responsible for creating the content, two are responsible for reviewing and editing the content, and one group has view-only access to the content. Unique site permissions will be granted to each of these groups, which means that all users within each group will have the same permissions.

It is important to understand the top-level site permissions and how your blog solution might differ in how it uses them. Given the creation of the new user groups, we recommend that you break permissions inheritance from the parent site and modify permissions to meet your security goals (to be covered later in the chapter). Separating classes of end users allows for greater control over your content authoring and approval process, ensuring that only defined users can approve content published to the blog.

Clarifying Workflow Activities

The solution will walk through the creation of a Microsoft SharePoint Designer workflow that helps automate the content review and approval process. However, because SharePoint has no field-level security, restricting the ability of content authors to publish their own content directly is difficult. Many content authors might also be able to provide peer reviews or even approve content to be published. The solution restricts the majority of blog visitors from creating or publishing content, but it still requires members of the specialized groups to adhere to the review and approval process as outlined.

Content Security

Depending on your environment and its content security requirements, this solution might not meet your needs. This solution assumes that all employees have access to the published content. If you have scenarios that include additional subsets of employees and want to publish content to different groups based on category, for example, then you should update the solution structure to account for the additional security requirements.

Solution Wireframes

The solution in this chapter uses the out-of-the-box blog template but adds some complexity for viewing, editing, and publishing content. The wireframes shown in this section will help project stakeholders better understand the scope of the project and the implications of permissions configurations before any development is completed.

Blog Home

This is the home page for the entire solution. From this page, users can access published blog content and, if they have permissions, create or review blog content.

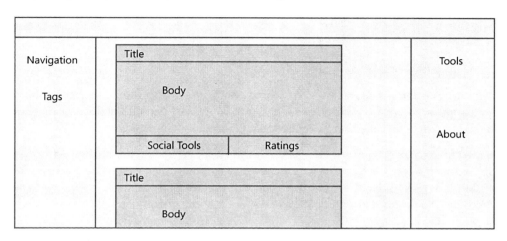

My Posts Page

On this page, content authors can see a list of their own drafts, pending reviews, and published content.

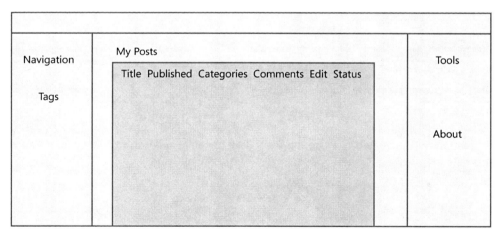

While these wireframes do not represent the final design of the blog (look and feel), they help build confidence in the solution with its stakeholders, ensuring the end results meet their expectations. As long as the project team verifies that you are moving in the right direction, you are good to proceed with building the solution.

Building the Solution

It is now time to start building the solution. The first step is to create the blog site collection. Once the site is created, permissions for the site will be modified, the primary content list will be created and customized, and the workflow will be generated. Finally, we will configure the blog with RSS and ratings information.

Build the Blog Site

The blog site collection will be created from Central Administration and should have the settings listed in the following table. If you don't have access to your farm's Central Administration pages, you should request that a site collection be created using the information listed.

You can also create a blog as a subsite as long as you have the correct permissions. In this solution, the approach is to create the blog as a parent site—as a corporate blog—controlling access through the creation and modification of specific user groups. If you use a subsite, there may be many more restrictions on who can read or participate, so be aware of those restrictions.

Create your blog with the following parameters.

Field	Value
Web Application	http://www.tailspintoys.com/
Title	Blog
Description	Team blog for all employees to learn about company objectives and initiatives.
URL	.../sites/blog
Template Selection	Blog
Primary Site Collection Owner	Wallace, Anne
Secondary Site Collection Owner	Duncan, Bart
Quota Template	Application_40GB

This solution will be created by using the Team Blog template and is likely to be considered part of the corporate intranet.

1. On the Central Admin home page, select Create Site Collections in the Application Management group.

2. Enter the information provided in the preceding table, and then click OK to provision the site collection.

3. Once the site has been provisioned, follow the link provided to open the new site collection.

Establish Blog Permissions

One of the easiest ways to control the management of your blog content, as well as who can view this content, is through permissions. Because this solution outlines a specific content-approval process that requires special user rights, we will walk through the steps of how to break inheritance from your portal permissions and set up unique permissions for the defined user groups.

Breaking Inheritance for the Blog Site

By default, the permissions for the blog are inherited from the parent site, unless the blog site is created with custom permissions. Because we will set unique permissions for the different blog roles, you need to break the permissions inheritance from the parent site and change the permissions settings. When you break inheritance, you simply create a copy of the existing permissions, which allows you to then customize them to meet your specific needs.

1. On the Site Actions menu, select the Site Settings link.

2. Select Users And Permissions, and then click Site Permissions. This displays the Permission Tools tab on a page listing the individuals and groups with current permissions.

3. If the site inherits permissions, select Stop Inheriting Permissions on the ribbon, and then click OK.

Creating New Groups and Setting Site Permissions for Blog Participants

Now that you have established unique permissions for your blog, you can set up permissions for the participants in your blog. The blog template comes with several groups already in place, which you can modify or remove. Because the differences between the standard groups—Blog Members, Blog Visitors, and Viewers—can be confusing, for this solution we will walk through the creation of four new groups with distinct functions and permissions.

To set up your new groups, follow these steps:

1. Go to Site Actions, Site Permissions to see a list of all current SharePoint groups and individuals that are part of the previously inherited site permissions.

2. Select Create Group on the ribbon.

The Create Group page opens.

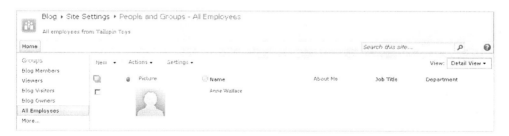

3. Create the All Employees group by using the following information, and then click Create.

The purpose of this group is to give all employees within your company view-only access to the blog. You might decide to restrict access to the blog. If this is the case, it might be easier to create an Active Directory group and manage this subset of users using Active Directory instead of SharePoint groups.

Field	Value
Name	All Employees
Description	All employees from Tailspin Toys
Owner	Your name and names of other group owners
Group Settings	Group members should be able to view membership of the group. Group owners should be able to edit membership of the group.
Membership Requests	Allow requests to join or leave this group. By default, auto-accept requests are not allowed, and no email is required for membership requests. Add email for join and leave requests.
Give Group Permission to This Site	View only

The new group is created. You will see the group membership page.

4. Add users to this group by selecting New, Add Users.

5. The Grant Permissions dialog box opens, which allows you to enter individual names or select from the directory. Search for the appropriate corporate or NT Authorized (authorized corporate users) group to allow all authorized employees to view the blog site.

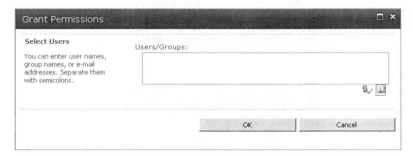

The new group now appears, as shown here:

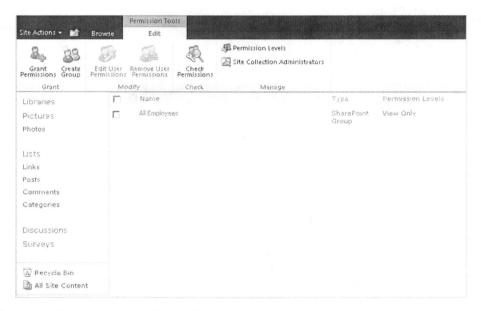

6. Repeat this step to create the Content Authors group.

Field	Value
Name	Content Authors
Description	Content authors from Tailspin Toys
Owner	Your name and the names of other group owners
Group Settings	Group members should be able to view membership of the group. Group owners should be able to edit membership to the group.

Field	Value
Membership Requests	Allow requests to join or leave this group. Do not allow auto-accept requests to join this group. Provide an email to receive membership requests.
Give Group Permission to This Site	Contribute access

When you add content authors to this group, select those individuals who will regularly and consistently post content to the site.

7. Create the Peer Reviewers group, following the same steps as earlier.

Field	Value
Name	Peer Reviewers
Description	Peer reviewers from Tailspin Toys
Owner	Your name and the names of other group owners
Group Settings	Group members should be able to view membership of the group. Group owners should be able to edit membership to the group.
Membership Requests	Allow requests to join or leave this group Do not allow auto-accept requests to join this group. Provide an email to receive membership requests.
Give Group Permission to this Site	Contribute access

Peer reviewers will likely include content authors or members of your organization who have an interest in the quality of content being published through the team blog and have accepted the responsibility of reviewing assigned workflow tasks in a timely manner.

8. Create the Content Approvers group, following the same steps as earlier.

Field	Value
Name	Content Approvers
Description	Content approvers from Tailspin Toys
Owner	Your name and the names of other group owners
Group Settings	Group members should be able to view membership of the group. Group owners should be able to edit membership to the group.
Membership Requests	Allow requests to join or leave this group. Do not allow auto-accept requests to join this group. Provide an email to receive membership requests.
Give Group Permission to This Site	Design access

Content approvers have the ultimate responsibility for managing the quality and accuracy of the content to be published on the team blog. Select users who, like peer reviewers, have accepted the responsibility of reviewing and approving assigned workflow tasks in a timely manner.

9. After all the groups have been created and individuals added to each group, use the breadcrumbs navigation links to go back to your blog site.

Note Name your groups appropriately. At any time, you can use the Group Settings dialog box to delete a group if it is no longer relevant. You can access this dialog box by going to Site Actions, Site Permissions, and then clicking on the relevant group name to gain access to the group profile. Then, under Settings, select Group Settings.

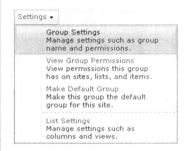

From here, you can also delete a group by clicking the Delete button at the bottom of the dialog box.

Enabling Anonymous Access to the Blog

Enabling anonymous access allows people, including authenticated users who have not been granted access to the site, to browse your blog without logging in. Setting up anonymous access is a two-step process. First, the server administrator must enable anonymous access to your site through Central Administration. Second, a content owner must also allow for anonymous access. For the purpose of this solution, and in the case of most intranet environments, enabling anonymous access is not a requirement.

See Also *For instructions and more information about enabling anonymous access, see* office.microsoft.com/en-us/sharepoint-server-help/configure-permissions-and-settings-for-a-blog-HA101919123.aspx.

Modify the Posts List

Now you need to modify the primary list (named Posts) that will be used for this solution. The modifications include creating a unique column, a custom view, and a workflow to reach the end results we want.

Creating a Column

For this list, you need to create one primary custom column to drive the content-management process. The column is described in detail in the following table. After the table, you'll find the steps you need to complete to create the column.

Field	Value
Column Name	Status
Type	Choice
Description	Review status of the blog post
Required	Yes
Enforce Unique Values	No
Choices to Include	Draft To be reviewed Reviewed Published
Display	Drop-down menu
Allow Fill-In Choices	No
Default Value	Draft
Add to Default View	Yes

The Status column is needed to drive our approval and notification workflow, help content reviewers and approvers identify incoming and outgoing (to be published) content, and for content authors to view the state of their content.

To create the column, follow these steps:

1. On the Site Actions menu, select View All Site Content.

2. Click the Posts link to open the list.

3. Click the List Tools List tab on the ribbon.

4. Click the Create Column link in the Manage Views group.

5. The Create Column dialog box opens. Enter the information based on the table shown earlier in this section.

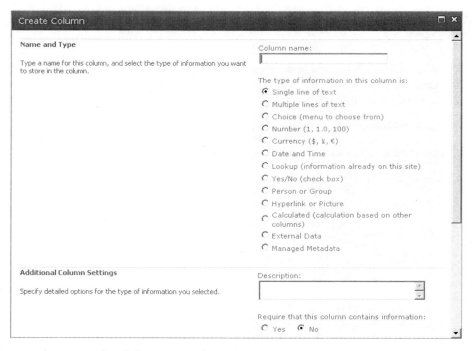

When you have completed the process, the Columns section on the List Settings page should appear as shown next. You can confirm this by going to Site Actions, Site Settings, selecting Site Libraries And Lists, and clicking the Posts list to see the detailed list information.

Columns		
A column stores information about each item in the list. The following columns are currently available in this list:		
Column (click to edit)	Type	Required
Title	Single line of text	✔
Body	Multiple lines of text	
# Comments	Lookup	
Category	Lookup	
Published	Date and Time	✔
Status	Choice	✔
Created By	Person or Group	
Modified By	Person or Group	

Create column
Add from existing site columns
Column ordering
Indexed columns

After the list has been modified, you are ready to create your workflow.

Creating the Review and Approval Workflow

Within SharePoint, your movements and the content you can access depend on site permissions. Earlier in this chapter, we broke the inherited permissions from the parent SharePoint site so that we could set up custom permissions to help drive the solution's review and approval process. This solution will help you create a simple process to restrict content creation, review, and approval to individuals with specific permissions. All other users will have view-only permissions. In addition, the solution will outline a workflow to notify peer reviewers and content approvers that new content is ready for them and also to alert content authors when their blog posts have been approved and published.

There are other ways that you can control the blog content creation and approval process. One method would be to create a Microsoft InfoPath–based solution that completely changes the author and reviewer interface. But for this solution, our goals are simplicity and to use out-of-the-box capability wherever possible, using permissions, notifications, and processes to guide content authors, peer reviewers, and content approvers.

The purpose of this workflow is to send an email notification to stakeholders when the state of the blog content changes. By default, all new content is defined with the status Draft. Content authors might have multiple posts at any given time in draft form. After the content author changes the status to the To Be Reviewed state, an email notification is sent to the Peer Reviewers group, letting them know there is new content to be reviewed. Likewise, when a peer reviewer changes the status to Reviewed, an email notification goes to the Content Approvers group, letting them know there is content to be reviewed and published. Both peer reviewers and content approvers have the ability to edit and modify the blog posts, or they can change the status back to Draft for the content author to once again review the post.

To create the review and approval workflow, follow these steps:

1. On the Posts list ribbon, select List Tools, and then click the Workflow Settings icon and select Create A Workflow In SharePoint Designer.

2. The Create List Workflow—Posts dialog box opens, prompting you to provide a name and description. Enter the name **Review and Approve** and a brief description, and then click OK.

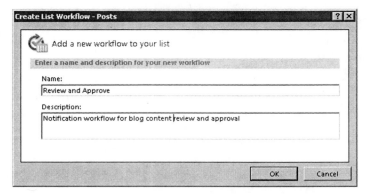

SharePoint Designer opens with a new table labeled Review And Approve and inserts a new step box in the editor.

3. Click Step 1 and rename it to **Content moved from Draft to Review**.

4. Using the ribbon, insert the condition If Current Item Field Equals Value.

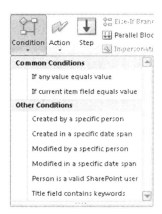

5. Select the box below the condition (the pulsing yellow line indicates that the workflow is ready for you to insert a condition or action), and insert the action Send An Email.

6. Click Field, and scroll through the options to select Status.

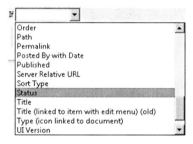

7. Now click Value, and select To Be Reviewed.

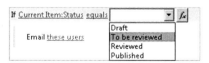

8. Finally, click These Users, and then complete the email message by using fields from the following table.

Field	Value
To	Peer Reviewers
CC	NA
Subject	New blog content to be reviewed
Body	Using the Add Or Change Lookup button, add the following fields to the email body: ■ Title ■ Permalink ■ Created By

The email message should look like this:

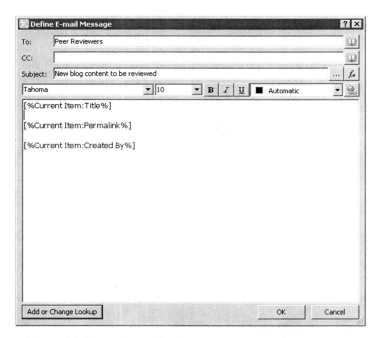

Additional fields can be added by using the Add Or Change Lookup button.

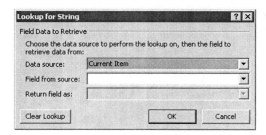

The final workflow step should appear as follows:

9. Click below and outside the workflow step to move the insertion point. On the ribbon, click Step to insert a second step in the process.

10. Click Step 2 and rename it to **Content moved from Review to Publish**, and then repeat the previous steps to insert the condition If Current Item Field Equals Value and the action Send An Email.

11. Change the condition field to CurrentItem:Status and the value to Reviewed.

12. Click the Email field and edit the workflow by using the following table.

Field	Value
To	Content Approvers
CC	NA
Subject	Reviewed content to be published
Body	Using the Add Or Change Lookup button, add the following fields to the email body: ■ Title ■ Permalink ■ Created By

The email message should look like this:

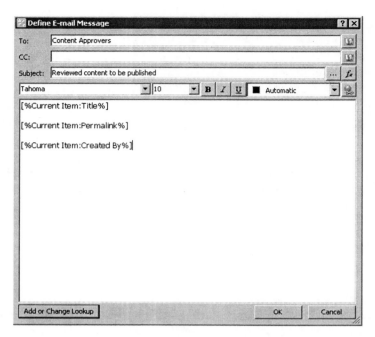

The final workflow step should appear as follows:

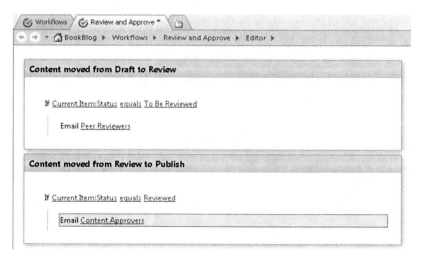

13. Click below and outside the second workflow step to move the insertion point. On the ribbon, click Step to insert a third step in the process.

14. Click Step 3, rename it to **Content moved from Publish to Published**, and then repeat the previous steps to insert the condition If Current Item Field Equals Value and the action Send An Email.

15. Change the condition field to CurrentItem:Status and the value to Published.

16. Click the Email field, and edit the workflow using the following table.

Field	Value
To	Created By (the content author)
CC	NA
Subject	Your blog post has been published
Body	Using the Add Or Change Lookup button, add the following fields to the email body: ■ Title ■ Permalink

The email message should look like this:

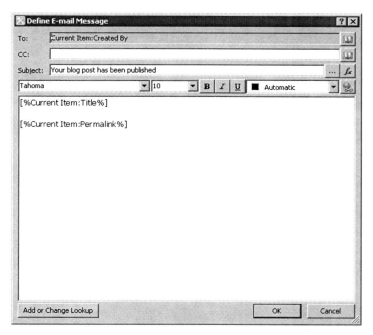

17. At the bottom of the third step, add one more action from the ribbon. Select Stop Workflow as the action. In the field, add the log item Approved And Published.

The final workflow step should look like this:

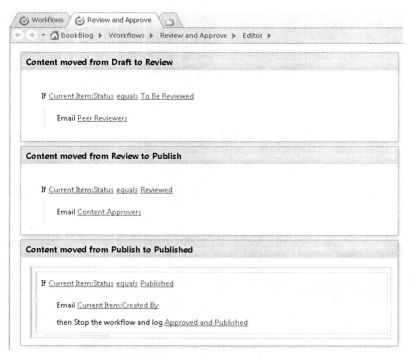

18. At the top of the workflow editor, under the tab title, click Review And Approve in the bread-crumbs navigation links to take you back a step to where you can manage settings for your workflow.

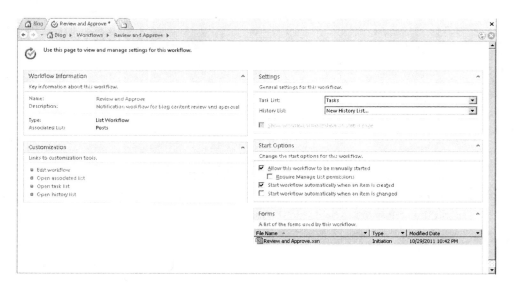

19. Under Start Options, select Allow This Workflow To Be Manually Started and Start Workflow Automatically When An Item Is Created.

20. After the workflow is complete, check for any errors in the logic by going to the ribbon and clicking Check For Errors.

If there are errors, the issues will be highlighted in your workflow in red, allowing you to quickly identify where changes need to be made. If there are no errors, a dialog box will open. Click OK to continue.

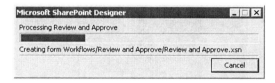

21. Save your workflow, and click Publish to make it available in the Posts list. SharePoint Designer will process the workflow, associate it with your site and list, and make it available in SharePoint.

22. Back in SharePoint, go to the Posts list by clicking Site Actions, View All Site Content, and then clicking Posts. To confirm that your workflow is in place, on the ribbon select List Tools, and then in the Settings group, click Workflow Settings and then select Workflow Settings again.

All running workflows will be visible on this page, as well as a count of the workflows in progress. In other words, this shows how many blog posts are currently in review.

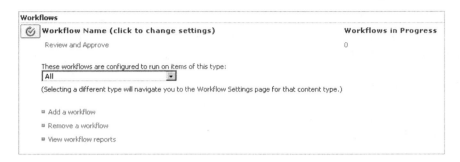

Creating the Personal View

After a blog post has been reviewed and approved, be aware that the content will not be visible in the blog until the defined publish date and time. Content might be approved several days before it has been scheduled to be published, which could cause some confusion after the content author receives an email notification that his or her content has been published.

One way to quickly verify where content is within the process is to create a personal view of all content created. This view shows content authors each post they have written, the current status of the post within the review process, and the final publish date.

To define the view, follow these steps:

1. On the blog home page, click Manage Posts on the right side of the page, or click Site Actions, View All Site Content, and then select the Posts list.

2. Select Site Actions, Edit Page.

3. In the Main area, click the Add A Web Part link.

4. From the category Lists And Libraries, select the web part Posts, and then click Add.

5. The web part is added to the page, essentially duplicating the list already on the page.

6. Select the check box at the far right to edit the new web part, which is labeled Posts [2]. This step changes the ribbon options. Under List Tools, click List, and then click Create View.

7. Under Start From An Existing View, select My Posts.

8. Use the following table to complete the new view.

Field	Value/Purpose
Name	My Post Status Check the option to make this the default view for the list
Audience	Create a public view
Columns	Title Status Published (the date you have selected to publish) Category # Comments Edit (link to edit item) Modified by
All other options	Leave default settings

9. Once you complete this step, click OK.

10. Click the Web Part Tools Options tab, and then click Web Part Properties.

11. The Web Part Properties menu opens at the far right, allowing you to modify your new list web part. Make the following two changes:

- Under List Views, change the Selected View to My Post Status.

- Under Appearance, change the Title to My Post Status.

12. Click Apply, and then click OK to close the dialog box.

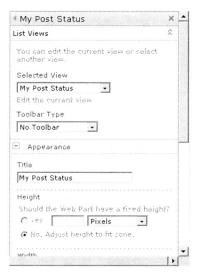

13. Once these settings are saved, you should have two views of the same list. One provides a snapshot of all blog posts in the system, and the other shows a personal view and the state of an individual's own blog posts.

14. Close the edit window, and you can see the new view and table on the Posts list page, which is accessible from the blog home page by clicking Manage Posts.

Modify Categories (Tags)

In the SharePoint blog paradigm, categories are your primary tag-based navigation tool. Some third-party vendors have extended the out-of-the-box SharePoint experience by adding additional tagging and navigation elements. Many of these third-party features are based on popular consumer blogging tools (for example, tag clouds). SharePoint categories are not complicated, and they provide basic navigation for a set of specific terms.

As part of your blog planning process, you should consider as a team how to build out your categories to ensure the maximum search benefits. You might, for example, set up a list of your business units and product or service areas. Or you might organize your categories by project names. Whatever convention you use, the categories can always be updated later and blog posts modified.

To configure your Categories list, do the following:

1. Select Categories in the left navigation area, and click Add New Item.

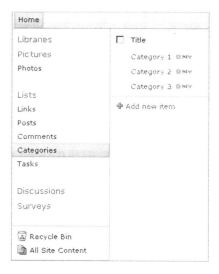

2. After adding your new categories, you can select the generic categories and use the context menu to delete them.

3. Going back to the home page, you will see your new categories in the left navigation area and can begin assigning them to existing or future content.

Add Ratings

Ratings are one more way that blog readers can share their feedback about content and that content authors and their managers can use to determine the success and impact of specific content on their audience. While SharePoint offers a simple, text-based version of ratings, this is not the standard that most social media platforms now provide. The following example will walk you through the steps to provide the more common star ratings within each blog post:

1. Go to the Posts list, and select Edit List.

2. Activate the ratings features under Settings, Rating Settings by selecting Yes.

3. Using SharePoint Designer, select Lists And Libraries, and then open the Posts list. At the right of the screen, right-click AllPosts and Edit In Advance Mode.

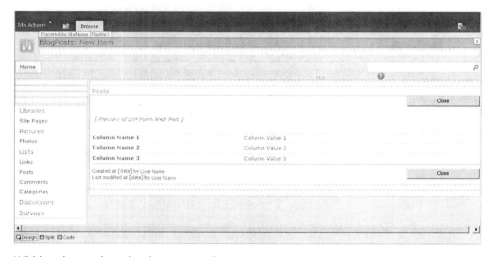

4. Within advanced mode, change to split view.

5. Add AverageRatingFieldControl to the PlaceHolderMain content control, as follows:

```
</WebPartPages:WebPartZone>
<div style="padding-bottom: 10px; vertical-align:middle">
    <div style="float:left;display: inline-block; margin-top: 2px; margin-right:10px">
        Rate this post
    </div>
    <SharePoint:AverageRatingFieldControl FieldName="5a14d1ab-1513-48c7-97b3-
657a5ba6c742"
        ControlMode="Display" runat="server"/>
</div>
<WebPartPages:WebPartZone runat="server" FrameType="TitleBarOnly" ID="LeftFooter"
    Title="loc:LeftFooter" AllowPersonalization="false">
<ZoneTemplate>
```

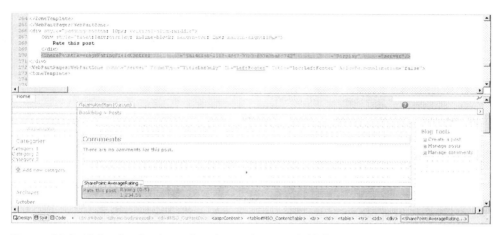

6. Next, add the following Register directive at the top of this layout page:

```
<%@ Register
    Tagprefix="SharePoint"
    Namespace="Microsoft.SharePoint.Portal.WebControls"
    Assembly="Microsoft.SharePoint.Portal, Version=14.0.0.0, Culture=neutral,
        PublicKeyToken=71e9bce111e9429c" %>
```

This step might require an IIS reset to activate. If so, you should see a message box immediately. If the message appears, click Yes.

Once this step is completed, if you create a new blog post in SharePoint, you will see the rating control appear on each page, allowing readers to provide a rating on each blog post.

You might need to use some trial and error to place the control on the page layout, but you can look for the comments near the bottom and add the code below them on the page, reviewing and adjusting as needed until the page layout meets your approval.

Note You might notice that when you click a rating and refresh the page that the rating does not show up yet. This feature is tied to an hourly timer job, and while it is correctly calculating, it will not refresh and show an accurate rating until after the next timer job is complete.

Configure RSS

One of the best ways to build blog readership is to push content to people and not rely on them to enter the site. Really Simple Syndication (RSS) in SharePoint is quick and easy to implement and will push a link to readers via Outlook for any newly published blog posts.

To ensure RSS is set up on your blog, follow these steps:

1. On the site's home page, click Site Settings on the Site Actions menu.

2. Select the RSS link in the Site Administration section.

3. On the RSS screen, select the Allow RSS Feeds In This Site Collection check box in the Site Collection RSS section.

4. Select the Allow RSS Feeds In This Site check box in the Enable RSS section.

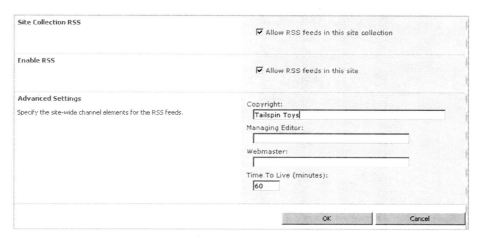

5. Enter any additional settings for the RSS feed in the Advanced Settings section. These settings apply to all RSS feeds created in the site collection.

6. Click OK.

7. To subscribe, simply select the RSS icon on the blog home page.

8. A subscription page opens. Select Subscribe To This Feed.

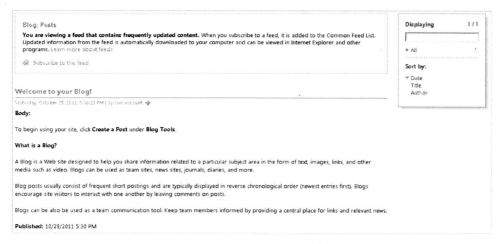

9. A Subscribe To This Feed dialog box opens. Confirm the name and location to which the feed will send notifications and specify whether to add the site to your browser's Favorites bar.

10. Click Subscribe.

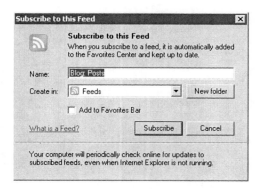

You are now subscribed to your blog. Email notifications of new content will be pushed to your inbox, providing another great reminder to stay connected with what your team is talking about.

Note If you receive the error message "RSS does not support authenticated feeds," you might have a conflict that requires additional steps. Please see your administrator.

Managing the Solution

Managing this solution should be a relatively low-key task that doesn't require much interaction. Although there is a process component, the solution by design is set up around roles that will help the process run smoothly and restrict access to those who should have access. This solution has not touched on look and feel—there are many options for design and further configuration based on the level of activity on your blog and the need to closely mirror the look and feel of your corporate environment. But from a management standpoint, this solution should give you what you need to get started, with minimal management needed on an ongoing basis.

Reviewing the Platform

The solution in this chapter was built using the features available within SharePoint Enterprise. In the remainder of this section, the different options available with the various other SharePoint licenses will be highlighted.

If You Are Using SharePoint Foundation or Standard

If you are using SharePoint Foundation, almost everything demonstrated here is available within the original blog template save the workflow capability. If you plan to use workflows to manage your content creation and approval process, you must use the Standard or Enterprise platform. While the blog template available across all versions has some limitations compared to public blogging platforms, the solution demonstrated here is fully functional.

If You Are Using SharePoint Online with Office 365

If you are using SharePoint Online with Office 365, your environment includes the enterprise features, which allows you to re-create everything demonstrated here. If you are building a public-facing blog, be aware that there are problems with anonymous access, and you might need to investigate third-party solutions before going live with your site.

Additional Customizations

In this chapter we covered quite a few customizations. However, many more features can be added to this solution. This information is being provided so that you can see some of the additional customizations that you may want to incorporate into your solution.

Additional Customization	Benefits
Tag clouds	The SharePoint blog template does offer a tag-cloud option, but it works differently from what is available in public blogging platforms, and it is not available in SharePoint Foundation. Aside from differences in look and feel, it draws its keywords from the entire SharePoint environment, not just from blog content. It also has timer-job limitations and does not update in real time (however, you can configure the timer jobs to better match your needed schedule). Several third-party vendors offer tag clouds as part of their custom templates and solutions.
Enterprise keywords	One of the configuration settings is to enable enterprise keywords. This is a great way to map your blog content to your structured keyword taxonomy, but it will take some additional planning and configuration to get it running properly. Unless you have a formal governance strategy to manage these keywords, it probably makes sense to stay with the default categories functionality.
Star ratings on your home page	As configured, the star ratings appear on the individual blog posting pages and are not visible from your blog home page. Someone from the SharePoint community (Henry Ong) has provided step-by-step instructions for how to extend the star ratings to be viewable from your home page. See his blog at *http:// blog.henryong.com/2011/10/28/adding-sharepoint-social-rating-stars-to-the-homepage-of-sharepoint-blog-sites/.*
Using Windows Live Writer	Posting to the blog is easy, using either the SharePoint user interface or Microsoft Word to create and edit your posts. Another option is to configure Windows Live Writer. Setup is easy. Simply add a new blog service by selecting SharePoint blog and providing the correct URL.
My Sites integration	Some blogging activity is integrated with My Sites. When you post to the blog, your activity shows up in the My Sites activity stream, but commenting does not appear. Several third-party vendors offer solutions that extend the My Sites integration, including comments.
Comments approval	An important content management option not covered in this solution is the ability to approve comments. There is no out-of-the-box method for managing comments, but there are several community members who have created solutions to do this and shared their methods on their blogs.

Summary

In this chapter we covered how to get the most from the out-of-the-box team blog features, helping SharePoint better meet your organizational expectations. This solution allows teams to manage blog content in a structured, peer-reviewed manner to ensure the quality and consistency of content. This chapter should serve as a guideline for you to implement a similar solution within your environment. Keep in mind as you implement your solution that you can easily tweak and modify the solution to fit any specific needs within your organization.

CHAPTER 8

Building an RFP Response Solution

I n this chapter, you will create a solution that coordinates responses to requests for proposals, or RFPs. The SharePoint 2007 platform included the Application Templates for Windows SharePoint Services 3.0 (the "Fab 40"), which included an RFP template designed for creating, releasing, and managing RFP submissions. The solution in this chapter is designed from a different perspective—that of a services company responding to an RFP.

The process of responding to RFPs is common in the services and consulting worlds. Depending on the services being offered, it can be time-consuming and challenging to coordinate the resources and expertise required to create an effective, accurate, and consistent response.

This solution creates a framework for the RFP-response process based on commonly used SharePoint functionality and can be used as a foundation for more elaborate solutions.

Identifying the Business Problems

The processes involved in responding to RFPs vary between organizations. The nature of the industry as well as the organizational maturity and experience of the company and staff play parts in determining how processes are developed and maintained. In some organizations, the process may be simple—with one or a small group of people involved who only respond to RFPs and do nothing else. In other organizations, many people are involved, and the process to get all the pieces in place may be complex. Communication is the key to the entire process.

The example used in this chapter is a medium-size technology services organization that offers services across a number of practice areas, where one or more practices might be called on for preparing each RFP.

The sales group generally takes the lead when it comes to finding and bringing RFPs to the company. They do a first-pass review of the request to determine whether the subject matter is something the company has the capabilities to respond to. The following questions are addressed:

- Does the RFP fit with the company's services?

- Can the company respond to the RFP in time?

- Does the company have the resources to act on the work if it is awarded, or can resources be obtained in time to deliver the solution?

If the RFP passes the first review, the sales group brings it to the organization for response. This is the first challenge: who to notify?

Notification of New Request

When a new RFP is submitted, someone needs to determine which teams need to be involved with generating the response. Sometimes, this can be done by a single person. In our example, each practice area needs to have a representative review the RFP to see whether the subject matter is related to their particular team and whether their practice or team is needed for any content or estimates.

Initiate the Response Content

Now that the practice areas are aware that they have tasks related to the RFP, they need to create the estimate and respond to any queries in the RFP in the allotted time. The salesperson who "owns" the RFP wants to be kept in the loop on the status of the work throughout and wants to be sure that sufficient time is available for all parties to review each other's content, make any additional changes, and prepare any materials needed to meet the RFP requirements.

Review and Approve the Response

Finally, once all the estimates and content have been compiled, practice representatives as well as management need to review the end product—the RFP response material—to make sure everything is correct before sending the response to the potential client.

Summarizing the Business Problems

Receiving, processing, and submitting RFPs should be a relatively simple process. Many organizations have it refined to a science, while others struggle. What makes it challenging are all the details involved with creating a complete RFP when so many people are involved with its creation and delivery.

Your focus is on RFPs that have passed the salesperson's initial review and that are being submitted to the practice areas and subject matter experts for review and response. This involves the following steps:

- Notifying the teams involved with reviewing incoming RFPs so that they are aware of the RFP and can determine whether their practice needs to be involved with the RFP response.

- Assigning the practices and teams that have tasks to complete for the RFP response.

- Review and approve the finalized RFP response product before sending it to the client.

There are many other potential aspects to the process that could be included or expanded on, but those will be saved for another time. Several of these enhancements will be discussed in "Additional Customizations" on page 312.

Gathering Information

With the high-level challenges identified, more specific information needs to be gathered in order to design the solution from the correct perspective and at the right depth.

System Users

The RFP process pulls together resources from a number of teams and departments within a company. Coordination and communication are key objectives. To understand the business needs of the solution, each team's requirements need to be understood. This information will then be used to design and develop the solution.

Sales

Salespeople or account managers capture the RFP details and submit them for a response. They are responsible for contact with the client and will oversee the response process, making sure the deliverable is completed on time. They also participate in the approval process.

Practice Leads

Representatives from each practice need to review each RFP to determine whether their respective practice is required to complete the RFP response. They also need to review the completed document to verify estimates and the availability of resources as well as the technical accuracy of any deliverables.

Estimators and Subject Matter Experts

Once team leads have identified which practices are required for the RFP response, members of the practice teams need to assemble the content for the response and estimate the work to be done. This information will be compiled into the RFP deliverable.

Approvers

Whatever the deliverable for the RFP response is, it needs to be reviewed and approved by all the applicable team leads before the response is finalized and delivered to the client.

Management

Management users are observers through the estimation process and approvers for the final deliverable. In a future iteration of this solution, management will be interested in reviewing RFP stats, although this is out of scope with the current initiative.

Process Flow

In addition to understanding the different users who are involved, it is useful to diagram the business process to verify it with users and to have a model as a reference when the solution is designed. A simple example is shown here:

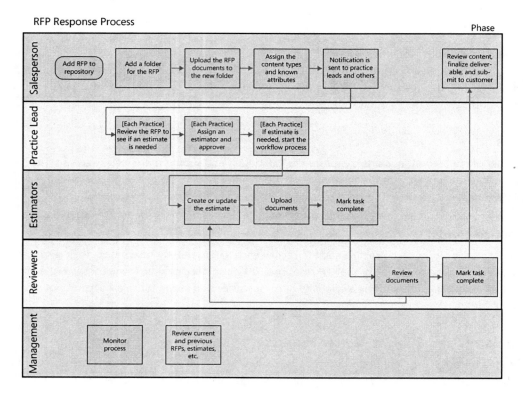

Solution Data

Several types of data are used in this solution. Some are related to the documents being used or created, and others serve as reference information to help pull the solution together. The primary data involves the RFP request and the deliverables.

RFP Request Documents

The RFP itself will have specific information that needs to be tracked. There may also be supporting documents, attachments, and addendums that accompany the RFP request document and need to be tracked:

- RFP name
- RFP description
- Account manager

- Notes

- Due dates

- Response status

- Submission instructions

- Company name

- Contact name

- Contact email

- Contact phone

- Practices

RFP Response Documents

The deliverable for each RFP will require a storage location as well as specific attributes. There might also be supporting documents, attachments, worksheets, and addendums that accompany the RFP response document and need to be tracked:

- Title

- Account manager

- Company name

- Notes

- Status

- Bid hours

- Bid estimate

Summarizing the Requirements Gathering Process

The goals of the scenario are to facilitate the timely preparation of RFP responses by including all the relevant participants in the estimating and content creation phase and to maintain the quality of RFPs through validation and approval.

Now the requirements identified will be aligned with SharePoint capabilities wherever possible and a solution design will begin to emerge.

Designing the Solution

The requirements that have been identified fit well with the SharePoint platform. So well, in fact, that a number of decisions need to be made regarding which direction to go technically. This section will walk through some of the decisions made for this particular scenario.

The RFP process is a good representation of how business processes should be addressed in SharePoint. Taking a business process and trying to jam it into the SharePoint platform is the wrong approach and often very frustrating. It's analogous to trying to fit a square peg in a round hole. What is effective, however, is to analyze a process and identify which steps fit into the SharePoint model and will deliver the most value. As initial automation steps are found to be successful, additional and potentially more challenging automation can be added at a later time. You will be addressing the first iteration of an RFP process in this chapter.

Design Decisions

One of the benefits of using SharePoint is that it provides so many ways to solve a particular problem. The challenge is picking the best approach possible for the specific instance and to start in a way that allows the solution to evolve over time.

Site Taxonomy

Where should the RFP content be stored? Should the libraries be part of an existing site alongside other lists and libraries, or should they be isolated in a site collection or a subsite? Each option has its pros and cons.

From a security perspective, a separate web or site for RFP content allows the separation of security settings from other content, which is common for estimates, bids, and proposals. The security for the separate web can stop inheriting the permissions of the parent and be managed independently.

Technically, the lists can be part of an existing web with other content, although creating the lists in their own site collection or web offers advantages in both navigation and security. From the navigation perspective, a new web allows the left navigation area to be used exclusively for RFP process functionality, so you avoid cluttering up an element that is also used for what may be many lists, libraries, and subsites.

Whether the solution is built as a stand-alone site collection or as a subsite is determined by the information architecture of the SharePoint environment. Either option allows for the necessary security isolation.

For this example, instead of allowing all users access to the content, you'll create a subsite of another site to accommodate specific security needs.

Site Templates

For this solution, both the Blank Site and Team Site templates work for the solution, although some features of blank sites that you might want to use for future enhancements are turned off. You will be using the Team Site template that is available in all SharePoint 2010 and Office 365 SharePoint Online versions.

The team site comes with the wiki functionality already enabled, but it also comes with a number of lists and libraries that aren't specifically called out in the example.

List Templates

List template selection for the solution is fairly straightforward. Most of the content will be managed in document libraries with additional configuration of new fields and views. Additional lists may be used for reference information (like companies) as needed.

In addition to the list template question is the question whether to use one or more libraries on the site to manage the content. Should all documents be stored in a single library using content types to allow different columns for each document type, or should separate libraries be used?

- Option 1: Single library

  - All documents related to RFPs: incoming documents and deliverable documents

  - Separate content types to allow for columns for specific document types.

  - Users need to select the document/content type when uploading documents

  - All documents related to an RFP can be grouped together in a folder

  - Consistent security across all documents unless folder or document-level security are also implemented.

- Option 2: Separate libraries

  - One library for RFP documents

  - One library for response and support documents

  - Supports unique security on each library

  - Documents from one library need to be associated somehow with related documents in the other library.

  - Users don't have to choose the content type when uploading docs.

At the cost of a little more effort for users to have to select the document type when uploading and security being the same for all content by default, Option 1 will be used in order to simplify relationship management between documents. In addition, folders will be used to keep related documents together.

Permissions

By using a subsite for the solution, you don't need to worry about inheriting users or groups, but you will set up at least one additional security group in addition to the default Visitors, Members, and Owners groups.

Data Thresholds/Scalability

The solution you build will involve a volume of documents that will grow larger over time, but the volume will not likely be so large as to cause concerns from a technical boundary (number of documents in a library), a database sizing, or a disaster recovery management perspective. If necessary, the site could be created as a site collection to isolate it in its own database, or a policy could be put in place to archive older documents to keep the size at a lower level (ongoing processes to archive older documents as newer documents continue to be added). These are both scenarios outside the scope of this chapter.

The solution will also be using workflows that will create both task and history lists, but neither should be so large as to cause concern. Lists and libraries can technically hold up to 30 million items per list. If each RFP workflow is creating two tasks and less than 10 history items, it would take a lot of RFP processes to even begin to challenge the technical limitations of the platform. Therefore, there isn't a threshold or scalability concern for this solution.

Solution Wireframes

Only the home page of the site will be built from multiple web parts. All other functionality will be accessible from views of the RFPs and Tasks lists and accessible from the Quick Launch or other web parts.

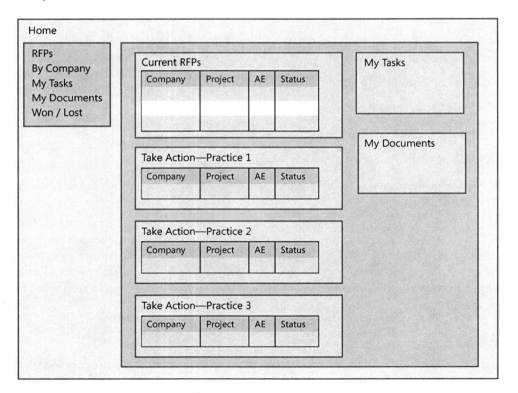

Building the Solution

Now it's time to start building the solution. The first step is to create the site that will contain the RFP request documents, the response deliverables, and the workflows required for the process. Once the site is created, the libraries, workflows, and other data stores will be created and customized using the web interface and SharePoint Designer.

Build RFP Site

The RFP site will be created as a subsite of another site—in many cases, a sales team site. A site administrator with access to create subsites can use the following information to build the site.

Field	Value
Template Selection	Team Site
Title	RFP Management
Description	Requests for proposals process site. Request and response deliverables are managed here.
URL	.../RFP
Permissions	Use unique permissions
Navigation—Quick Launch	Yes
Navigation—Top Link Bar	No
Navigation Inheritance	Yes

1. Navigate to the site that will be the parent of the RFP site.

2. On the Site Actions menu, select the New Site link.

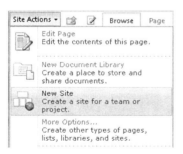

3. To configure more than just the name and URL for the new site, select Browse All to get the full selection of sites and lists.

4. Select the Team Site template, and then click More Options.

5. Use the site option information in the preceding table to configure the site. Note that any of these settings can be updated later if changes need to be made.

6. Click Create.

7. Because unique permissions were selected for the site, permissions must be configured for the site. The RFP Owners and RFP Members groups are automatically created. These groups and their members can be used as the site is being configured. If other people are assisting with the site configuration, they need to be added to the RFP Owners group. Once the site has been configured, permissions will be updated to allow access to others.

8. Select Create A New Group under Visitors To This Site and give it the name **RFP Visitors**.

9. Click OK.

Creating an RFP Notification Security Group

When creating the site, the Visitors, Members, and Owners security groups are created for the site. In addition to these, an additional group should be created to allow for more functionality throughout the site.

1. On the Site Actions menu, select the Site Settings link.

2. Under Users And Permissions, select the People And Groups link.

3. Select the Groups link in the left navigation bar.

4. From the New menu, select New Group.

5. Create a SharePoint group with the following settings.

Field	Value
Name	RFP Notification
Description	(Leave blank since the title is self-descriptive.)
Who Can View	Everyone
Who Can Edit	Group Owner
Allow Requests	Yes
Auto-Accept Requests	No
E-mail Address	Add the site owner email address
Permissions	Read

6. Click Create.

Create Site Columns and Content Types

It's easier to create the content types you need ahead of time so that when the document library is added a few steps from now, the new content types are ready to be added to the library.

Practices, Estimates, and Approvers

Part of the design that will vary from implementation to implementation is the groups that are tasked with providing estimates and approvals for the estimates. In the example you are building, the groups are simply called Practice 1, Practice 2, and Practice 3.

In a Microsoft software services company, these might be the following:

- Application Development (.NET) Practice

- SharePoint/Information Worker Practice

- Design and Branding Practice

In a home building and renovation company, they might be:

- Architecture

- Engineering

- Design

These practices are the different groups that each have their own staff, their own criteria for providing estimates, and their own approvers. There may be more or less than three practices, but the same model will be needed for each. Three columns need to be added to the RFP content type for each practice. A separate workflow will also need to be created.

Creating the Site Columns

For the RFPs library you need to create several additional columns that will be used to build the content types for RFP documents and deliverables. The content type columns will be used to track RFP details, drive processes, and create views.

1. On the Site Actions menu, select the Site Settings link.

2. In the Galleries section, select Site Columns.

Galleries
Site columns
Site content types
Master pages

3. On the Site Columns page, select Create, and then add each of the columns described in the following table. The columns should be added to the existing group Custom Columns.

Column Name	Field	Value
RFPDescription	Type	Multiple Lines of Text
	Description	Short description of the RFP
	Required	No
	Allow Unlimited Length	No
	Number of Lines for Editing	6 (default)
	Type of Text to Allow	Plain text
	Append Changes	No
AccountManager	Type	Person or Group
	Description	Person responsible for customer relationship and communication.
	Required	Yes
	Enforce Unique	No
	Allow Multiple	No
	Allow Selection Of	People Only
	Choose From	All Users
	Show Field	Name (with presence)
Notes	Type	Multiple Lines of Text
	Description	Additional notes and details
	Required	No
	Allow Unlimited Length	No
	Number of Lines for Editing	6 (default)
	Type of Text to Allow	Plain Text
	Append Changes	No
RFPDueDate	Type	Date and Time
	Description	Date RFP response is due to the customer
	Required	Yes
	Enforce Unique	No
	Date and Time Format	Date Only
	Default Value	(None)

Column Name	Field	Value
EstimateDueDate	Type	Date and Time
	Description	Date estimate is due for internal review and approval
	Required	No
	Enforce Unique	No
	Date and Time Format	Date Only
	Default Value	(None)
ApprovalDueDate	Type	Date and Time
	Description	Date internal approval is due (Note: Additional time may be required to prep deliverables.)
	Required	No
	Enforce Unique	No
	Date and Time Format	Date Only
	Default Value	(None)
RFPStatus	Type	Choice
	Description	Status of RFP
	Required	Yes
	Enforce Unique	No
	Choices	New Submitted Did not submit
	Display Choices Using	Drop-down menu
	Allow Fill-in choices	No
	Default Value	Choice: New
Instructions	Type	Multiple Lines of Text
	Description	Detailed instructions for submitting the RFP response
	Required	No
	Enforce Unique	No
	Number of Lines for Editing	6
	Type of Text	Plain Text
	Append Changes	No

Column Name	Field	Value
CompanyName	Type	Single Line of Text
	Description	Name of organization requesting proposals
	Required	Yes
	Enforce Unique	No
	Max Number of Characters	255 (default)
	Default Value	(Leave blank)
ContactName	Type	Single Line of Text
	Description	(Leave blank since the column title is self-descriptive.)
	Required	No
	Enforce Unique	No
	Max Number of Characters	255 (default)
	Default Value	(Leave blank)
ContactEmail	Type	Single Line of Text
	Description	(Leave blank since the column title is self-descriptive.)
	Required	No
	Enforce Unique	No
	Max Number of Characters	255 (default)
	Default Value	(Leave blank)
ContactPhone	Type	Single Line of Text
	Description	(Leave blank since the column title is self-descriptive.)
	Required	No
	Enforce Unique	No
	Max Number of Characters	255 (default)
	Default Value	(Leave blank)
BidHours	Type	Single Line of Text
	Description	(Leave blank since the column title is self-descriptive.)
	Required	No
	Enforce Unique	No
	Max Number of Characters	255 (default)
	Default Value	(Leave blank)

Column Name	Field	Value
BidPrice	Type	Single Line of Text
	Description	(Leave blank since the column title is self-descriptive.)
	Required	No
	Enforce Unique	No
	Max Number of Characters	255 (default)
	Default Value	(Leave blank)
BidStatus	Type	Choice
	Description	Status of RFP Bid
	Required	No
	Enforce Unique	No
	Choices	In Process Submitted Did not submit Won Lost
	Display Choices Using	Drop-down menu
	Allow Fill-in Choices	No
	Default Value	(Leave blank)
Practice1Status	Type	Choice
	Description	Status of the Practice 1 estimate
	Required	Yes
	Enforce Unique Values	No
	Values	New Assigned Estimated Approved NA
	Display Choices Using	Drop-down menu
	Allow Fill-in Choices	No
	Default Value	New

Column Name	Field	Value
Practice1Estimator	Type	Person or Group
	Description	Person assigned to estimate the proposal from Practice 1
	Required	No
	Enforce Unique	No
	Allow Multiple	No
	Allow Selection	People and Groups
	Choose From	SharePoint Group: Practice 1
	Show Field	Name (with presence)
Practice1Approver	Type	Person or Group
	Description	Person assigned to review and approve the proposal from Practice 1
	Required	No
	Enforce Unique	No
	Allow Multiple	No
	Allow Selection	People and Groups
	Choose From	SharePoint Group: Practice 1
	Show Field	Name (with presence)

Repeat the Practice 1 columns for Practice 2 and Practice 3 so there are a total of 9 columns: 3 each for Status, Estimator, and Approver.

4. Click OK.

Creating the RFP Content Type

When the site columns have been created, add the two content types and add the new site columns to the appropriate content type.

1. On the Site Actions menu, select the Site Settings link.

2. In the Galleries section, select Site Content Types.

3. On the Site Content Types page, select Create.

4. Complete the New Content Type form as shown in the following screenshot.

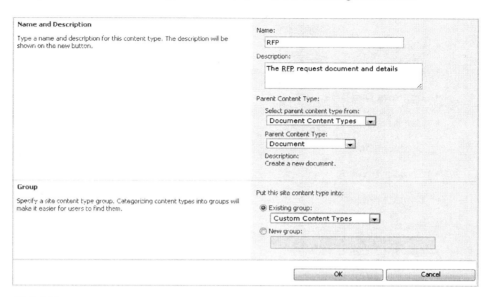

5. Click OK.

Now you need to add the content type columns:

1. On the Site Content Type Information page, select Add From Existing Site Columns.

2. Set Select Columns From to Custom Columns.

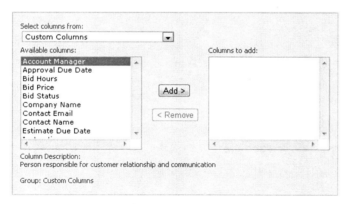

3. In the following order, add the site columns to the content type:

    • ˙RFP Description

    • RFP Due Date

    • Account Manager

- RFP Status

- Notes

- Instructions

- Estimate Due Date

- Approval Due Date

- Company Name

- Contact Name

- Contact Email

- Contact Phone

- Practice 1 Status

- Practice 1 Estimator

- Practice 1 Approver

- Practice 2 Status

- Practice 2 Estimator

- Practice 2 Approver

- Practice 3 Status

- Practice 3 Estimator

- Practice 3 Approver

4. Leave the setting for Update All Content Types Inheriting From This Type at the default Yes.

5. Click OK.

Creating the Deliverable Content Type

Create the Deliverable content type and add the new site columns.

1. On the Site Actions menu, select the Site Settings link.

2. In the Galleries section, select Site Content Types.

3. On the Site Content Types page, select Create.

4. Complete the New Content Type form as shown in the following screenshot.

Name and Description

Type a name and description for this content type. The description will be shown on the new button.

Name:

Deliverable

Description:

Final document sent as the RFP response.

Parent Content Type:

Select parent content type from:

Document Content Types

Parent Content Type:

Document

Description:
Create a new document.

Group

Specify a site content type group. Categorizing content types into groups will make it easier for users to find them.

Put this site content type into:

⦿ Existing group:

Custom Content Types

○ New group:

[OK]   [Cancel]

5.   Click OK.

Now add the content type columns:

1.   On the Site Content Type Information page, select Add From Existing Site Columns.

2.   Set Select Columns From to Custom Columns.

3.   In the following order, add these site columns to the content type:

   • Account Manager

   • Company Name

   • Notes

   • Bid Hours

   • Bid Price

   • Bid Status

4.   Leave the setting for Update All Content Types Inheriting From This type at the default, Yes.

5.   Click OK.

Creating a Notification Workflow for RFPs

Rather than rely on alerts, which users can deactivate, you will create a quick workflow to send notifications to people who should be aware of incoming RFPs and review them to determine whether their practice areas need to provide estimates. The email sent to this group will also have more information than a common alert, making the notice more relevant and effective. This workflow will satisfy the first of the identified business needs.

Because all the documents are being stored in a single document library and you want notifications to be sent only for new RFPs, you will create a content type–specific workflow in SharePoint Designer.

1. On the Site Actions menu, select Edit In SharePoint Designer.

Note This link may not work in some browsers. If that is the case, open SharePoint Designer and then open the site directly.

2. Once SharePoint Designer is loaded, select Workflows in the left navigation area.

3. On the Workflows tab, in the New group, select Reusable Workflow.

4. Enter the workflow details as shown here:

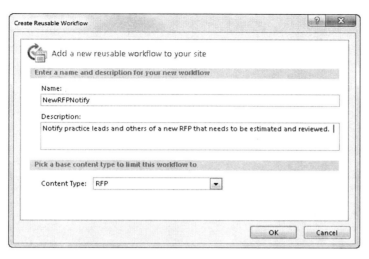

5. Click OK.

SharePoint Designer will display a new workflow with a single step. You don't need to set any conditions or additional steps. Just create a single action step that will automatically send an email as new items are added to the library.

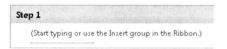

6. With the Step 1 control selected, click the Action menu and select Send An Email.

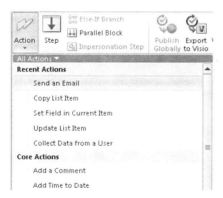

7. The step now changes. Click These Users to build the email.

8. A blank email message template opens. Click the Select Users icon (the book icon shown in the following screenshot) for the To field.

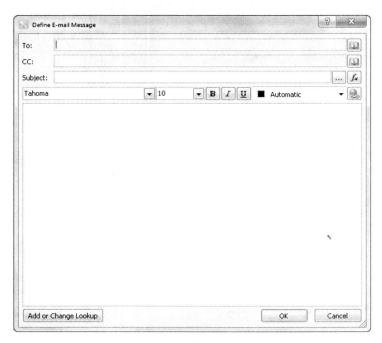

9. The Select Users dialog box is displayed. Select People/Groups From SharePoint Site, and then click Add.

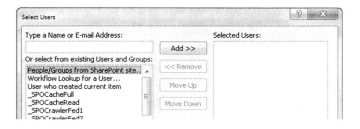

10. The Select People And Groups dialog box opens. Select SharePoint Groups, and then type **RFP** in the search field. Click the search icon.

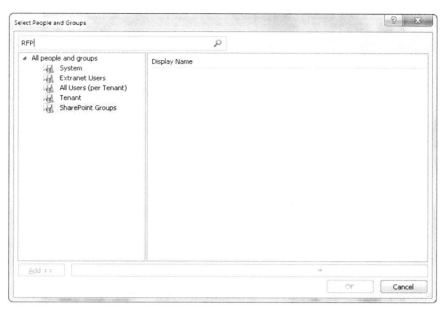

11. The search results should show the RFP Notification group that was created earlier. Select the RFP Notification group, and then click Add.

12. Click OK.

13. The RFP Notification group should be displayed in the Select Users dialog box. Click OK.

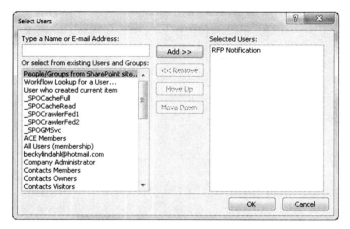

14. Enter the following value for the email Subject line: **New RFP for review**.

15. Now create the body of the email message. You will use a number of values from the library item to make the content more specific and useful. When completed, the content should look like the following screenshot.

When a value from the RFP item is needed for the message, follow the steps provided after the screenshot.

Values from the RFP item that are displayed in the message look similar to [%Current Item:Account Manager%].

16. Click the Add Or Change Lookup button in the lower-left corner of the dialog box shown in the preceding screenshot.

17. Select the field you want (such as Account Manager), and then click OK.

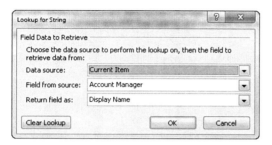

18. When you finish adding all the content and field values, click OK.

19. When the email message is complete, click the Publish button and the workflow will be validated and published to the library.

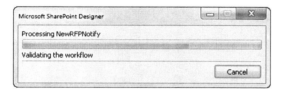

The workflow now shows up in the library once the RFP content type has been added. A specific instance of the workflow will be created at that time.

Create RFPs Library

A single document library is used for storing RFP documents, deliverable documents, any supporting documents, and tracking the RFP and deliverable details. As RFP request documents are acquired, they are uploaded to the library and placed in a new folder that matches the RFP name. A simple naming convention can be used to include the company name as the first element in the RFP's name. Management uses the list, details, and status to keep an eye on what is being worked on, won, and lost.

There are a lot of columns to track in the library, but they all have their purpose. Some of the fields track content that management wants to see to get a high-level view of all the RFPs coming through. Other fields are needed to facilitate the estimation and approval process. Forms for adding and updating documents can be edited to simplify data entry as needed.

Content Types

Two content types will be added to the library in addition to the default Document content type. These content types will be used to group and manage additional properties of the specific documents. The three content types will be:

- Document (default). No additional columns will be added. Support documents will be associated with the RFP by storing them in the same folder.

- RFP

- Deliverable

Creating the Library

Use the information provided in the following table to create the RFPs library.

Field	Value
Library Name	RFPs
Type	Document Library
Description	This library contains RFP documents from customers requesting bids.
Navigation	Yes
Document Version History	No
Document Template	Leave as default Word document

1. On the Site Actions menu, select the More Options link.

2. Locate the Document Library template, and then click the More Options button.

3. Enter the information from the preceding table, and then click Create.

Configuring the Library for Content Types

Two additional content types will be added to the library:

1. In the Settings group on the ribbon, select Library Settings.

2. Under General Settings, select Advanced Settings.

3. For the Content Types setting, select Yes.

4. Click OK.

5. In the Content Types section, select Add From Existing Site Content Types.

6. Select site content types from the list of custom content types.

7. Select the RFP and Deliverable content types, and then click Add.

8. Click OK.

9. Select Change New Button Order And Default Content Type, and then complete the Content Type Order settings as shown here.

10. Click OK.

Creating the Views

The RFPs library provides the core data for the solution and will have a number of views that can be used for management of the information. These views will also prove to be useful throughout the process. For this library you need to create several custom views. Settings for each of the views are detailed in the following table. After the table, you'll find the steps to follow to edit and create the views.

View Name	Field	Value
By Company	View Format	Start from All Events
	Default View	Yes
	Columns	Type (icon linked to document) Name (linked to document with edit menu) Modified Modified By
	Sort	Name
	Filter	Show all items in this view
	Inline Editing	No
	Tabular View	Yes
	Style	Default
	Folders	Show items inside folders
	Item Limit	30, display in batches
	Mobile	Enable, 3
All Recent	View Format	Start from All Events
	Default View	No
	View Type	Public
	Columns	Name (linked to document with edit menu) Account Manager Modified
	Sort	Modified
	Filter	None
	Inline Editing	No
	Tabular View	Yes
	Group By	None
	Totals	None
	Style	Default
	Folders	Show all items without folders
	Item Limit	30, display in batches
	Mobile	Enable, 3

View Name	Field	Value
Won/Lost	View Format	Start from Standard View
	Default View	No
	View Type	Public
	Columns	Name (linked to document w/Edit) Company Name RFP Name Account Manager Bid Hours Bid Price
	Sort	Modified
	Filter	Content Type is equal to Deliverable AND Bid Status is equal to Won OR Bid Status is equal to Lost
	Inline Editing	No
	Tabular View	Yes
	Group By	Bid Status
	Totals	None
	Style	Default
	Folders	Show all items without folders
	Item Limit	30, display in batches
	Mobile	Enable, 3
My Docs	View Format	Start from Standard View
	Default View	No
	View Type	Public
	Columns	Name (linked to document w/Edit) Account Manager Company Name Modified
	Sort	Modified
	Filter	Modified By is equal to [Me]
	Inline Editing	No
	Tabular View	Yes
	Group By	None
	Totals	None
	Style	Default
	Folders	Show all items without folders

View Name	Field	Value
My Docs, *continued*	Item Limit	30, display in batches
	Mobile	Enable, 3
New—Practice 1	View Format	Start from Standard View
	Default View	No
	View Type	Public
	Columns	Name (linked to document w/Edit) Account Manager Company Name Modified Practice 1 Status
	Sort	Modified
	Filter	Practice 1 Status is not equal to NA AND Practice 1 Status is not equal to Approved AND RFP Status is equal to New AND Content Type is equal to RFP
	Inline Editing	No
	Tabular View	No
	Group By	None
	Totals	None
	Style	Default
	Folders	Show all items without folders
	Item Limit	30, display in batches
	Mobile	Enable, 3

Repeat the New—Practice 1 view for each practice (Practice 2, Practice 3, and so on) by starting with the New—Practice 1 view and changing the displayed column as well as the filter columns.

To create a new view, follow these steps:

1. On the Site Actions menu, select the View All Site Content link.

2. Click the RFPs link to open the library.

3. Select the Library tab on the ribbon.

4. Click the Create View icon in the Manage Views group.

5. Enter the information for each new view shown in the preceding table.

Creating a Notification Workflow

Since a content type–specific reusable workflow was created for the RFP content type, now you only need to create an instance of it in the library:

1. Navigate to the RFPs library.

2. Select the Library tab on the ribbon.

3. Click the Library Settings icon in the Settings group.

4. Under Permissions And Management, select Workflow Settings.

5. On the Workflow Settings page, select Add A Workflow.

6. Unless RFP was selected in the drop-down on the Workflow Settings page, the notification workflow will not yet be visible as an option. On the Add A Workflow page, in the Content Type section, select RFP from the Run On Items Of This Type list.

   Once RFP has been selected, the reusable workflow created for the RFP content type will be visible and selectable.

7. Complete the rest of the form using the values in the following table.

Field	Value
Content Type	RFP
Workflow	NewRFPNotify
Name	New RFP Notification
Task List	Tasks (default)
History List	Workflow History (default)
Start Options	Allow this workflow to be manually started Start this workflow when a new item is created

8. Click OK.

Creating a Process Workflow

For each practice that might have estimates to create and approvals to procure before the company sends the RFP bid/deliverable to the client, you will create a workflow that notifies estimators and approvers that they have been assigned a task. You will use the out-of-the-box Three-State workflow for this.

These workflows will not be started automatically but be initiated by the team leads who are reviewing the RFP to determine if their practice is contributing to the estimate. If the practice is creating an estimate, the team lead will assign an estimator and an approver and then manually start the process workflow.

1. On the Site Actions menu, select the View All Site Content link.

2. Click the RFPs library link to open the library.

3. Select the Library tab on the ribbon.

4. In the Settings group, select Library Settings.

5. Under Permissions And Management, select Workflow Settings.

6. On the Workflow Settings page, select Add A Workflow.

7. Fill out the form using the following values:

Field	Value
Content Type	RFP
Workflow	Three-state
Name	Practice 1 Estimate and Approval Process
Task List	Tasks (default)
History List	Workflow History (default)
Start Options	Allow to be started manually (checked)

8. Click Next.

9. Complete the next form using the following values:

Field	Value
Choice Field	Practice 1 Status
Initial State	Assigned
Middle State	Estimated
Final State	Approved
Title: Custom Message	RFP estimate workflow initiated:
Include List Field	Keep selected: RFP Name
Description: Custom Message	An RFP workflow has been initiated on the following list item:
Include List Field	Keep selected: RFP Name
Insert Link to List Item	Keep selected
Due Date: Include List Field	Keep selected: Estimate Due Date
Assigned To: Include List Field	Keep selected: Practice 1 Estimator
Send Email Message	Keep selected
To	Blank (keep selected)
Subject	Blank (keep selected)
Body	Keep selected: Please estimate the Practice 1 component of the RFP.
Title: Custom Message	RFP approval task
Include List Field	Keep selected: RFP Name
Description: Custom Message	An RFP review task has been initiated on the following list item:
Include List Field	Keep selected: RFP Name
Insert Link to List Item	Keep selected
Due Date: Include List Field	Keep selected: Approval Due Date
(Assigned to) Include List Field	Keep selected: Practice 1 Approver
Send Email Message	Keep selected
To	Blank (keep selected)
Subject	Blank (keep selected)
Body	Keep selected: Please review and approve the Practice 1 component of the RFP.

10. Click OK.

11. Repeat the process to create a workflow for each practice (Practice 2 and Practice 3).

Create Pages

Once the underlying lists, libraries, and functionality have been created, the home page that users typically use as an entry point to the solution needs to be built and configured. Depending on the requirements and wireframing that was done, a number of web parts and text can be added to the page to make it intuitive and useful for the various user groups.

Additional pages are sometimes added when too much is going on within a single page or when user requirements demand role-specific pages. We are only configuring the home page for our example here.

Configuring the Home Page

The home page created by the Team Site template includes the wiki page functionality but doesn't really do much of what we want it to do for our solution, so we need to clean it up a bit by adding information for users and quick links for access to frequently used functionality and selected views of the data.

1. On the home page of the site, select the Page tab on the ribbon.

2. Select Check Out.

3. Select Edit.

   You will make edits to this page:

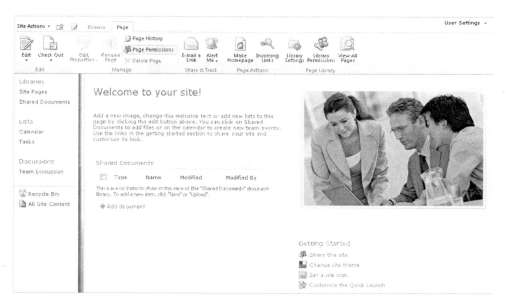

4. Remove the default image by clicking it and then pressing Delete.

5. Remove the Getting Started section by selecting the text and then pressing Delete.

6. Delete the Shared Documents web part by selecting the Web Part menu and clicking Delete.

7. Change the welcome text header and content to something more appropriate for the RFP solution, as shown here.

> Welcome to the RFP site!
>
> This site is used to manage and store RFPs and estimates/bids created by the various practices.

8. Now add four instances of the RFPs Library web part to the left zone. First, position the cursor where the web part will be added.

9. On the ribbon, select the Insert tab.

10. Open the Document Library menu, and select the RFPs library.

11. Repeat steps 8 through 10 three more times. Each web part will be configured with a different view.

12. Add a User Tasks web part to the right zone. Select Insert and then More Web Parts, which opens a dialog box.

13. Select the User Tasks web part.

14. Click Add.

15. Add a Relevant Documents web part to the right zone, under the User Tasks web part. Select Insert, More Web Parts to open the selection dialog box.

16. Select the Relevant Documents web part.

17. Click Add.

18. Edit the User Tasks web part in the right zone. Point to the upper-right corner, select the drop-down, and then click Edit Web Part. Make the changes listed in the following table.

Field	Value
Columns	Name (linked to document with edit menu) Modified
Sort	Modified (descending order)
Filter	Modified By is equal to [Me]
Tabular View	(Do not select)
Item Limit	10

19. Expand the Appearance section and change the web part title to **My Tasks**.

20. Click Apply.

21. Edit the Relevant Documents web part in the right zone. Point to the upper-right corner, select the drop-down, and then click Edit Web Part.

22. Change the web part title to **My Documents**.

23. Click Apply.

24. Edit the first (top) RFPs web part in the left zone. Point to the upper-right corner, select the drop-down, and then click Edit Web Part.

25. Change the web part title to **Current RFPs**.

26. Click Apply to save the change and continue editing the Current RFPs web part.

Now we need to edit the current view. Follow these steps:

1. Select Edit The Current View.

2. Use the following table to set the view.

Field	Value
View Name	RFPs Home Page
View Format	Start from Standard View
Default View	No
View Type	Public
Columns	Name (linked to document w/Edit) Account Manager Company Name RFP Status Modified
Sort	Modified
Filter	Content Type is equal to RFP
Inline Editing	No
Tabular View	No
Group By	None
Totals	None
Style	Default
Folders	Show all items without folders
Item Limit	30, Display in Batches
Mobile	Enable, 3

3. Click OK on the Edit View page.

4. Click OK.

5. Edit the second RFPs web part in the left zone. Point to the upper-right corner, select the drop-down, and then click Edit Web Part.

6. Change the web part title to **Practice 1—RFP Actions**.

7. Click Apply.

8. Change the setting for Selected View to New—Practice 1.

9. Click OK.

10. Edit the third RFPs web part in the left zone. Point to the upper-right corner, select the drop-down, and then click Edit Web Part.

11. Change the web part title to **Practice 2—RFP Actions**.

12. Click Apply.

13. Change the setting for Selected View to New—Practice 2.

14. Click OK.

15. Edit the last (bottom) RFPs web part in the left zone. Point to the upper-right corner, select the drop-down, and then click Edit Web Part.

16. Change the web part title to **Practice 3—RFP Actions**.

17. Click Apply.

18. Change the settings for Selected View to New—Practice 3.

19. Click OK.

20. Click Check In.

Customizing the Quick Launch

Because the Team Site template was used to create the site, a few lists and libraries were created and added to the Quick Launch that aren't being used initially. Cleaning up the Quick Launch will help users not get distracted. The lists and libraries will remain on the site for future use and will still be accessible via the All Site Content page, but the links will be removed from the Quick Launch for simplicity.

1. On the Site Actions menu, select the Site Settings link.

2. In the Look And Feel section, select the Quick Launch link.

3. For each of the navigation links listed here, select the link icon and then click the Delete button:

   • Site Pages

   • Shared Documents

   • Lists

   • Discussions

We also want to get rid of the Libraries heading and create a new heading with the title RFPs.

1. Select the RFPs link and copy the URL value.

2. Delete the Libraries heading. The RFPs link goes with it.

3. Create a new heading for RFPs, and paste in the URL.

4. Add a new navigational link for each of the views listed here:

- By Company
- My Tasks
- My Documents

Managing the Solution

After the solution is built, a few more configuration tasks need to be attended to by whoever is managing the solution. These include, but are not limited to, managing security permissions and training users so that they understand the system and their roles.

Permissions Management

Permissions for the site can be managed through the existing SharePoint security groups as well as the new RFP Notification group. All users that require access—sales, leads, estimators, and reviewers—need to have Contributor level access to do the work they are required to do. Other users can be given View access if the organization allows this. Other users who want to be notified when new RFPs are submitted can be added to the RFP Notification group and will get an email message.

The Business Process

The RFP response solution is a good example of applying a business to the SharePoint platform because while some automation has been provided by SharePoint, users still need to perform some activities. Users need to be trained in how to use the system.

- Account managers need to know how to create folders, upload documents, and assign a content type and other attributes.

- Practice leads need to know how to access the RFP records, how to assign estimators and approvers, set the status, and initiate the workflow.

- Estimators and approvers need to know how to add and update the estimate, bid, and deliverable documents; complete tasks; and set properties.

Reviewing the Platform

This RFP response solution is built with capabilities that are available in any version of SharePoint 2010. The site template, the list features, and the configuration made with SharePoint Designer 2010 allow it to be used just about everywhere.

Higher-level versions of SharePoint 2010, such as SharePoint Enterprise or SharePoint Online (Office 365) Enterprise, offer additional capabilities that could extend or improve this baseline site.

Additional Customizations

The solution created in this chapter is only the tip of the iceberg when it comes to the complete estimation and RFP process. Several other additions, configurations, or customizations could be addressed and added to this foundation going forward. Several examples are listed in the following table.

Additional Customization	Benefits
Upgrade from folders to document sets	Document set functionality offered by higher-level versions of SharePoint would allow for better metadata management and organization for the bids.
Update the default RFP view to group by content type	SharePoint Designer is required to create this solution, but the solution would be more user-friendly if users could easily see the original RFP and the deliverable/bid documents separately.
Additional automation	There are several areas in which additional automation or notifications could be added. These would take some rework or require stitching together several workflows to operate. Additional automation might involve, for example, notifying the account manager when all approvals have been gathered or dealing with approvers rejecting an estimate or requesting changes.
Content reuse and document assembly	This customization would integrate processes to build the bid or deliverable document from stock content and involve maintaining a library of repeatable content for quicker and more consistent document creation.
Connect to a CRM solution with company and contact information	Rather than using stand-alone company and contact names, a connection to a CRM system would allow for more data aggregation. The CRM system would be able to see the list of RFPs and bids.
Add structure or automation to the estimation processes.	The estimation process or processes for each practice could also be standardized or provided with automation tools.

Summary

In this chapter, we looked at a method for building a solution to manage RFP responses within an organization. The solution enables users who want to be kept in the loop to be notified when RFPs have been submitted and need to be worked on. Based on information submitted by the account manager and practice leads, the resources responsible for compiling, reviewing, and approving estimates are assigned tasks and notified of the required work. Through this process, higher-quality deliverables should be created on a timeline that meets the RFP requirements.

The solution in this chapter is also built using the lowest common denominator for SharePoint platforms—allowing broad usage and setting a foundation for solutions on the SharePoint Server platform and Office 365 Enterprise platform.

CHAPTER 9

Building a Contact Management Solution

In this chapter, you will create a basic contact management solution that goes beyond the standard SharePoint Contacts list but not as far as more full-featured customer relationship management (CRM) products. The solution will be based on core SharePoint components available in SharePoint Foundation 2010 and Office 365 for Professionals and Small Businesses, including lists, views, and no-code customizations.

There are a wide variety of products in the contact management or CRM markets, including a very robust offering from Microsoft Dynamics. But when you don't need the feature depth, don't have the budget, and already have access to SharePoint, you've got the makings for an efficient and cost-effective contact or customer relationship solution that can be used for contact management today, and extended to other solutions later.

Identifying the Business Problems

Keeping track of contacts and managing the business processes for them can be time-consuming and cumbersome without the proper tools. In an organization driven by sales of products or services, these contacts and relationships are a significant value to the organization, as are the methods used to extend and capitalize on the data.

Organizations large and small keep track of people and partner organizations they deal with for a wide variety of reasons. Because of the wide variety of users and needs, there are usually many different data repositories or contact lists, none of which are standardized or consistent. A common contact management example is a business keeping track of clients and partners as a CRM-like solution. There are, however, plenty of other related scenarios, such as churches keeping track of members and clubs or user groups keeping track of their membership.

Some issues are merely logistical, like having multiple users that need access to a consolidated data source instead of each employee maintaining his or own. SharePoint Foundation or SharePoint Online through Office 365 can address this issue because they are server-based platforms. Decision makers need to determine which platform better suits the needs of their organization, although both have the technical capabilities to meet the requirements for contact management. Once the platform decision has been made, building or extending a solution suited to the particular needs of the organization is the next step.

This chapter focuses on three areas of concern around a small company's collection of contacts.

Consistent and Available Data

Employees at a company who need to track contact data do so using their own methods and storage—as individuals and as teams rather than as a company. Data stored unconventionally is not backed up, not sharable between people or teams, and is not protected as the valuable company asset that it is.

Tracking Activity

Users are not collecting information about contacts beyond the traditional "Rolodex" information—the core name, address, and contact information. When multiple employees interact with the same contacts, it is critical to know the history of those interactions and quickly collect and communicate ongoing activity to maintain consistency between the company and its contacts.

Personalization of Data

Default "Rolodex" types of contact management solutions provide a list of users that is typically ordered alphabetically. However, a number of different users and roles work with a contact management solution, and they each have their own needs when using it.

Summarizing the Business Problems

Understanding the business needs allows you to prioritize the solution so that it aligns your needs with the capabilities of the tool. With contact management, we'll be focusing on the following:

- Consistent and available data

- Tracking activity

- Personalization of data

Customer relationship management (CRM) tools engage these needs at a number of levels and scopes, but they can be expensive for some organizations. They are most often associated with sales and marketing but can also see wider adoption across an organization.

When considering CRM options, organizations sometimes find that "best of breed" CRM solutions have more bells and whistles than are required to meet their needs, that they don't want to spring for the more expensive licensing costs, and that with SharePoint already in place, they already have the makings for a simple and useful CRM solution.

Gathering Information

With the high-level challenges identified, more specific information needs to be gathered to design the solution from the correct perspective and at the right depth.

System Users

The solution being designed will have several different user scenarios. Knowing what information they are dealing with, where it comes from, what they do with it, and where it goes will be critical to understanding how these requirements align with the platform the solution will be built on.

All Users

All users of the system will come looking for core contact information: the lists of people working with an organization, information about the organization in general, and contact details for both the organization and the associated individuals. These users need to do the following:

- Browse organizations or companies

- Browse contacts

- Search for companies or contacts

- Update company or contact information

Sales Resources

Salespeople are responsible for client contact and are the key users and managers of information in the contact or customer relationship system. They are the people adding new contacts and working with them to make sales and manage relationships over time. Salespeople need to do the following:

- Add new contacts

- Manage existing contacts

- Track historical interactions with contacts

Solution Data

There are two key types of data used in this solution: individual contacts and the company or organization. The following individual contact data will be stored:

- Last name

- First name

- Company

- Job title

- Email address

- Business phone

- Mobile phone

- Fax number

- Address information

- Notes

- Journal

- Follow-up flag

- Tickler file date

- Status

- Contact type (Prospect, Client, Partner, Vendor, Networking)

The Journal field will be used to capture information about contact events: when contact was made, what was discussed, resolved, or left for a later date, and so on. The Follow-up Flag field will be used when new contacts are found and need to be contacted. The Tickler File Date field will be used to help salespeople know when to reconnect with contacts who they are not in constant communication with. The Status field will help determine which activities should be taking place for a particular contact.

The following list shows the information that will be stored for company data:

- Company name

- Description

- Address information

- Billing contact

- Billing information

- Billing address information

- Website

- Journal

- Status

- Account owner

For contacts that represent a company at which activity is happening and a relationship exists, additional information may be required about the company.

Summarizing the Requirements Gathering Process

With information about the users of the system and the data that will be tracked, the solution design can begin to take shape. A high-level summary looks like the following:

- Salespeople were consulted on the type of information they need to collect about contacts and companies as well as what views of the information would be useful for their job responsibilities.

- All users were consulted to find out how they find the contacts they're looking for and if the information provided is sufficient to meet their needs.

Now the requirements identified will be aligned with SharePoint capabilities wherever possible and a solution design will begin to emerge.

Designing the Solution

The requirements that have been identified fit well with the list approach used by the SharePoint platform. A few decisions need to be made regarding which direction to go technically. This section walks through some of the decisions that were made for this particular scenario.

Design Decisions

One of the benefits of using SharePoint is that it provides many ways to solve a particular problem. The challenge is picking the best approach possible for the specific instance and to start in a way that allows the solution to evolve over time.

Site Taxonomy

Where should the contacts content be stored? Should the lists be part of an existing site alongside other lists and libraries, or should they be isolated in a site collection or a subsite? Each option is technically feasible and has its own pros and cons. Ultimately, two of the bigger decision factors are the overall environment architecture and security requirements.

For larger organizations and environments, architecture approaches might dictate that a contact management solution demands its own site collection for reasons of data management and security management. In a smaller organization, ease of use may be a higher priority, so nesting the contact solution within a root site might be more beneficial.

From a security perspective, it's easy to lock down a whole site, whereas locking down specific lists and pages would take a little more effort and understanding of the solution design to be sure everything is correctly secured.

Navigation might also be a consideration. With a self-standing site or web, the Quick Launch (left navigation bar) is available for use specifically for the solution. When the solution is nested in another site or web, the Quick Launch is likely already being used, and adding new links for contact management might be restricted.

For our example, we'll create a subsite of another site because our scenario is a smaller-scale contacts repository that a team might use, rather than an enterprise-wide solution that might be housed in a site collection.

> **Note** For the most part, the same solution could be built as part of an existing site or web or as a stand-alone site collection. With the solution as part of an existing web, the differences would lie in the management of the Quick Launch and how web parts are displayed on a default page rather than a secondary page.

Site Templates

Once the decision to use a separate site is made, the site template needs to be determined. The two leading candidate templates are the Blank Site template and the Team Site template because they are both out-of-the-box options that provide a good starting point to the solution. Knowing that we want to use multiple pages to accommodate different user scenarios, or dashboards, we will select the Team Site template. The Team Site template has the wiki feature turned on and won't cause you to run into issues with nonprovisioned features, as the Blank Site template does sometimes when you try to use more advanced (enterprise) features such as content-type publishing.

The Team Site template does come with some preconfigured lists and libraries that won't be used in our example, but they can be deleted after the site is built.

List Templates

Two lists are used in this solution. SharePoint comes with a Contacts List template that is a good starting point for the main data used in the solution, although a number of fields will be added as well. You will also be creating a custom Company list from the Custom List template.

Permissions

As mentioned in the site taxonomy discussion earlier, one of the advantages of using a separate site is allowing for a separate security model, which is needed for the contacts site. There isn't an immediate need for special groups for the site, but you will break inheritance on the site so that future changes to the main site won't inadvertently add inappropriate permissions to the contacts site.

The default Visitors, Members, and Owners groups can be created and used for the site initially. A Sales security group will be used to help isolate column values in the Company table. More role-specific groups could also be created in the future as needs arise.

Data Thresholds/Scalability

Since the solution isn't used to store a number of documents anywhere near SharePoint's list limitations or content that would take up large volumes of space that would affect content database architecture, the solution is being created as a site of another site collection. There are no concerns about scalability and data thresholds.

If a more feature-rich contact management solution were being built rather than purchased, creating the solution as a site collection would be more appropriate so that farm administrators could manage the site collection and database as needed. However, also note that while SharePoint does a wonderful job managing data in lists, it is very limited when it comes to relational data, only allowing very simple lookup-like relationships, not the many-to-many relationships that are required for building robust CRM solutions.

Solution Wireframes

Wireframes for this solution include a main entry page and a page for displaying contacts who are associated with each company. Other pages will use the default list views for each list.

Home

With the solution having its own site, an entire default page will be dedicated to the Contacts list and activities associated with it. If the solution was built within another site, some of the web parts could still be added to a home page, but others would likely need to be added to a new wiki or web part page to avoid cluttering up existing pages.

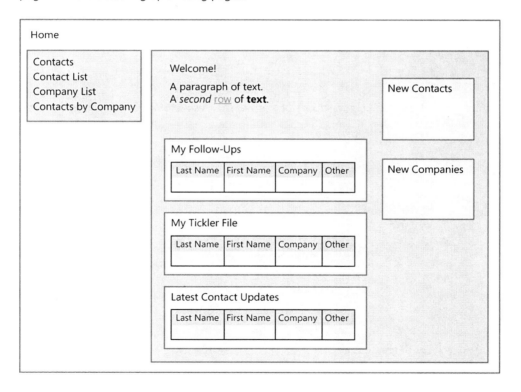

Company Information

Rather than have just a single listing of companies, for each company it would be convenient to display the list of contacts within the organization.

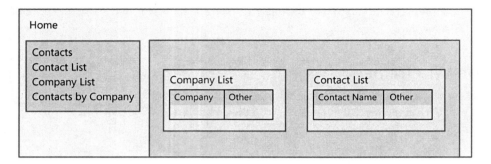

Building the Solution

Now it's time to start building the solution. The first step is to create the site or site collection that will contain the contacts lists and pages. Once the site is created, the lists, pages, and forms will be created and customized using the web interface and SharePoint Designer.

Build the Contacts Site

The contacts site will be created as a subsite of another site. A site administrator with access to create subsites can use the following information to build the site:

Field	Value
Template Selection	Team Site
Title	Contact Management
Description	Contact information for customers, vendors, and partners
URL	.../Contacts
Permissions	Use unique permissions
Navigation—Quick Launch	No
Navigation—Top Link Bar	Yes
Navigation Inheritance	Yes

Follow these steps to create the site:

1. Navigate to the site that will be the parent of the contacts site.

2. Select Site Actions, New Site.

3. Since you don't see all the options you need, click Browse All to display the full selection of sites and lists.

4. Select the Team Site template, and then click More Options.

5. Use the site information in the preceding table to configure the site. Any of these settings can be updated later if changes need to be made.

6. Click Create.

7. Because unique permissions were selected for the site, permissions must be configured for the site. The default settings can be used initially as the site is being configured. If other people are assisting with the site configuration, they need to be added to the Contacts Owners group. Once the site has been configured, permissions will be updated to allow access to others.

8. Note that users in the existing site Visitors group have access to view the site by default. To keep these users out of the site, select Create A New Group under Visitors To This Site. Leave the members of the Visitors group blank for now.

9. Click OK.

You now have a team site and are taken to the home page.

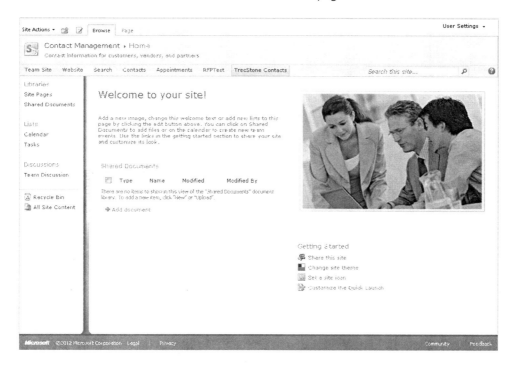

Creating the Sales Security Group

The Visitors, Members, and Owners SharePoint security groups are defined for the site during the site's creation. In addition to these, a group for Sales should be created to allow for additional functionality throughout the site:

1. On the Site Actions menu, select the Site Settings link.

2. Under Users And Permissions, select People And Groups.

3. Click the Groups heading in the left navigation bar.

4. From the New drop-down, select New Group.

5. Create a SharePoint group using the following settings:

Field	Value
Name	Sales Group
About Me	(Leave blank since the title is self-descriptive.)
Group Owner	Default (current user)
Who Can View	Group Members (default)
Who Can Edit	Group Owner (default)
Allow Requests	No
Add to Default View	No (unchecked)
Permissions	Contribute

6. Click Create.

Create the Company List

The first list you'll create is for storing company contact information. Companies will be connected to contacts using a lookup field and will act as a parent record when multiple contacts for the same company exist in the list. Additional functionality might be added later as needed. From a technical perspective, it's nice to add the Company list first so that when the Company lookup field is created in the Contacts list later, the Company list will be ready to be configured.

Creating the List

Use the information provided in the following table and procedure to create the Company list:

Field	Value
List Name	Company
Type	Custom
Description	This list contains company information for contacts
Navigation	Yes

1. On the Site Actions menu, select the More Options link.

2. Locate the Custom List template, and then click the More Options button.

3. Enter the information from the preceding table, and then click the Create button.

4. When the new list is displayed, select the List Settings option on the ribbon.

5. Click the Title, Description And Navigation link in the General Settings group.

6. Update the list name to **Company List**, and then click Save.

 Note The new title wasn't used when you created the list so that the shorter name, Company, would be used in the URL for the list. Using the new list name initially would have created a longer URL and included additional characters for the space between the words. When you change the name of a list or library, the original URL is kept but the displayed list name is updated.

7. Click the Versioning Settings link.

8. Under Item Version History, select Yes for Create A Version Each Time.

 Note Turning on versioning for the list enables the Journal field to append each change to the field's value to keep a running record of updates.

9. Click OK.

Creating the Columns

For this list you need to add or create several additional columns. Since you are starting from a custom list template, most fields don't yet exist. You will add columns from scratch by using the details and steps listed here.

Each custom column is described in detail in the following table. After the table you'll find the steps you need to complete to create each of the columns.

Column Name	Field	Value
Address	Type	Single Line of Text
	Description	(Leave blank since the column title is self-descriptive.)
	Required	No
	Enforce Unique	No
	Max Number of Characters	255 (default)
	Default Value	(Leave blank)
	Add to Default View	No (not selected)
City	Type	Single Line of Text
	Description	(Leave blank since the column title is self-descriptive.)
	Required	No
	Enforce Unique	No
	Max Number of Characters	255 (default)
	Default Value	(Leave blank)
	Add to Default View	No (not selected)
State/Province	Type	Single Line of Text
	Description	(Leave blank since the column title is self-descriptive.)
	Required	No
	Enforce Unique	No
	Max Number of Characters	255 (default)
	Default Value	(Leave blank)
	Add to Default View	No (not selected)
Zip/PostalCode	Type	Single Line of Text
	Description	(Leave blank since the column title is self-descriptive.)
	Required	No
	Enforce Unique	No
	Max Number of Characters	255 (default)
	Default Value	(Leave blank)
	Add to Default View	No (not selected)

Column Name	Field	Value
Country/Region	Type	Single Line of Text
	Description	(Leave blank since the column title is self-descriptive.)
	Required	No
	Enforce Unique	No
	Max Number of Characters	255 (default)
	Default Value	(Leave blank)
	Add to Default View	No (not selected)
Description	Type	Multiple Lines of Text
	Description	(Leave blank since the column title is self-descriptive.)
	Required	No
	Number of Lines	6
	Specify Type of Text	Rich text (bold, italics, text alignment, hyperlinks)
	Append Changes to Existing Text	No
	Add to Default View	No (not selected)
BillingInformation	Type	Multiple Lines of Text
	Description	(Leave blank since the column title is self-descriptive.)
	Required	No
	Number of Lines	6
	Specify Type of Text	Rich text (bold, italics, text alignment, hyperlinks)
	Append Changes to Existing Text	No
	Add to Default View	No (not selected)
BillingContact	Type	Single Line of Text
	Description	(Leave blank since the column title is self-descriptive.)
	Required	No
	Enforce Unique	No
	Max Number of Characters	255 (default)
	Default Value	(Leave blank)
	Add to Default View	No (not selected)

Column Name	Field	Value
BillingAddress	Type	Single Line of Text
	Description	(Leave blank since the column title is self-descriptive.)
	Required	No
	Enforce Unique	No
	Max Number of Characters	255 (default)
	Default Value	(Leave blank)
	Add to Default View	No (not selected)
BillingCity	Type	Single Line of Text
	Description	(Leave blank since the column title is self-descriptive.)
	Required	No
	Enforce Unique	No
	Max Number of Characters	255 (default)
	Default Value	(Leave blank)
	Add to Default View	No (not selected)
BillingState/Province	Type	Single Line of Text
	Description	(Leave blank since the column title is self-descriptive.)
	Required	No
	Enforce Unique	No
	Max Number of Characters	255 (default)
	Default Value	(Leave blank)
	Add to Default View	No (not selected)
BillingZip/PostalCode	Type	Single Line of Text
	Description	(Leave blank since the column title is self-descriptive.)
	Required	No
	Enforce Unique	No
	Max Number of Characters	255 (default)
	Default Value	(Leave blank)
	Add to Default View	No (not selected)

Column Name	Field	Value
BillingCountry/Region	Type	Single Line of Text
	Description	(Leave blank since the column title is self-descriptive.)
	Required	No
	Enforce Unique	No
	Max Number of Characters	255 (default)
	Default Value	(Leave blank)
	Add to Default View	No (not selected)
Website	Type	Hyperlink or Picture
	Description	(Leave blank since the column title is self-descriptive.)
	Required	No
	Format URL as	Hyperlink
	Add to Default View	No (not selected)
Journal	Type	Multiple Lines of Text
	Description	Track information about each conversation or connection event over time. New entries will be date stamped and appended to the record.
	Required	No
	Number of Lines	6 (default)
	Specify Type of Text	Rich text (bold, italics, text alignment, hyperlinks)
	Append Changes to Existing Text	Yes
	Add to Default View	No
Status	Type	Choice
	Description	Tracks company status for sorting and filtering purposes
	Required	Yes
	Enforce Unique Values	No
	Values	Active Inactive
	Display Choices Using	Drop-down
	Allow 'Fill-in' choices	No
	Default Value	Active
	Add to Default View	No

Column Name	Field	Value
AccountOwner	Type	Person or Group
	Description	Person responsible for the company from a sales and contact perspective
	Required	No
	Enforce Unique Values	No
	Allow Multiple	No
	Allow Selection	People Only
	Choose From	SharePoint Group: Sales Group
	Show Field	Name (with presence)
	Add to Default View	No (not selected)

1. While still on the List Information page for the Company list, select Add From Existing Site Columns in the Columns section.

2. Add the column details from the preceding table.

3. Click OK.

Changing Column Order

While still on the List Information page, change the order of the columns as follows:

1. Select Column Ordering.

2. Assign the Position From Top settings to match the following column order:

Column (click to edit)	Type
Title	Single line of text
Description	Multiple lines of text
Account Owner	Person or Group
Website	Hyperlink or Picture
Journal	Multiple lines of text
Address	Single line of text
City	Single line of text
State/Province	Single line of text
Zip/Postal Code	Single line of text
Country/Region	Single line of text
Billing Information	Multiple lines of text
Billing Contact	Single line of text
Billing Address	Single line of text
Billing City	Single line of text
Billing State/Province	Single line of text
Billing Zip/Postal Code	Single line of text
Billing Country/Region	Single line of text
Status	Choice
Created By	Person or Group
Modified By	Person or Group

3. Click OK.

Creating the View

The view you need to create is detailed in the following table. After the table, you'll find the steps you follow to create the view.

Field	Value
View Name	Active Companies
Format or Existing View to Start From	All Items
Default View	Yes
Columns	Title (linked to item with edit) Description Account Owner Website
Sort	Title
Filter	Status = Active
Inline Editing	No
Tabular View	Yes
Style	Default
Folders	Show items in folders
Item Limit	30, display in batches
Mobile	Enable, 3

To create a new view, follow these steps:

1. On the Site Actions menu, select the View All Site Content link.

2. Click the Company List link to open the list.

3. Select the List tab on the ribbon.

4. Click the Create View icon in the Manage Views group.

5. Enter the information for the view shown in the preceding table.

Create the Contacts List

The Contacts list is the main list for the solution. You will use the Contacts List template as a foundation, with a few configuration changes and additional fields to add the view and functional capabilities required.

Creating the List

Use the information provided in the following table to create the Contacts list.

Field	Value
List Name	Contacts
Type	Contacts
Description	Contact information for customers, partners, and vendors
Navigation	Yes

1. On the Site Actions menu, select the More Options link.

2. Locate the Contacts List template, and then click the More Options button.

3. Enter the information from the preceding table, and then click the Create button.

4. When the new list is displayed, select the List Settings option on the ribbon.

5. Click the Title, Description And Navigation link in the General Settings group.

6. Update the title to **Contacts List**, and then click Save.

7. Click the Versioning Settings link.

8. Under Item Version History, select Yes for Create A Version Each Time.

9. Click OK.

Creating the Columns

Using the Contacts List template saves time by creating many of the fields for you, but you also need to create several custom columns. Each column is described in detail in the following table. The steps you complete to create each of the columns are provided after the table.

Column Name	Field	Value
Journal	Type	Multiple Lines of Text
	Description	Track information about each conversation or connection event over time. New entries will be date stamped and appended to the record.
	Required	No
	Number of Lines	6 (default)
	Specify Type of Text	Rich text (bold, italics, text alignment, hyperlinks)
	Append Changes to Existing Text	Yes
	Add to Default View	No

Column Name	Field	Value
Contact Type	Type	Choice
	Description	Type of contact for sorting and filtering purposes.
	Required	Yes
	Enforce Unique Values	No
	Values	Prospect Client Partner Vendor Networking
	Display Choices Using	Drop-down
	Allow Fill-in	No
	Default Value	General
	Add to Default View	Yes
Status	Type	Choice
	Description	Tracks contact status for sorting and filtering purposes.
	Required	Yes
	Enforce Unique Values	No
	Values	Active Inactive
	Display Choices Using	Drop-down
	Allow Fill-in	No
	Default Value	Active
	Add to Default View	No
Follow-up Flag	Type	Yes/No (check box)
	Description	Flag to indicate that the contact should be contacted soon as a follow-up to some contact event (conversation, email, phone call, etc.).
	Default Value	No
	Add to Default View	No
Tickler File Date	Type	Date and Time
	Description	Date to set for longer-term reminder to touch base with a contact.
	Required	No
	Enforce Unique	No
	Date and Time Format	Date Only
	Default Value	Calculated Value: [Today] + 90
	Add to Default View	No

To create each of the columns, follow these steps:

1. On the Site Actions menu, select the View All Site Content link.

2. Click the Contacts List link to open the list.

3. Select List on the List Tools tab.

4. Select the List Settings item in the Settings group.

5. Click the Create Column link in the Columns section.

6. Enter the information based on the preceding table, and then click OK.

7. Repeat the process for all the columns identified.

Remove the original Company field so that you can add a new Company field that is a lookup to the Company list:

1. While still using the List tab, select List Settings in the Settings group.

2. Select the Company column.

3. Select Delete.

4. A confirmation dialog box opens. Click OK.

5. Add the new Company field by following the steps provided earlier for adding columns, and use the details shown in the following table.

Field	Value
Name	Company
Type	Lookup
Description	Company associated with the contact
Required	No
Enforce Unique Values	No
Get Information From	Company List
In This Column	Title
Add a Column to Show	None
Add to Default View	Yes
Relationship	Keep selected: Restrict Delete

6. Select Column Ordering.

7. Change the Position From Top setting for the Company column to place it in its original position (7).

8. Click OK.

Using the Journal Field

Why did you add a Journal field when the Notes field is usually sufficient?

By default, changes made to a Notes column over time would look like this:

Notes	Initial Meeting Talked about new products Talked about online marketing

Essentially, the contents of the Notes field changes to whatever is the latest version, with users tweaking the content as needed. You will still use a Notes column, but it will be more of a static value describing the contact. A new column will be used to track contact events over time.

With list versioning turned on and Append Changes configured, a Journal column will provide more of a historical view and look something like this:

Notes	Wes Preston (10/13/2011 12:21 PM): Talked about online marketing Wes Preston (10/13/2011 12:21 PM): Talked about new products Wes Preston (10/13/2011 12:18 PM): Initial Meeting

Creating the Views

For this list, you need to create several custom views. Each view is detailed in the following table. After the table, you'll find the steps you complete to create the views.

View Name	Field	Value
Active Contacts	Format or Existing View to Start From	All Items
	Default View	Yes
	Audience	Public View
	Columns	Last Name (linked to item with edit menu) First Name Company Business Phone E-mail Address Contact Type Journal
	Sort	Last Name (ascending) First Name (ascending)
	Filter	Status = Active
	Inline Editing	Yes
	Tabular View	Yes
	Group By	None
	Totals	None
	Style	Default
	Folders	Show items in folders
	Item Limit	12, display in batches
	Mobile	Enable, 3

View Name	Field	Value
My Follow-Ups	Format or Existing View to Start From	Active Contacts
	Default View	No
	Columns	Last Name First Name Company Business Phone E-mail Address Journal
	Sort	Last Name First Name
	Filter	Status is equal to Active Follow-up Flag is equal to Yes Modified By is equal to [Me]
	Inline Editing	Yes
	Tabular View	Yes
	Style	Default
	Folders	Show items in folders
	Item Limit	30, display in batches
	Mobile	Enable, 3
My Tickler File	Format or Existing View to Start From	My Follow-Ups
	Default View	No
	Columns	Last Name First Name Company Business Phone E-mail Address Tickler Date
	Sort	Tickler Date (ascending) Last Name (ascending)
	Filter	Status is equal to Active Tickler Date is not equal to (leave blank) Modified By is equal to [Me]
	Inline Editing	Yes
	Tabular View	Yes
	Style	Default
	Folders	Show items in folders
	Item Limit	30, display in batches
	Mobile	Enable, 3

View Name	Field	Value
Latest Modifications	Format or Existing View to Start From	All Items
	Default View	No
	Audience	Public View
	Columns	Last Name (linked to item with edit menu) First Name Company Business Phone E-mail Address Contact Type Journal
	Sort	Modified (descending)
	Filter	Status = Active
	Inline Editing	Yes
	Tabular View	Yes
	Group By	None
	Totals	None
	Style	Default
	Folders	Show items in folders
	Item Limit	12, display in batches
	Mobile	Enable, 3

To create a new view, follow these steps:

1. On the Site Actions menu, select the View All Site Content link.

2. Click the Company List link to open the list.

3. Select the List tab on the ribbon.

4. Click the Create View icon in the Manage Views group.

5. Enter the information for the views shown in the preceding table.

Now would also be a good time to add some sample data to the list so that you can test the views. You can do this by using the ribbon to create new items.

Creating a Custom Edit Form

Users want a quick and simple method for adding a journal entry for a contact without needing to see all the other contact information. You'll create a form for this purpose in this section.

1. On the Site Actions menu, select the View All Site Content link.

2. Click the Contacts List link to open the list.

3. Select the List tab on the ribbon.

4. In the Customize List group, click Edit List In SharePoint Designer.

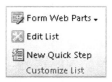

SharePoint Designer will open and may prompt for site credentials.

 Note If you are not using Internet Explorer, SharePoint Designer and a connection to the site and list may need to be opened manually.

5. Once SharePoint Designer is open, select New in the Forms area.

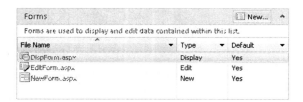

6. Fill in the Create New List Form dialog box with the following values:

Field	Value
Name	JournalEntry
Type of Form	Edit item form
Set as Default	No (not selected)
Content Type	Contact
Create a Link	Yes (selected)
Link Name	Journal Entry

7. Click OK.

8. Make sure that at least one record appears in the Contacts list. The SharePoint Designer form doesn't do well with empty data sets.

9. In the Forms section, select the new JournalEntry form and give the form a few seconds to load fully.

10. At the bottom of the SharePoint Designer page, select the Design tab to see more of the form and hide the code.

11. Select and remove each column title and field other than the Full Name and Journal columns.

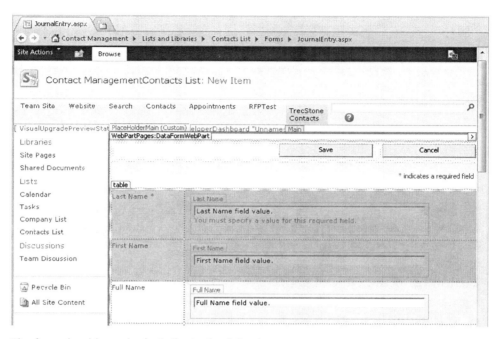

The form should now look similar to the following:

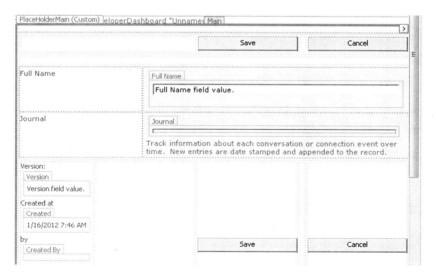

12. Save the form and close SharePoint Designer.

The item drop-down for the contact should now include the Journal Entry option:

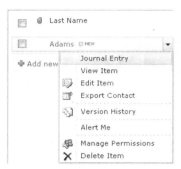

Create Pages

The original home page created for the team site doesn't do much of what we want it to do for our solution, so we need to clean it up a bit by adding some information for users and quick links to access frequently used functionality and selected views of the data.

Customizing the Quick Launch

The links in the Quick Launch are defaults for the Team Site template. A bunch of the links aren't necessary for the contacts solution, and these will be removed. Users will still be able to access the lists and libraries these links refer to through the View All Site Content command.

First we will add the Contacts header and page links:

1. On the Site Actions menu, select the Site Settings link.

2. In the Look And Feel section, select the Quick Launch link.

3. Select the New Heading link.

4. For the URL, type **/Team-Site/Contacts/SitePages/Home.aspx** for the web address and **Contacts** for the description.

5. Click OK.

6. Select the Contacts List link.

7. Change the heading to **Contacts**.

8. Click OK.

9. Select the Company List link.

10. Change the heading to **Contacts**.

11. Click OK.

Now you can remove the links you don't need:

1. Select the Libraries link.

2. Click Delete.

3. In the confirmation dialog box, click OK.

4. Repeat these steps to remove the Lists link and the Discussions link.

Adding Web Parts to the Home Page

Within the page itself, you will update the title and description text, remove the rest of the content, and add new content that is appropriate for the contacts solution.

1. On the home page of the site, select the Page tab on the ribbon.

2. Select Check Out.

3. Select Edit.

4. Remove all the content from the right zone by selecting it and then pressing Delete.

5. Point to the Shared Documents web part header to display the drop-down control.

6. Select Delete to remove the web part from the page.

7. In the confirmation dialog box, click OK.

8. Change the content of the welcome text to something more appropriate to the solution.

9. The page should now look something like this:

10. Place the cursor at the top of the right zone.

11. Select the Insert tab on the ribbon.

12. Open the Contacts web part drop-down and select Contacts List.

13. Press Enter.

14. On the Insert tab on the Ribbon, select More Web Parts.

15. Select Company List.

16. Click Add.

Editing the Views of the Web Parts

You've added the web parts to the page, and now you need to edit the views of the new web parts.

Instead of creating a permanent view for the list, as you did previously when the list was created and configured, you'll be editing the current views of the web parts to create a page-specific view of the list.

1. Open the Contacts List web part menu, and then select Edit Web Part.

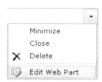

2. In the Contacts List tool pane, expand the Appearance section and change the Title to **New Contacts**.

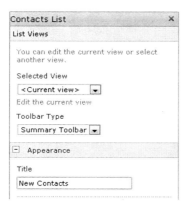

3. Click Apply.

4. Select the Edit The Current View link in the tool pane.

5. Configure the view using the following values:

Field	Value
View Name	Current View
Columns	Edit (linked to edit item) Full Name Company
Sort	Created (descending)
Filter	Show all items in this view
Inline Editing	No
Tabular View	No
Group By	None
Totals	None
Style	Default
Folders	Show items in folders
Item Limit	12, display in batches
Mobile	Enable, 3

6. Click OK.

7. Open the Company List web part menu, and then select Edit Web Part.

8. In the Company List tool pane, expand the Appearance section and change the Title to **New Companies**.

9. Click Apply.

10. Select the Edit The Current View link in the tool pane.

11. Configure the view using the following values:

Field	Value
View Name	Current View
Columns	Title (linked to item with edit menu) Account Owner
Sort	Created (descending)
Filter	Show all items in this view
Inline Editing	No

Field	Value
Tabular View	No
Group By	None
Totals	None
Style	Default
Folders	Show items in folders
Item Limit	12, display in batches
Mobile	Enable, 3

12. Click OK.

The other web parts on the page will use views created for the lists:

1. Place the cursor below the text in the main (left zone) section of the page.

2. Select the Insert tab on the ribbon.

3. Open the Contacts web part drop-down and select Contacts List.

4. Press Enter.

5. Repeat steps 2 and 3 twice. You should have three Contacts List web parts on the page.

Now you can change the view and web part titles for each one so you are providing different facets of the same list data:

1. Open the first Contacts List web part menu and select Edit Web Part.

2. In the Contacts List tool pane, expand the Appearance section and change the Title to **My Follow-Ups**.

3. In the Contacts List tool pane, open the Selected View drop-down and select My Follow-Ups.

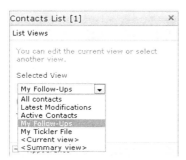

4. Click OK.

5. Open the second Contacts List web part menu and select Edit Web Part.

6. In the Contacts List tool pane, expand the Appearance section and change the Title to **My Tickler File**.

7. In the Contacts List tool pane, open the Selected View drop-down and select My Tickler File.

8. Click OK.

9. Open the third Contacts List web part menu and select Edit Web Part.

10. In the Contacts List tool pane, expand the Appearance section and change the Title to **Latest Contact Updates**.

11. In the Contacts List tool pane, open the Selected View drop-down and select Latest Modifications.

12. Click OK.

13. On the Page tab, click Save And Close.

14. On the Page tab, click Check In.

15. Add any comments you want, and then click Continue.

Adding Conditional Formatting to Tickler Dates

To make information on the home page a little easier to read and sort through, it's helpful to implement some conditional formatting on the data. The Tickler File Date view can be tweaked to show different colors based on whether the date is in the future or the past.

1. On the home page, select the Page tab on the ribbon.

2. In the Edit group, select Check Out.

3. Open the Edit drop-down and select Edit In SharePoint Designer.

4. Click through the dialog boxes.

5. Give SharePoint Designer a few seconds to load the page and data. Once it has, the home page should be displayed.

6. A lot is going on in the SharePoint Designer interface. Covering all the capabilities is beyond the scope of this book, but here you will make a relatively simple change to the Tickler File Date view by using conditional formatting capabilities. This change lets users see when they have reached or are past a date set in the list items.

7. Select the Tickler File Date data.

8. Under Filter, Sort And Group on the ribbon, open the Conditional Formatting drop-down and select Format Selection.

9. Set the field values as shown in the following screenshot. You are defining a condition for when the value of Tickler File Date is today.

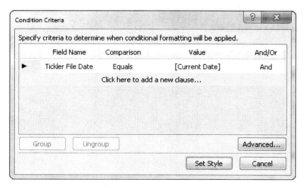

10. Click Set Style.

11. For today's date, you will highlight the date to capture the user's attention. Select Background in the Category list on the left and set the background color.

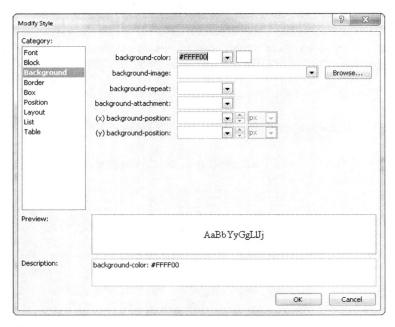

12. Click OK.

13. Repeat the steps to add a second condition for when the date has passed, as shown here:

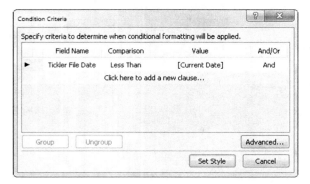

14. Set the formatting to change the text to red.

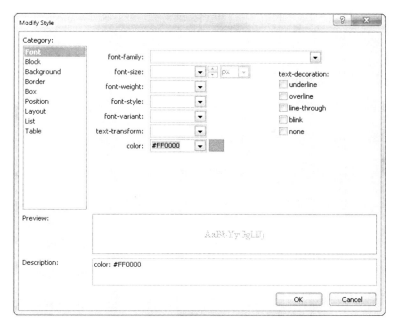

15. Save the page and exit SharePoint Designer.

16. Return to the browser and refresh the page.

17. In the Edit section, click Check In.

18. Add any comments to the page version, and then click Continue.

The Tickler File Date view should now have conditional formatting that highlights the date when it equals the current date and changes the font to red when the date has passed.

Creating the Contacts By Company Page

In addition to the Contacts list views and Company list views, one last page and view need to be configured to display contacts by the company they are a part of:

1. On the Quick Launch, select All Site Content.

2. Select the Site Pages document library.

3. Under Library Tools, select the Documents tab on the ribbon.

4. In the New group, select New Document.

5. Name the page CompanyContacts.

6. Click Create.

You now have a clean wiki page, but it has only a single area to work in and you need two columns:

1. In the Layout group on the ribbon, open the Text Layout drop-down and select the Two Columns layout.

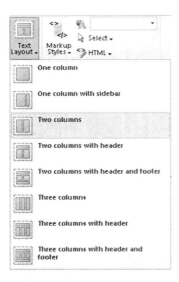

2. The cursor is already placed in the left column. Under Editing Tools, select the Insert tab.

3. In the Web Parts group, select More Web Parts.

4. Select the Company List web part, and then click the Add button.

5. Put the cursor in the right column.

6. In the Web Parts group on the ribbon, open the Contacts drop-down and select Contacts List.

You now have two web parts side by side on the page. The functionality you are looking for to make this page different from the existing views comes from connecting the two web parts so that you can select a company name and get a listing of the contacts for that company.

1. On the Company List web part, open the web part properties drop-down and select Edit Web Part.

2. Select the web part properties drop-down again, and a new Connections option is available. Point to Connections, select Send Row Of Data To, and then select Contacts List.

3. A dialog box then prompts you to select a connection type. Select Get Filter Values From, and then click Configure.

4. A second dialog box then asks about the values that are being connected. Select the values as shown in the following screenshot, and then click Finish.

5. A new Select column is now displayed in the Company List web part. When the Select icon is clicked for a company item, the corresponding contacts are displayed in the Contacts list.

 Note The default views were used when you added the web parts to the page. You may want to edit the views used on the page to meet your specific needs.

6. Copy the URL of the page.

7. On the Site Actions menu, select Site Settings.

8. In the Look And Feel group, select Quick Launch.

9. Click New Navigation Link.

10. Paste the URL in the Web Address field.

11. Add the description **Contacts by Company**.

12. For the Heading, select Contacts (the default value) from the drop-down.

13. Click OK.

Managing the Solution

After the solution is built, only a few additional tasks need to be completed to deliver the solution and start using it. First, permissions need to be configured for the users of the site. Second, users should be trained and expectations should be set in order to have successful user adoption.

Permissions Management

Managing permissions for the solution site is generally the same as for other sites within your Share-Point environment. The standard SharePoint groups are used for permissions in addition to the Sales group that was added.

The Sales group is used as a way to filter the users who can be selected for the account owners of company records. No additional permissions are granted to the group at this time.

Communication and Training

Keeping users informed and enabling them for success with the solution are both key governance concepts. It's important to have a communication plan in place to keep users involved throughout the entire process both for feedback purposes and to allow them to plan for the new functionality. Once the solution has been completed, it's important not only to provide training on how to use the solution for users at that time, but to have ongoing materials available to bring new users up to speed on the solution as well.

Reviewing the Platform

The contact management solution in this chapter is built using capabilities that are available in any version of SharePoint 2010—from the site template, to the list features, to configuration performed with SharePoint Designer 2010—which allows it to be used in SharePoint Foundation 2010, SharePoint Server, or SharePoint Online in Office 365.

When using more advanced versions of SharePoint, the additional capabilities made available by these versions can be used to continue building on this solution. A few examples are listed in "Additional Customizations," but there are many opportunities for improvements.

Access Services

The contacts solution could also be built using Access Services if it is available via SharePoint Server Enterprise or the E3 and E4 plans in SharePoint Online. If you need additional data and connections between tables and lists, Access Services may provide the additional capabilities required without you having to make the move to a more robust .NET solution.

Additional Customizations

The solution created in this chapter only scratches the surface of the functionality available in CRM products and what could eventually be built using the SharePoint platform. There are plenty of additional capabilities in SharePoint (both out of the box and custom) that could be used to create both broader and deeper solutions.

Additional Customization	Benefits
New view and edit forms	More complex view and edit forms could be created that look more like traditional contact or CRM forms, with the fields arranged more intuitively. For example, you could group all the address fields together, and so on.
Enhance the follow-up and tickler file functionality	Rather than just using fields in the contacts table, add functionality to create new tasks or appointments specific to users.
Additional metadata	Depending on the needs of the organization, additional fields could be added to the Contacts or Company lists and used for additional views.

Additional Customization	Benefits
Contact type–driven activities	More specific solutions could be configured and built to accommodate type-driven activities: vendor-specific versus client-specific.
Search	In upgraded platforms that include Search Server, SharePoint Server, or Office 365 Enterprise accounts, solution-specific search capabilities could be added to the site to allow searches by specific metadata in the Company and Contacts lists.

Summary

In this chapter we looked at a method to build a contact management solution for keeping track of customers, clients, partners, and other types of contacts, as well as information about interactions with them. This solution is not a full-featured CRM solution, but it does illustrate a number of approaches and techniques that can be used in other solutions and provides a foundation from which more robust solutions can be built.

CHAPTER 10

Building a Resource Scheduling Solution

In this chapter, you will create a solution that can be used for scheduling resources. Resources are people, places (meeting rooms), or equipment such as tools, vehicles, and projectors. In environments in which Microsoft Exchange is available, Exchange calendars are the preferred method for this type of scheduling. However, not all organizations have Exchange as an option, so here you'll build a SharePoint-only solution using features in SharePoint Foundation and the Small Business P1 plan in Office 365.

The solution you'll build in this chapter is relatively simple, and concepts demonstrated here might also be applied in environments that use Exchange for departments, teams, or scenarios for which adding resources to Exchange doesn't fit best practices.

Identifying the Business Problems

Small organizations have limited resources, but they still need to track people and resources effectively in order to deliver the level of customer service they desire. Many of these organizations have distributed workforces, with off-site staff or staff with no central office at all, but they still need visibility into where people are located and what their schedules look like and the ability to make assignments. They also need to be able to take actions quickly in response to customer needs.

In the past, a single person staffing a phone could be the point of contact for running an organization—scheduling and distributing communications. Now, most of these activities can be performed remotely by more than one person accessing a single calendar or schedule. In the past, a physical scheduling book was needed as the single point of truth, which made it difficult for more than one person to manage schedules, let alone more than one person at separate—sometimes geographically dispersed—locations. Using a SharePoint site, either in the cloud or on an externally facing on-premises server, can allow multiple people to manage appointments while also providing a place for the people doing the work to see the details of their schedules as they are populated.

This chapter focuses on three areas of concern for a small service organization tracking appointments for customers and technicians.

Multiple Off-Site Schedulers

The main business need is to allow more than one scheduler in different locations to see resources' calendars and be able to assign resources to customer appointments. With a tool like SharePoint, this should be easy. Unfortunately, creating the solution is not quite as intuitive as it should be with the normal tools and list templates that users are accustomed to. Schedulers need an online and easily available "schedule book" that they can work with to capture customer appointment requests and avoid double-booking technicians.

Send Appointment Confirmation

Moving from a manual scheduling book to an online solution also allows the organization to consider stepping up the customer-service experience in other ways. When appointments were made the old way, appointment reminders were also likely sent the "old way"—through manual mailings—if they were sent at all. Expectations now are for immediate verification of an appointment via email. With the schedule online, the organization also wants to automate the appointment verification process where possible.

Daily Assignments Reports

Finally, daily assignments for technicians were summarized in the past by a single scheduler manually reviewing the calendar and writing up orders for the day for each technician. This could be a time-consuming and labor-intensive process, prone to human error and dependent on the single scheduler being available to hand out the assignments.

Summarizing the Business Problems

Understanding the business needs allows you to prioritize the solution so that it aligns your needs with the capabilities of the tool. With the resource planning solution, we'll be focusing on the following:

- Building a calendar with functionality to determine resource availability and set appointments

- Sending appointment confirmations to customers

- Identifying daily appointment schedule for technicians

With the resource scheduling solution, everything is based on the appointment schedule. The other business issues will be addressed by building additional functionality on top of that calendar.

Gathering Information

With the high-level challenges identified, more specific information needs to be gathered in order to design the solution from the correct perspective and with the required depth.

System Users

Our solution is going to be built based primarily on the needs of one group, although two other groups might also be involved as the solution matures. To fully understand the needs of the solution, each user group needs to provide information about the specific tasks that group needs to complete within the system. This information will then be used to design and develop the solution.

Administrators/Schedulers

There will be one or more schedulers in one or more locations. From the business perspective, this allows for flexibility and redundancy, but it means that the schedule needs to be maintained in a location that all schedulers can access.

Schedulers take calls from customers and create appointments in the system. They need to see what's in the appointment calendar and which technicians are available so that appointments can be made.

Schedulers also prepare the daily work assignments for the technicians.

Technicians

Technicians won't directly access the system in the initial deployment described in this chapter, but they can and likely will be more involved in subsequent phases as capabilities are added.

Technicians need to see what work has been assigned to them and what the details are for the customer and the work to be done. For this most basic scenario, they will get their daily appointments from the schedulers who produce reports based on the overall schedule.

Building a more mature solution requires technicians to be registered users of the system so that they can access their specific calendars and assignments. Other functionality is also available for technicians, which we'll cover in the section "Reviewing the Platform" on page 382.

Solution Data

There are two key types of data used in this solution: the technicians being scheduled and the appointments themselves.

Resources

The technicians being scheduled will be managed in a list of their names and with descriptions of the skills and services they offer:

- Name

- Description

The Resources list will primarily be a lookup or reference list for the appointment data that drives the rest of the functionality.

Appointments

Appointments are the main data elements you'll be dealing with in this solution. You need to be able to capture the core elements of an appointment as it is set up with a customer, while also scheduling it at a time they request that is also available in your technicians' schedule:

- Customer name

- Address or location of the work

- Contact phone number

- Contact email address

- Start date/time

- End date/time

- Category of work

- Description of work

- Technician assigned

Summarizing the Requirements Gathering Process

The primary need for this scenario is to replace the old scheduling book with an online scheduling solution that multiple people can maintain. After that core piece is created, other improvements can be implemented that directly affect customer service and communications.

Now the requirements identified will be aligned with SharePoint capabilities wherever possible, and a solution design will begin to emerge.

Designing the Solution

The requirements that have been identified fit well into the list approach used by the SharePoint platform, but they do run into some stumbling blocks when you try to manage the scheduling piece with traditional lists.

Design Decisions

One of the benefits of using SharePoint is that it provides so many ways to solve a particular problem. The challenge is picking the best approach possible for the specific instance and to start in a way that allows the solution to evolve over time.

Site Taxonomy

Where should the appointments content be stored? The Appointments list and supporting lists can technically go anywhere. Should the lists be part of an existing site alongside other lists and libraries, or should they be isolated in a site collection or a web? Both options have pros and cons. Adding the new functionality to an existing site is clean and simple since there aren't a lot of moving pieces to the solution. Creating a web provides more opportunity for managing security (if needed) and for creating additional pages without disrupting an existing home page.

For this example, you'll be activating the new features and building a solution in an existing site, and not creating a new subsite.

Site Templates

For this solution, the choice of site template isn't a critical decision because you'll be building on top of an existing site. The solution is fairly simple and can live within any SharePoint 2010 or Office 365 SharePoint Online site template. In this scenario, you will be activating a specific site feature that is probably not turned on by default on the site being used.

List Templates

There are two main list templates used in this solution. Both are based on out-of-the-box list templates, although they might not look like it to the casual user. The Resources list is available only when you activate the Group Work Lists feature. You won't be doing any further adaptation of this list for your scenario.

The second list is based on the standard Calendar list template, but it has a few additional fields that are also made available through the Group Work Lists feature. These fields enable specific capabilities in the Calendar list settings that are available only when the site feature is activated. Finally, a few other fields will be added to the list to capture additional content and enable additional capabilities.

Permissions

Permissions for the solution are fairly straightforward. The default groups for a site could be used, but you will be creating a separate security group for schedulers for the sake of clarity when managing the solution and to make extending the solution easier in the future.

All other users of the solution can gain access to view or edit the site as a member of the Viewer or Contributor group.

Data Thresholds/Scalability

Since you aren't doing anything with documents or attachments, the space used by the list won't grow that fast and won't have an impact on the content database that includes the list. If or when it comes time to revisit the list size or number of items, a policy could be put in place to remove old list items for easier list management.

Solution Wireframes

Wireframes for this solution are pretty basic. Because the solution is being built on top of an existing site, the home page is likely to be already defined. If real estate is available, a single web part can be added to the page to show upcoming appointments. Additional quick links can be added for access to the new lists or new item forms.

Home Page

The home page will stay in its current state with the potential addition of a single web part and new navigational elements in the Quick Launch (left navigation) area.

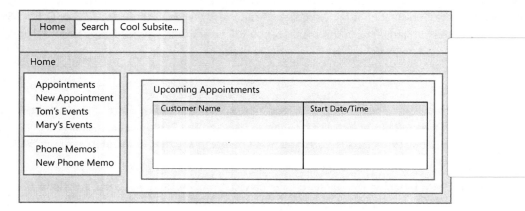

Appointments

Calendar lists default to the calendar view. This can be confusing to users when they use the scheduling functionality, so you'll change the default view to a list view.

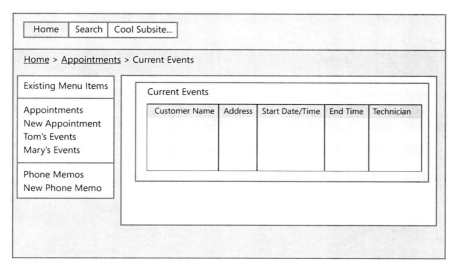

And that's it. Add and edit forms are created by the lists themselves and remain in the out-of-the-box configuration, with the exceptions of reordering fields and adding additional descriptions to assist users.

Building the Solution

Now it's time to start building the solution. The first step is to identify or create the site or site collection that will contain the required lists and pages. The solution can be built within an existing site or in a new site. Once the site has been identified, the lists and pages will be created and customized using the web interface and SharePoint Designer. Site Owner or Site Administrator permissions are required for many of the following steps.

Configure the Site

For this scenario, you're using an existing site and adding functionality specific to appointment keeping.

Enable Site Features

To use the reservation functionality for the site, you need to enable the site feature called Group Work Lists:

1. On the site home page, select Site Actions, Site Settings.

2. On the Site Settings page, under Site Actions, select Manage Site Features.

3. For the Group Work Lists feature, click the Activate button.

The Group Work Lists feature creates the Phone Call Memo, Resources, and Whereabouts lists.

4. Click Home on the top navigation bar to return to the home page.

Populate the Resources List

When the Group Work Lists site feature is activated, SharePoint creates a Resources list. This list will be used as a lookup to select the technicians or other resources that will be assigned to an appointment and tracked to be sure that no overlaps or dual bookings occur. Add some or all of your resources to this list to see how it works. These resources will be available when you add an item to the Appointments list, which you'll create in the next section.

1. On the Site Actions menu select the View All Site Content link.

2. Select the Resources list.

3. If you open the New Item drop-down on the ribbon, you can create a resource or a resource group. Clicking the Add New Item link or the New Item button on the ribbon (without opening the drop-down list) creates a new resource, which is what you want to do for this example.

Note If you have a lot of resources, you might want to create groups for them to make finding them easier when schedulers create appointments. One example is to create the groups Work Week Technicians and After-Hours/Weekend Technicians. Technicians can belong to more than one resource group. Along these same lines, if you have a lot of resources, you can also create alphabetical-listing groups: single letters or a range of letters.

4. Add a new resource to the list. The description value is optional.

5. Click Save.

6. Repeat steps 3 through 5 a few times to add resources to the list.

Create the Appointments List

The main list is a calendar list that will store all of the service appointments. Once the calendar is created, you'll configure a few additional pieces of the list as well.

Create the List

Use the information provided in the following table to create the Appointments list.

Field	Value
List Name	Appointments
Type	Calendar
Description	This calendar contains customer appointment times and details
Navigation	Yes
Use This Calendar to Share Member's Schedule?	No
Use This Calendar for Resource Reservation?	Yes

1. On the Site Actions menu, select the More Options link.

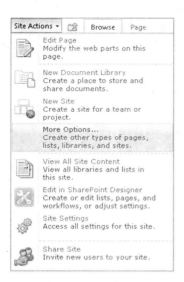

2. Locate the Calendar template, and then click the More Options button.

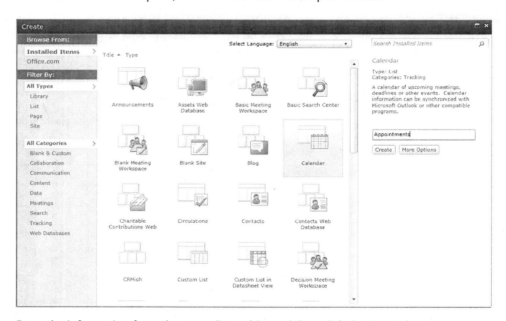

3. Enter the information from the preceding table, and then click the Create button.

Update the Title Column

The default Title field is going to be used to record the customer, client, or event name, but the purpose of the field might not be clear to users when they first use the form. To mitigate this, you can add a description to the field so that users understand how to use it.

1. Navigate to the Appointments list.

2. On the ribbon, select the Calendar tab. (If the default view has been changed to a noncalendar view, you need to select the List tab instead of the Calendar tab.)

3. In the Settings group on the ribbon, select List Settings.

4. In the Columns section, select the Title column.

5. Change the column's name to **Name**.

6. Add the following description: **Customer, client or event name**.

   The New and Edit forms will now show the description, as shown here:

7. Click OK.

Update the Location Column

As with the Name field, the use of the Location field is made clearer by adding a description to the field.

1. In the Columns section, select the Location column.

2. Add the following description: **Address where work will be done**.

3. Click OK.

Update the Category Column

The default Category field has some generic calendar-like options that should be replaced with more service-oriented options.

1. In the Columns section, select the Category column.

2. In the Type Each Choice On A Separate Line box, select all and delete the selection.

3. Enter options that are more appropriate for the scenario. Place each on a separate line as directed:

   - Service Check

   - Installation

   - Repair

4. Change the Allow Fill-In Choices option to No.

5. Click OK.

Create Confirm Email Column

If the customer setting up the appointment wants to receive an email confirmation of the new appointment, you'll need the customer's email address. You need to add a column to collect this information that you'll act on later:

While still on the List Information page for the Appointments list, do the following:

1. In the Columns section, select Add From Existing Site Columns.

2. Add a new field with the following values:

Field	Value
Column Name	Confirm Email
Type	Single Line of Text
Description	Email address used to send appointment confirmation information to customer.
Specify Type of Text	Rich text (bold, italics, text alignment, hyperlinks)
Required	No
Enforce Unique Values	No
Maximum Number of Chars	255 (default)
Default Value	Text (default)

Field	Value
Add to All Content Types	Yes (unchecked)
Add to Default View	Yes (checked)

3. Click OK.

4. Now you want to change the order of the fields so that the Confirm Email field is just after the Location (Address) field. In the Content Types section, select Reservations.

5. On the List Content Type Information page, select Column Order.

6. For Confirm Email, change Position From Top to 3.

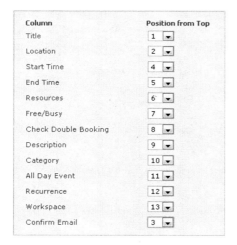

7. Click OK.

The field is now available in the forms to collect an email address from a customer when a scheduler collects the other appointment information.

Create Phone Column

When setting up an appointment, the scheduler captures the phone number of the customer calling so that the customer can be contacted for any schedule changes or if the technician has any questions.

While still on the List Information page for the Appointments list, do the following:

1. In the Columns section, select Add From Existing Site Columns.

2. Add a new field with the following values:

Field	Value
Column Name	Phone
Type	Single Line of Text
Description	Customer phone number
Required	No
Enforce Unique Values	No
Maximum Number of Chars	255 (default)
Default Value	Text (default)
Add to All Content Types	Yes (checked)
Add to Default View	Yes (checked)

3. Click OK.

4. Now you want to change the order of the fields so that the Phone column is just after the Location (Address) field. As shown in the previous step 4, in the Content Types section, select Reservations.

5. On the List Content Type Information page, select Column Order.

6. For the Phone field, change Position From Top to 3.

7. Click OK.

The field is now available in the forms to collect the phone number from a customer while a scheduler collects the other appointment information.

Change Order of Columns

A few more columns should be reordered to make the forms more intuitive and easier for the schedulers to use:

1. On the List Content Type Information page, select Column Order.

2. Set Category to 5.

3. Set Description to 6.

4. Click OK.

Create and Edit the Views

Calendar and event lists in SharePoint have some neat features, namely their ability to show an events list in a traditional calendar view. Unfortunately, this takes a little SharePoint "magic," and it sometimes doesn't work quite as expected. In this example, the Group Work Lists feature gives you the ability to assign appointments to users or resources and allows users to view the calendar for an individual user or resource. It does not, however, provide a combined calendar view for all users and resources. In fact, the default calendar view shows *none* of them, which is slightly confusing to users.

For this list you need to edit one existing view and create a custom view. Settings for each of the views are detailed in the following table. After the table, you'll find the steps you follow to edit and create the views.

View Name	Field	Value
Current Events (edit)	Default View	Yes
	Columns	Title (linked to item) Location Phone Start Time End Time Resources
	Sort	Title
	Filter	Show all items in this view
	Inline Editing	No
	Tabular View	No
	Style	Default
	Folders	Show items in folders
	Item Limit	30, Display in Batches
	Mobile	Enable, 3

View Name	Field	Value
Today's Events (new)	View Format	Start from All Events
	Default View	No
	View Type	Public
	Columns	Title Location Start Time End Time Resources Category Description
	Sort	Start Time
	Filter	Start Time is equal to [Today]
	Inline Editing	No
	Tabular View	No
	Group By	None
	Totals	None
	Style	Boxed
	Folders	Show items in folders
	Item Limit	30, Display in Batches
	Mobile	Enable, 3

To edit an existing view, follow the steps outlined here:

1. On the Site Actions menu, select the View All Site Content link.

2. Click the Appointments link to open the list.

3. Select the List tab on the ribbon.

4. In the Manage Views section, select the name of the view to be edited and click Modify View.

5. Enter the information for the Current Events view shown in the preceding table.

To create a new view, follow these steps:

1. On the Site Actions menu, select the View All Site Content link.

2. Click the Appointments link to open the list.

3. Select the List tab on the ribbon.

4. Click the Create View icon in the Manage Views section.

5. Enter the information for the Today's Events view shown in the preceding table.

One quick note about the Today's Events view: You could create a specific view for each resource to define a Today's Events for [PersonX] view, but you can get similar functionality by creating a quick link for the Today's Events view with a filter, which is then added to the query string. You will see how to do this in the section "Customize the Quick Launch" on page 371.

Configure Security

Because you are creating the lists directly on the main site, they will inherit the permissions of the site by default. However, the lists you are creating are more utility lists than lists that all your users should be adding data to. So, you are going to lock them down a bit by creating a special security group and removing unnecessary permissions from the lists.

Create a Schedulers Security Group

In addition to the security groups being used on the site, a group for schedulers should be created to allow for intuitive management of the scheduling functionality.

1. Navigate to the site that will contain the new scheduling functionality.

2. On the Site Actions menu, select the Site Settings link.

3. Under Users And Permissions, select the People And Groups link.

4. Select the Groups link in the left navigation bar.

5. From the New drop-down, select New Group.

6. Create a SharePoint group with the following settings:

Field	Value
Group Name	Schedulers
Description	Leave blank since the title is self-descriptive.
Who Can View	Everyone
Who Can Edit	Group Owner
Allow Requests	No
Add to Default View	No (unchecked)

7. Click Create.

Configure Resources List Security

Configuring the security for the Resources list will have the following high-level steps:

1. Remove the inheritance of the list security from the security of the site it is contained in.

2. Add the Schedulers security group to the list as contributors.

3. Change the Members group permissions to view.

The detailed steps are as follows:

1. Navigate to the Resources list.

2. On the List Tools tab, select List.

3. In the Settings group on the ribbon, select List Settings.

4. In the Permissions And Management section of the List Information page, select Permissions For This List.

5. On the ribbon, select Stop Inheriting Permissions.

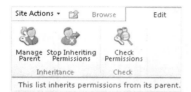

6. Click OK when prompted with a message box.

Note that the options available on the ribbon have changed.

7. Select Grant Permissions on the ribbon.

8. When selecting the users, select the Schedulers group, and then click the Check Names button to verify the name.

9. Select Grant Users Permissions Directly, and then select the Contribute permission level.

10. Clear the Send Welcome E-Mail option.

11. Click OK.

12. On the permissions page, select the Members group, and then click Edit User Permissions on the ribbon.

13. For the Members group, clear the Contribute permission and select the Read permission.

14. Click OK.

Configure Appointments List Security

Repeat the steps you just followed for the Resources list security for the Appointments list security. Break the security inheritance from the site, add the Schedulers security group as contributors, and change Members group permissions to view only.

Customize the Quick Launch

Now that you've got the lists and features enabled, you want the schedulers to be able to access the new appointment feature quickly, so you'll add a link to a more convenient location in the Quick Launch (left navigation) bar.

Add New Appointment Header and Link

To make the navigation easier to use, you're going to create an Appointments header to replace the existing link and then create a few additional links to specific views and a new appointment form.

1. Under Site Actions, select Site Settings.

2. Under the Look And Feel Section, select Quick Launch.

3. Edit the Appointments link to copy the web address.

4. Click Delete to remove the existing link while you're here.

5. Click New Heading.

6. Paste the URL in the address field, fill in the description as shown here, and then click OK.

7. Navigate to the existing Appointments list by using the link in the Quick Launch (left navigation) bar.

8. Right-click the Add New Event link and copy the link. The link will be unique for each list.

9. Under Site Actions, select Site Settings.

10. Under the Look And Feel Section, select Quick Launch.

11. Click New Navigation Link.

12. Paste the copied shortcut into the web address field, enter **New Appointment** in the description field, select Appointments from the Heading drop-down, and then click OK.

Quick Links to Filtered Views

If you have a favorite filtered view that you want to get to quickly, without having to follow as many steps as it takes to display the view manually, you can do the following. For this scenario, you are creating a link for each of the resources so that the schedulers can quickly see and print the day's appointments.

1. Navigate to the existing Appointments list by using the link in the Quick Launch (left navigation) bar.

2. Select the Today's Events view from the List tab on the ribbon.

3. In the Resources column header, select the resource to filter the list by.

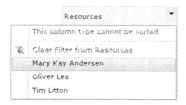

4. Copy the URL from the browser, which now includes the filter criteria.

5. Under Site Actions, select Site Settings.

6. Under the Look And Feel section, select Quick Launch.

7. Click New Navigation Link.

8. Paste the URL shortcut into the address field, fill in the description field as shown in the following screenshot, and select Appointments from the Heading drop-down. Click OK.

9. Repeat the process for any filtered views that are needed regularly. You might want to create one for each resource if the list isn't too long.

Add New Phone Message Header and Link

Because you're making changes to the left navigation and also have the Phone Call Memo list that comes with the Group Work Lists feature, you can also add a link to create a new memo. First, change the existing link to a section header, and then add the Add New link.

1. Under Site Actions, select Site Settings.

2. Under the Look And Feel Section, select Quick Launch.

3. Edit the Phone Call Memo link to copy the web address.

4. Click Delete to remove the existing link while you're here.

5. Click New Heading.

6. Paste the URL in the address field, fill in the description as shown here, and then click OK.

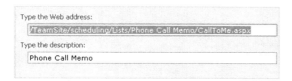

7. Navigate to the existing Phone Call Memo list by using the link in the Quick Launch (left navigation) bar.

8. Right-click the Add New Item link and copy the link.

9. Under Site Actions, select Site Settings.

10. Under the Look And Feel Section, select Quick Launch.

11. Click New Navigation Link.

12. Paste the URL shortcut into the address field, fill in the description field as shown in the following screenshot, and select Phone Call Memo from the Heading drop-down. Click OK.

Remember, these links can work from anywhere in the site or outside the site as long as the user clicking them has access to the site. They can be placed on an intranet home page or even in email signatures if needed.

Extend the Core Functionality

With the lists created, the core functionality of the scheduling solution is in place. The organization has a new scheduling tool and process, but there is a lot more the organization can do with the information. The next step you'll take is to create a quick workflow to send a confirmation email to customers about their new appointments. This better serves customers by communicating with them—and it only takes a click, if that.

Create a Send Confirmation Workflow

If you collect an email address from the customer at the time an appointment is scheduled, you can create a short and easy workflow that sends the customer an email with the appointment details so that the customer knows you've gotten it right:

1. Navigate to the Appointments list.

2. If the ribbon is not already visible, click the List tab.

3. In the Customize List group, select Edit List In SharePoint Designer.

4. Once SharePoint Designer is loaded, in the Workflows section, select New.

5. Enter the workflow details as shown here:

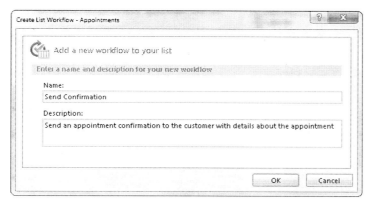

6. Click OK.

7. SharePoint Designer will display a new workflow with a single step. You don't need to set up any conditions or multiple steps. You'll just be creating a single action step to send the email using the information from the appointment.

8. With the Step 1 control (shown previously) selected, click the Action drop-down and select Send An Email.

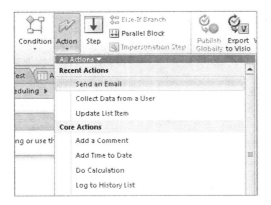

Step 1 changes to look like the following:

9. Click These Users to build the email. The message will look like the following before any content is added:

10. Click the Select Users icon (the book) for the To field. The Select Users dialog box is displayed. Select Workflow Lookup For A User, and then click Add.

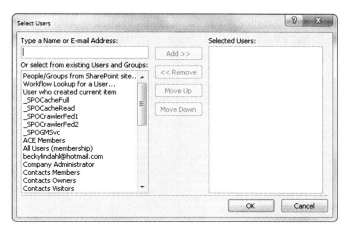

11. When you click Add, the dialog box you use to select the field value is displayed. Leave the Data Source field as Current Item. For Field From Source, click the drop-down and select Confirm Email. This setting takes the email address value for the current appointment and populates the To field. Assuming the email is valid, a message will be sent to the address via the workflow.

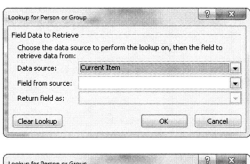

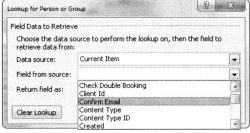

12. Click OK in the Lookup For Person Or Group dialog box.

13. Click OK in the Select Users dialog box.

14. Enter the following value for the email Subject line: **Appointment Confirmation Details**.

15. Now, you need to build the body of the email message that will be sent out. As you've already seen in working with the To field, you have the option to use values from the list item to personalize the content. You'll be using a few more fields now as well. Use the following screenshot to direct you. To create the other list item–specific values, click the Add Or Change Lookup button in the lower-left corner of the dialog box. These values will look similar to [%Current Item:Title%], with the field name (for example, Title) included.

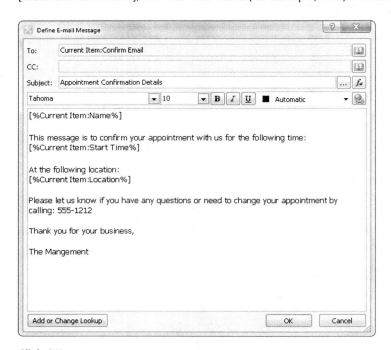

16. Click OK.

17. When the email message has been completed, click the Publish button, and the workflow will be validated and published to the list.

18. Select the Appointments tab to return to the list details.

19. You might need to click the Refresh button for the workflow to show up. When it does, it should be listed as follows:

The workflow is now attached to the list and should function as designed, but you want to add one more step to make the workflow even easier to access. You'll accomplish this by using a custom action, which you'll define in the next section.

If you want to verify or see the workflow in action at this point, you can fire it by doing the following:

1. On the list, edit an item to include an email account in the Confirm Email field that you have access to.

2. Back on the list view, select the same item, and then select Workflows from the drop-down menu for the item or on the ribbon. Both options are shown here.

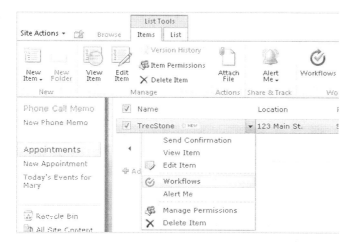

3. On the workflow page, click the Send Confirmation link to start the workflow.

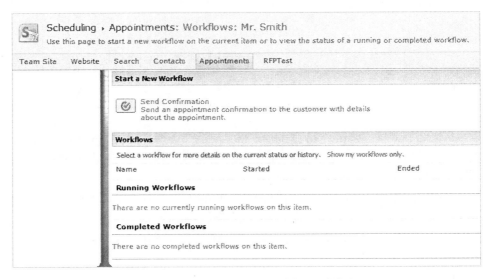

4. You will see one more confirmation to start the workflow. Click Start.

5. The email should be sent immediately. Once received, you should see the values for the fields that were called out in the design: customer name (Title column), Start Time, and Location.

Well done!

Create a Send Confirmation Action

Now that you have a workflow in place, you want to make it a little easier for the scheduler to send the email. You can do this by using a custom action, which you also define in SharePoint Designer.

1. Back in SharePoint Designer, find the section called Custom Actions. It will not have any items listed in it initially. Click the New button.

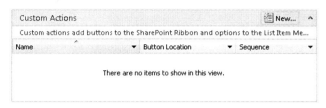

2. The Create Custom Action dialog box opens. Fill in the Name and Description fields as shown in the following screenshot. The value of the Name field will show up in the item drop-down in the list after the custom action is created.

3. Under Select The Type Of Action, select the Initiate Workflow option and verify that the Send Confirmation workflow has been selected.

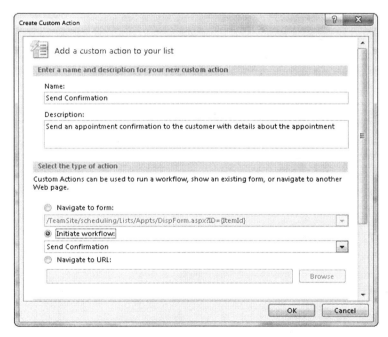

4. Click OK.

5. Return to the Appointments list in your web browser and refresh the page.

6. Select a list item and open the drop-down menu to see the new custom action.

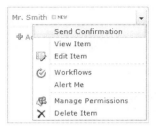

The scheduler will still see the final workflow confirmation and need to select Start, but he will not need to dig down a few screens to initiate the workflow.

Managing the Solution

Managing this solution should be very easy because it has only a few moving parts that need to be tended to from time to time.

Permissions Management

Permissions for the lists can be managed through the existing SharePoint security groups. If additional people need access to view the data, they can be added to the Members group. If additional scheduling resources are added to the system, they can be added to the Schedulers security group.

View Management

If you choose to add a link per technician to the Quick Launch, additional links will need to be created as new technicians are added. If that list gets too long, you might need to cease that particular practice and instead use the actual filter in the list header row or create a new view that uses Group By functionality to show all upcoming appointments for all technicians in more practical ways.

Reviewing the Platform

The scheduling solution is based on the Group Work Lists site feature in SharePoint, which is available on all the various platforms from Office 365 Small Business through the SharePoint Server Enterprise edition.

If you find the scheduling functionality useful, it might be worth your time to look into the other lists that are created as a part of this feature: Phone Call Memo, Whereabouts, and Time Card (via SharePoint Designer).

Additional Customization	Benefits
Domain users	Although the scheduling piece works by using the Resources list, it could also work with actual system users. System users would allow for more audience targeting and other useful views and functionality. One of the other lists, Phone Call Memo, could also be directed to those same users as needed.
CRM or contacts list integration	You could integrate a contacts list or CRM system to be the source of the Title field, which could automatically feed the Confirm Email field and keep a log of communications like the confirmation email if needed.

Summary

In this chapter we looked at a method for building a scheduling solution that keeps track of resources from a central location—moving beyond the older, more manual methods. You used a relatively underused feature of SharePoint called Group Work Lists, which has some interesting capabilities. As with many SharePoint solutions, this solution provides a basic result that can be built on and extended further, as time allows.

Resources

As you work through this book, it is likely that you will come across items that you are unfamiliar with or items that you need to research further to gain a greater understanding. This resources appendix is provided to help point you to some of the authors' favorite reference materials. You should be able to use these items to help get you up to speed and ready to build solutions such as those created in this book.

Microsoft Content

Microsoft provides a large amount of online content that is focused on end user and power user functions. This content can be found on the Microsoft Office website (*office.microsoft.com*). This site is a large repository of different types of help files. You can find videos, tutorials, and text articles on many different products. One good way to find content on this site is by using the powerful search engine. To get you started, here are some links to some helpful articles found on this site:

- "Make the Switch to the SharePoint 2010 User Interface"

  office.microsoft.com/en-us/sharepoint-server-help/make-the-switch-to-the-sharepoint-2010-user-interface-RZ101806469.aspx?CTT=5&origin=HA101859255

- "Share Information in a Central Place"

  office.microsoft.com/en-us/sharepoint-server-help/share-information-in-a-central-place-RZ101827926.aspx?CTT=5&origin=HA101859255

- "Manage Documents and Content in Microsoft SharePoint Server 2010"

  office.microsoft.com/en-us/sharepoint-server-help/manage-documents-and-content-in-microsoft-sharepoint-server-2010-RZ101828001.aspx?CTT=5&origin=HA101859255

Books and Publications

In addition to the content you can find online from Microsoft, several books are available that can familiarize you with the functionality in SharePoint. The following list outlines some of the books that we recommend.

Title	Authors	ISBN
Beginning SharePoint 2010: Building Business Solutions with SharePoint	Amanda Perran, Shane Perran, Jennifer Mason, Laura Rogers	978-0-470-61789-2
SharePoint 2010 Six-in-One	Chris Geier, Cathy Dew, Becky Bertram, Raymond Mitchell, Wes Preston, Kenneth Schaefer, Andrew Clark	978-0-470-87727-2
Beginning SharePoint Designer 2010	Woodrow W. Windischman, Bryan Phillips, Asif Rehmani, Marcy Kellar	978-0-470-64316-7
Microsoft SharePoint 2010 Plain & Simple	Johnathan Lightfoot, Chris Beckett	978-0-7356-4228-7
Microsoft SharePoint Designer 2010 Step by Step	Penelope Coventry	978-0-7356-2733-8
Microsoft SharePoint Foundation 2010 Step by Step	Olga M. Londer, Penelope Coventry	978-0-7356-2726-0

Community Content

Finally, in addition to the content provided by Microsoft and the content created through book publications, we want to point you to content that is created and maintained by the community. This content is created by community contributors and is typically peer-reviewed before it is posted. The following is one of the community sites we recommend:

- Nothing But SharePoint for End Users

    https://www.nothingbutsharepoint.com/sites/eusp/Pages/default.aspx

Index

Symbols

A

About the Authors

 JENNIFER MASON has more than eight years of SharePoint experience and is a frequent blogger, speaker, author, and community contributor about SharePoint products and technologies. Her primary focus is helping organizations get the most value from SharePoint through building solutions that bring immediate ROI by using the tools provided out of the box. Her main goal when looking at any problem is to truly understand the issues from the business's prospective and then map the tools available in SharePoint to create the best solution possible. In 2011, Jennifer was awarded the Microsoft MVP award for her continued contributions to the community. You can find more content from Jennifer on her blog at *blogs.sharepoint911.com/blogs/jennifer* and on Twitter *@jennifermason*.

 CHRISTIAN BUCKLEY is a SharePoint Server MVP and director of product evangelism for Axceler, a SharePoint ISV, where he helps drive partner and community development. An international speaker and author, he previously worked at Microsoft as a senior program manager on the enterprise-hosted SharePoint platform team (now part of Office 365), and also managed an engineering team in advertising operations. Prior to working at Microsoft, Christian participated in several startups, working with some of the world's largest hi-tech and manufacturing firms to build and deploy collaboration and supply-chain solutions. He is coauthor of three books on software configuration management and defect-tracking solutions, regularly contributes to sites such as AIIM.org and CMSWire, and can be found online at *www.buckleyplanet.com* and *www.twitter.com/buckleyplanet*.

 BRIAN T. JACKETT is a premier field engineer for Microsoft specializing in SharePoint, Project Server, and PowerShell. He has worked with SharePoint for more than four years on both development and administration projects for numerous companies and industries. Brian is also active in the SharePoint community by organizing community conferences, such as SharePoint Saturday Columbus, as well as local user groups. He also holds several Microsoft Certified Technology Specialist (MCTS) certifications for SharePoint-related technologies. You can find his blog at *www.brianjackett.com*.

 WES PRESTON is a SharePoint Server MVP and an independent SharePoint consultant. He works primarily as a SharePoint product specialist and solution designer, helping align business needs with the SharePoint platform and guiding organizations through the use of best practices. Wes has been a developer, IT pro, consultant, and technology evangelist for more than

15 years. He is coauthor of *SharePoint 2010 Six-in-One* and a speaker and community leader in the Twin Cities (Minnesota). He can be found online at *www.idubbs.com/blog*, *www.TrecStone.com*, and *www.twitter.com/idubbs*.

About the Technical Editors

SHANNON BRAY is a SharePoint evangelist and Microsoft Certified Master (MCM) for SharePoint Server 2010. He is currently employed with Planet Technologies as its chief SharePoint architect. Shannon specializes in architecture design and solution development using Microsoft technologies. He is the president of the Colorado SharePoint User's Group, and has presented SharePoint topics at Microsoft's TechReady, TechED, and SPC11. In addition to being an MCM, Shannon is also an MCITP and MCPD for SharePoint 2010. During his spare time, Shannon teaches scuba diving and enjoys running. He also operates a non-profit for wounded veterans (*kicksforwarriors.org*).

GEOFF EVELYN has published many articles, guides, and books about SharePoint. He is a SharePoint MVP, with over 25 years of experience in information systems. He is a Fellow of the Institution of Analysts and Programmers, a Fellow of the Institute of Computer Technology, a Member of the Institute for the Management of Information Systems, a PRINCE2 Practitioner, with MCDST, MCSD, MCTS, MCITP Microsoft certifications, and is MOS (Microsoft Office Specialist) Certified.

What do you think of this book?

We want to hear from you!

To participate in a brief online survey, please visit:

microsoft.com/learning/booksurvey

Tell us how well this book meets your needs—what works effectively, and what we can do better. Your feedback will help us continually improve our books and learning resources for you.

Thank you in advance for your input!

CPSIA information can be obtained at www.ICGtesting.com
Printed in the USA
LVOW072052080612

285310LV00011B/29/P